Simply WordPerfect

An Introductory Guide to Version 5.0

Steven J. Bennett
and
Peter G. Randall

Brady
New York

BRADY

Simon & Schuster, Inc.
Gulf + Western Building
One Gulf + Western Plaza
New York, New York 10023

Distributed by Prentice Hall Trade

Manufactured in the United States of America

10 9 8 7 6 5 4 3 2

Library of Congress Cataloging-in-Publication Data
Bennett, Steven J., 1951-
    Simply WordPerfect : an introductory guide to version 5.0 /
Steven J. Bennett and Peter G. Randall.
      p.   cm.
    1. WordPerfect (Computer program) 2. Word processing.
I. Randall, Peter G., 1951-   . II. Title.
Z52.5.W65B46 1988
652'.5--dc19   88-7642
                                      CIP

ISBN 0-13-965450-X

Contents

SECTION I: GETTING STARTED

SECTION II: WORDPERFECT FUNDAMENTALS

SECTION IV: PRINTING

ACKNOWLEDGEMENTS

First and foremost, we'd like to thank Burt Gabriel, our editor, and Michael Mellin, Associate Publisher, for their support and encouragement. We'd also like to thank Steve Dyson of WordPerfect Corporation for reviewing the manuscript and suggesting helpful changes and corrections. In addition, we're grateful to Pamela D'Arcangelo of Ciba Corning Diagnostics for testing the manuscript in the field and helping us to make it more useful to the people who use WordPerfect every day. Finally, we'd like to express our appreciation to Geraldine Ivins and her staff at Brady for guiding us through the production of this book.

PRODUCTION NOTE

This book was designed and produced by PageWorks, Inc., located in Cambridge, MA. It was printed on a QMS PS 810 laser printer. All figures were created with HOTSHOT Graphics, manufactured by Symsoft, Inc, Mountain View, CA.

LIMITS OF LIABILITY AND DISCLAIMER OF WARRANTY

TRADEMARK ACKNOWLEDGEMENTS

INTRODUCTION

The Origin of Software Species
(With apologies to Charles Darwin)

A New Breed of Software

Every major software maker puts its products through a continual evolution to provide new features and improve existing ones; as in the biological world, constant change in the microcomputing marketplace is the key to survival. Sometimes the change is small, involving minor cosmetic surgery, the fixing of minor bugs, or the addition of a few features. This is usually accompanied by a fractional change in the version or release number of the program, say from 1.0 to 1.1. Other times, the changes represent a quantum leap and in effect create a whole new product, in which case the version jumps from 1.0 to 2.0, 2.0 to 3.0, and so on.

WordPerfect is no exception; version 5.0 represents a major departure from version 4.2, adding scores of new features that make it one of the most powerful word processors available. Actually, with its laser printer control and new formatting commands, WordPerfect 5.0 lies somewhere in the software kingdom between a word processor and a desktop publishing program. The resulting hybrid might therefore best be called a "document processor."

However you describe WordPerfect 5.0, one thing is certain; with its added power comes a steep learning curve. New users may find a seemingly overwhelming number of functions and concepts to learn. And those familiar with version 4.2 might be a little dismayed to find that a number of familiar key strokes have been changed. The good news is that despite WordPerfect 5.0's enormous power, a relatively easy-to-manage subset of the program's functions enable you to easily handle day-to-day use of the program for creating correspondence, memos, reports, manuscripts, and other basic documents.

A Shortcut

Simply WordPerfect is designed to guide you through the essential WordPerfect functions. Some of the special functions for which you may only have occasional use are also briefly described in Appendix A. Rather than drag you through a tutorial in which you create a silly letter or memo, then manipulate it a hundred ways, the book strives to match the mental processes you'll probably go through from the moment you open the box to the first time you print a document. As you read along, you can experiment with your own text and create documents relevant to your own pursuits. Here's the flow of logic:

Installing the program

Installing the printer

Finding your way around the keyboard

Learning the use of each function key

Personalizing the program

Creating and formatting text

Editing text

Checking your spelling

Printing your document

Saving and retrieving your document

Now that you see the logic flow of *Simply WordPerfect*, let's see how it translates into the individual chapters—this will help you decide what portions of the book are most relevant to your needs.

SECTION I: GETTING STARTED

Chapter 1: Installing, Starting and Exiting the Program. Version 5.0 has an automated installation routine. This chapter explains how and when to use the routine, as well as how and when to manually install each disk to avoid tying up your hard disk with unnecessary files. It also lists the minimum hardware requirements for running the program. In addition, step-by-step instruction is provided for installing a printer.

SECTION II: WORDPERFECT FUNDAMENTALS

Chapter 2: Navigating through WordPerfect: the Keyboard and Screen Display. There are many ways to move the cursor in WordPerfect 5.0; by space, by word, by screen, by page, and by document. You also have a number of options for deleting words, lines, and pages. You'll find all of the cursor and editing key movements described in this chapter.

Chapter 3: The Function Keys. WordPerfect 5.0 makes extensive use of the special function keys, labeled F1 through F10 and located either to the left of or at the top of your keyboard. By combining the 10 function keys with the (Ctrl), (Shift), and (Alt) keys, WordPerfect offers 40 primary functions. Many of these functions offer menus with five or more options, bringing the total number of functions well into the hundreds. This chapter describes the basic use of each function key.

Chapter 4: Setup. WordPerfect 5.0 allows you to personalize a number of aspects of the program, such as whether the screen is measured in inches, centimeters, points, or character units (as was used in version 4.2).

SECTION III: DOCUMENT PROCESSING

Chapter 5: Creating a Document from Scratch. Once you know the keyboard layout and understand the concept behind the function keys, you're ready to create a document. This chapter covers how to use WordPerfect 5.0's powerful formatting features to set margins and tabs, line spacing, assign page numbers, etc.

Chapter 6: Column Formats. An important capability of WordPerfect 5.0 is column formatting. This chapter explains how you can create striking effects for newsletters, reports, and directories.

Chapter 7: Footnotes & Endnotes. WordPerfect has extensive features for creating footnotes and endnotes. You can vary the appearance and placement of your notes to comply with any academic or business writing style guides. This chapter explains everything you'll need to know to draw on WordPerfect's footnote and endnote features.

Chapter 8: Editing Your Document. The main advantage of a word processor over a typewriter is that it allows you to continually revise your work without retyping, or cutting and pasting scraps of paper together. WordPerfect allows you to electronically manipulate your document through a number of editing functions, such as electronic "cut and paste" and "search and replace." In this chapter, you'll learn how to use these and other features to quickly alter the content and appearance of your documents.

Chapter 9: Fine Tuning Your Document. WordPerfect includes an extensive Thesaurus to help you find synonyms, and a spell checker for picking up and correcting typographical errors. In this chapter, you'll learn how to use both features to make your final documents as clean and professional as possible.

SECTION IV: PRINTING

Chapter 10: From Screen to Paper: Printing Your Document. WordPerfect 5.0 offers exquisite printer control, allowing you to print a whole document, a single page of a document, or a series of non-continuous pages. You can also queue up a stack of print jobs and then expedite a particular job without starting all over again. You can specify how many copies will be printed, and even let the program adjust for the binding width of the document. All key printer functions are discussed in this chapter.

SECTION V: FILE MAINTENANCE

Chapter 11: Storing and Retrieving Your Document. Built in to WordPerfect 5.0 is a sophisticated file manager that allows you to retrieve, rename, and delete files. You can even ask WordPerfect to list files containing a specific word or group of words. All of the file management functions are explained in this chapter, along with tips for backing up your work—just in case...

APPENDICES

Appendix A: Exploring WordPerfect's Special Features. While the preceding chapters describe the basic functions you'll use on a daily basis, this Appendix briefly describes WordPerfect's mail merge and sorting function, outliner, and macro generator. As you become more proficient, you can explore these features in greater detail and incorporate them into your day-to-day routines.

Appendix B: Installing an HP LaserJet Series II Printer. The LaserJet Series II makes an ideal companion for WordPerfect 5.0. Whereas Chapter 1 provides a simple installation for any printer, this Appendix provides step- by-step instruction for installing a Laserjet Series II along with optional font cartridges and soft fonts.

Appendix C: Changing Fonts. If you've installed a printer that has built-in fonts or uses plug-in font cartridges or soft fonts, you can use WordPerfect to create professional looking documents with a typeset look and feel. This appendix covers the basics of changing fonts for new and existing text.

Appendix D: WordPerfect File Summary.

Appendix E: Summary of Commands.

Appendix F: Summary of Codes.

How to Use this Book

New Users. If you're staring at a small mountain of WordPerfect program diskettes, wondering what to do, start with Chapter 1 and work through the following chapters sequentially. Experiment with each feature you read about, entering your own sample text as you proceed.

Version 4.2 Users. As mentioned above, a number of the keystrokes and concepts you inherited from 4.2 simply won't work in version 5.0, so you've got some adapting to do in 5.0's new and more complex environment.

For example, in all versions of WordPerfect prior to 5.0, line margins were calculated from the left edge. Therefore a margin setting of 10,70 meant a left margin 10 characters from the left side of the page, and a right margin 70 characters from the left side of the page. In 5.0, the margins are calculated from their respective edge of the paper, so to achieve a margin of 10 characters on each side you must set the left margin at 10, and the right margin at 10. If you set your margins at 10,70 in version 5.0, you will wind up with a strange looking beast. Many other such pitfalls await you, too.

The solution? Browse through the function key explanation in Chapter 3, scanning the summary table for each key. The summary table lists the keystroke combinations used to execute function key commands.

Typographical Conventions

Throughout this book, you'll be shown various combinations of keystrokes used to activate WordPerfect commands. They are represented in nearly the same style as that used in the WordPerfect reference manual. Here's a summary:

1. Special keys that do not represent characters are enclosed in parentheses and are abbreviated as they are on the keyboard. The Delete key, for example, appears as:

    (Del)

2. Some keys have symbols, but are spelled out with the name of the function.

    a. The four keys with arrows on the numeric keypad move the cursor. In this book, they are referred to as:

        (Right Cursor)

        (Left Cursor)

        (Up Cursor)

        (Down Cursor)

    b. The key located in the upper right portion of the keyboard, designated by a large arrow pointing left, is referred to as:

        (Backspace)

    c. The long key at the bottom of the keyboard is referred to as:

        (Spacebar)

    d. The key marked by a "hooking" left arrow (E) is variously referred to by people as "enter," "return," or "carriage return" (a holdover from the days of manual typewriters). In this book it is referred to as:

        (Enter)

3. When a special key must be pressed and held while a second key is pressed, the two keys are separated by a minus (-) sign. For example:

        (Shift-F1)

means press and hold the shift key, then press the key marked F1, and finally release both keys. Another example would be:

        (Ctrl-Left Cursor)

which means press the key marked "Ctrl," then press the left cursor once, and release both keys.

4. When keys are to be pressed one at a time in sequence, they are separated by a plus (+) sign, as in:

        (Home) + (Home) + (Up Cursor)

which means press the key marked home two times, then press
the key with the arrow pointing up.

5. Finally, when commands are listed, such as,

   "Type: **CD \WP50** (Enter)"

they are listed in upper case, for clarity only; you can enter all
commands in lower- or uppercase, as you please.

Regardless of your previous computing experience, *Simply WordPerfect* can help you make an evolutionary leap in your word processing
efforts, so you'll work more efficiently and effectively. And in the race
for productivity, it's survival of the fittest.

Installing, Starting, and Exiting WordPerfect 5.0

PRE-INSTALLATION CHECKLIST

Few things are more annoying than opening a new software package only to be told to stop and consider all possible alternatives for setting up the program on your system. WordPerfect 5.0 does not make you jump through any major installation hoop, because most of the options are set later via an internal setup option (more on that in Chapter 4).

Nevertheless, there is some information you must gather before carrying out the installation. This includes:

— the amount of available memory

— the size of your hard disk, if you plan to use one

— the type of monitor and graphics card you're using

— the type of printer you're using

A detailed checklist form is provided in Table 1.1 to help you organize the information. Each of the categories on the form are explained below.

1

TABLE 1.1 PRE-INSTALLATION INFORMATION

Memory

Amount of *available* RAM _____

Disk Space (For hard disk users)

2 Megabytes of Hard Disk (Y/N) _____

Display

Monitor type _____

Graphics adapter _____

Printer

Make/Model # _____

    Font Cartridges _____

    Soft Fonts _____

Printer Interface (Serial/Parallel) _____

    If Serial Interface:

    Baud Rate _____

    Parity (none, even, odd) _____

    Stop Bits (1 or 2) _____

    Data Bits (7 or 8) _____

Forms Feed (Continuous/Manual Feed Sheet Feeder)

    If Sheet Feeder: _____

    Brand Name _____

Number of Paper Bins _____

Once you complete the form, you're ready to move onto the actual installation procedure. It is divided into two sections: one for hard disk users, one for floppy users. If you understand all of the categories on the Pre-Installation Checklist, fill out the form and proceed to the installation section below.

Available RAM Memory

WordPerfect 5.0 requires significantly more memory than its predecessors. The size of the program is one of the major trade-off for added capabilities. The additional size requires more of the computer's "volatile" or random access memory ("RAM," which only works when the computer is on) as well as more permanent storage space (floppy or hard disk). WordPerfect 5.0 requires 384K of *available* RAM memory; that is, memory not already used for DOS or "RAM Resident Programs," such as Sidekick. (Programs like Sidekick can always "pop up" for use because they reside in RAM. The trade-off: they reduce the amount of available RAM). If your system only has a total of 384K of RAM, you cannot run the program, since DOS uses 40K or more. WordPerfect recommends a minimum of 512K of RAM to allow for DOS and any RAM resident programs. In general, WordPerfect 5.0 performs better with additional memory.

The easiest way to determine how much available RAM you have left on your system for WordPerfect is to run the CHKDSK utility from DOS. This program lists the total amount of disk storage you have left on the specified disk, and also lists the amount of Total RAM on your system and the amount of RAM still available. To run the CHKDSK program:

1. Start up your computer from scratch and load all the RAM resident programs that you plan to be using when you run WordPerfect 5.0.

2. If you are using a hard disk system, make sure you have the C:> prompt; if you are using a floppy disk-based system, you will be at the A:> prompt. Either way, type:

   CHKDSK (Enter)

   The system response looks something like this:

   ```
   31768576        bytes total disk space
   165888          bytes in 9 hidden files
   137216          bytes in 55 directories
   20858880        bytes in 1548 user files
   20480           bytes in bad sectors
   ```

```
10586112              bytes available on disk
655360                bytes total memory
524288                bytes free
```

(Note: the actual numbers displayed on your screen will undoubtedly differ, as they will reflect the particular memory situation of your computer.) The last line indicates the amount of available RAM. If you do not have at least 384K of available RAM, you either have to reduce the number of RAM resident programs loaded with WordPerfect, or you must add more memory to your computer to run this program. Contact your dealer or the person responsible for configuring computers in your company for information about increasing your available memory.

Hard Disk

In addition to requiring more RAM memory, WordPerfect 5.0 requires a great deal of disk storage. While it is technically possible to run WordPerfect 5.0 on a floppy disk-based system, we strongly recommend that you use a hard disk for this program. If you run the program on a dual-drive floppy system, many functions are slowed considerably. Worse, you'll find yourself doing a lot of disk swapping, since the program can't all fit on one disk. This can break your concentration and thought flow. The slow speed and disk swapping are not only annoying, but in the Age of Cheap Hard Disks and Disk Cards, they're unnecessary. While you'll find a complete explanation of how to set up a floppy disk-based system later in this chapter, if you can spring for a hard disk, do yourself a great favor and upgrade your computer. You'll not only operate WordPerfect 5.0 at a whole new level, but you will see dramatic performance improvements in *all* your applications.

Required Hard Disk Space

If you do have a hard disk, be aware that the complete WordPerfect 5.0 package requires about 2.5 megabytes (2.5 million bytes) of

III BradyLine

Insights into tomorrow's technology from the authors and editors of Brady Books.

You rely on Brady's bestselling computer books for up-to-date information about high technology. Now turn to BradyLine for the details behind the titles.

Find out what new trends in technology spark Brady's authors and editors. Read about what they're working on, and predicting, for the future. Get to know the authors through interviews and profiles, and get to know each other through your questions and comments.

BradyLine keeps you ahead of the trends with the stories behind the latest computer developments. Informative previews of forthcoming books and excerpts from new titles keep you apprised of what's going on in the fields that interest you most.

- Peter Norton on operating systems
- Jim Seymour on business productivity
- Jerry Daniels, Mary Jane Mara, Robert Eckhardt, and Cynthia Harriman on Macintosh development, productivity, and connectivity

Get the Spark. Get BradyLine.

Published quarterly, beginning with the Summer 1988 issue. Free exclusively to our customers. Just fill out and mail this card to begin your subscription.

Name _____

Address _____

City _____ State _____ Zip _____

Name of Book Purchased _____

Date of Purchase _____

Where was this book purchased?   *(circle one)*

    Retail Store   Computer Store   Mail Order

F R E E

Mail this card for your free subscription to BradyLine

Brady Books
One Gulf+Western Plaza
New York, NY 10023

hard disk space. If you plan to use the auto-install routine provided with the program, you'll transfer the whole nine yards, so you'd better plan to have the space. To find out how much space you have left, repeat the CHKDSK command described above. This time, you're interested in the last line of the top set of numbers, which indicates:

```
[X]    bytes available on disk
```

If you don't have at least two megabytes available, you have two options: 1) eliminate obsolete files from your disk or transfer them to floppies to clear up the space; or 2) manually install WordPerfect so that you only copy essential files. By eliminating "drivers" for hardware that you don't use, graphic samples, and the learning files, you can reduce the hard disk requirements to about 1.5 megabyte. By removing the little used programs and files you can push the requirement to just under one megabyte. It's even technically possible to run an absolute minimum WordPerfect configuration with just over one half a megabyte. Manual program installation is discussed below.

Graphics Monitor/Adapter

One of the great enhancements of WordPerfect 5.0 over its predecessors is its ability to use a graphics monitor (either color or monochrome) to display before printing an accurate preview of a document including graphic elements and special fonts. With the use of special "RAM fonts," some monitor adapters can even display the different sized and shaped fonts while in text mode. The monitor adapter is a card that occupies a slot in your computer and translates the data into a form for display on screen. At the very least, a system must have a monochrome adapter to run a monochrome monitor and display text.

While a graphics monitor and adapter are necessary to display the advanced features cited above, they are not required to run the basic WordPerfect 5.0 program. You can even use WordPerfect 5.0's graphic capabilities when you print (provided your printer supports the desired effects)—you just won't be able to see them on the screen. A relatively inexpensive solution is to purchase one of the many monochrome graphics adapters, which will add graphics capability to your existing monochrome monitor.

WordPerfect automatically figures out what kind of monitor and display adapter you're using and selects the correct driver. If you don't want to clog up your hard disk with drivers for hardware you're not using, you must know which drivers you need for your monitor and adapter. Therefore, if you're planning a "sparse" manual installation, make sure you know the brand of your monitor and adapter. Table 1.2 of the Manual Installation section of this chapter shows which files you need to run the major monitor and adapter brands.

Printer

Before you can print with WordPerfect, you must indicate what printer you're using, even if you do not have one connected to your computer at this time. You can always change your printer selection later. If you do have a printer and wish to install it when you install the program, you need to know some basic information in addition to the brand name and model. This includes whether or not you plan to use additional font cartridges or software-based fonts. You also need to know the *interface*; that is, whether the printer uses a *serial* or *parallel* port, or both. The port contains a plug that connects to a cable, which in turn connects to your computer. If your printer can only be run through a serial port, you must gather four pieces of technical information: the *Baud Rate*, or speed at which data is transmitted, and the *Parity, Stop Bits*, and *Data Bits,* which determine how the print data is "packaged" for transmission to the printer. Finally, if you have a separate sheet feeder, you need to know the brand name and the number of paper bins it contains.

If all this sounds like arcane techno jumbo, far removed from word processing, be assured, it is. Nevertheless, you need the information to complete the installation. A quick call to your dealer or your computing department should provide answers. Also, most of the newer printers use a parallel interface, or give you the choice of a using the parallel or serial interface. The parallel connection is simpler and actually transmits data faster between the computer and printer. This is covered more fully under the printer installation section in this chapter, as well as Appendix B, which gives a step-by-step guide to the installation of a LaserJet Series II.

At this point, your pre-installation checklist should be complete and you're ready to begin installing the program. If you're using a hard disk, continue reading. If you have a dual drive floppy system, turn to page 23. After you install the system on your hard disk or floppy disk system, read the sections in this chapter on starting WordPerfect, installing a printer, and exiting WordPerfect.

HARD DISK INSTALLATION

If you have a hard disk, you have to decide two things before installing the program: 1) where, on the hard disk, do you want to keep the program files and data files; and 2) do you want WordPerfect to automatically copy the files, or do you wish to do the copying yourself (it's not as obvious a choice as it sounds). Once you make those decisions, use the following procedure:

1. Copy the program files (either automatically or manually).

2. Modify or create an AUTOEXEC.BAT file to include the "PATH" command.

3. Modify or create a "CONFIG.SYS" file.

If this sounds complicated, don't worry—step-by-step instructions are provided, and the whole operation only takes five to ten minutes, depending on your proficiency. Besides, once it's done, you won't have to do it again.

Pre-installation Consideration #1: Program and data directories.

A hard disk is so large that you can't efficiently scatter files anywhere and expect the computer to instantly find them. Instead,

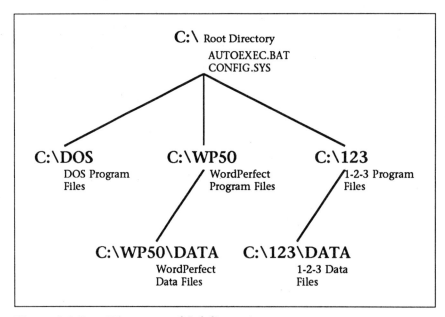

Figure 1.1 *Root Directory and Subdirectories*

hard disks are organized by areas called *directories*. Every hard disk must contain a *root directory*. The root directory, like the root system of a tree, branches into other directories (see Figure 1.1). Directories themselves can be split into *subdirectories*. You can create and name any directory or subdirectory you wish, as explained below. The key concept, though, is that WordPerfect files should be kept in one directory, spreadsheet or database files in another, communication programs in another, etc. The idea is that each program has its own special place on the hard disk. This helps you organize what would be an otherwise impossible mess, and helps the computer find your files more quickly.

With WordPerfect, it's important to separate the WordPerfect program files (the actual word processing files) from your data files (letters, reports, and other documents that you create). There are two reasons for this hard disk strategy. First, it permits you to easily back up your data files, which change frequently, without wasting time and space to backup the program files, which only change when

WordPerfect issues a new release. If your data resides in its own directory by itself, you can copy the entire directory with one command. Second, when you want to list the files in your data directory to retrieve a document you've been working on, you don't want to have to find your letter to mom by sorting through program files with names like "HRF12.FRS."

You are therefore well advised to install your program files in one directory, called WP or WP50 or some other appropriate name. Set up a separate directory called DATA or WPDATA or any other name you choose as a subdirectory of the program file directory, or as a totally independent directory branching from the root directory. Specific instructions for creating the directories are described below.

CAUTION: If you already have WordPerfect 4.2 installed on your hard disk system, do not delete it yet. Save it until you are certain WordPerfect 5.0 is up and running correctly. Then archive 4.2 to floppies to hold as a backup for an appropriate period of time (one or two months). In any case, if you choose to put your WordPerfect 5.0 program files in a directory called WP, rather than WP50, as suggested in this chapter, make sure no WordPerfect 4.2 files remain in the WP directory. Otherwise, WordPerfect 5.0 may become confused by the extraneous files. Copy the WordPerfect 4.2 program files to another directory until you are ready to delete them.

Pre-installation Consideration #2:
Manual vs Automated Copying of Files to Your Hard Disk

WordPerfect 5.0 is shipped with an install routine that takes care of creating directories and copying the program files from your floppy drive to your hard disk. While this is easy, as we mentioned earlier, it has a high price in terms of disk space; the routine copies all files, except the printer drivers, to a directory called WP50. This means that in addition to the necessary program files, WP50 will contain the tutorial program and sample graphics files, as well as drivers for equipment that you aren't using, for a grand total of nearly 2.5 megabytes.

If you have plenty of disk space, and just want to get on with word processing, then the auto-install routine may be perfectly acceptable for you (see Auto-Install below). If, however, disk space is at a premium, you have two choices: run the auto-install and delete unnecessary files (see Table 1.2), or manually install the program, copying only those files you need or want. The latter strategy makes more sense if you want to conserve disk space, and is explained under the Manual Installation section below.

Step #1a: Copying the Files: Automated Installation

To run the automated installation routine, insert the Learning Disk in the A: drive and type:

A:INSTALL (Enter)

The program will ask you to confirm that you have a hard disk, after which it will begin copying files, prompting you to change disks as required. That's all there is to it. You now need only to install your printer and set up your system parameters as described below and you are ready to go. You should also create or modify the PATH command in your AUTOEXEC.BAT files, also described below. You do not need to create or modify your CONFIG.SYS file since the automated installation program does that for you.

Step #1b: Copying the Files: Manual Installation

Selecting files

You need only the WP.EXE and WP.FIL files to run the basic WordPerfect program on most systems. Your system may, however, require one or more of the ancillary files to run a graphics, color or other high resolution monitor. You are likely to want some of the additional features of WordPerfect 5.0 such as the spell checker or thesaurus, which require still more files. Table 1.2 shows the required files and recommended files for a manual hard disk installation.

(See Appendix D for a complete listing and description of all the files supplied with the program.)

TABLE 1.2

Location	File Name	File Size	Status
WordPerfect 1	WP.EXE	245K	Required
WordPerfect 2	WP.FIL	299k	Required
WordPerfect 1	WPHELP.FIL	48K	Recommended
WordPerfect 1	WPHELP2.FIL	52K	Recommended
WordPerfect 2	WP.MRS	4K	Recommended
WordPerfect 2	KEYS.MRS	5K	Recommended
Speller	WP{WP}US.LEX	292K	Recommended
Thesaurus	WP{WP}US.THS	362K	Recommended
Fonts/Graphics	WP.DRS	73K	Recommended *
Printer 1-4	Printer Driver	1-60K	Recommended **

* You must use either the WP.DRS or the WPSMALL.DRS for the Print Preview function. We recommend that you use the more comprehensive WP.DRS version unless you absolutely can't spare the additional space.

** You must select the appropriate printer driver for your printer when you first install it. You can select the generic printer driver STANDARD.PRS, but we don't recommend that you bother. As soon as you install the correct driver, the STANDARD.PRS just hangs around taking up space.

Creating a new directory

Before manually copying the required and recommended files to your hard disk, you must first create the directory into which you want to place WordPerfect. This is done with the command (at the C:> prompt):

MD \[Directory Name] (Enter)

Since you are going to create the directory yourself, you can name it anything you wish, although WP50 is a logical choice for WordPerfect 5.0 (Hint: When you name directories, come up with names that make sense so they're easy to remember. You can have a maximum of eight alphanumeric characters in a directory name).

Copying files

Once you have created the new directory, use the DOS COPY command to copy the required and recommended files from the floppy disks to the hard disk. For example, place the WordPerfect 1 disk in drive A: and enter the command:

   COPY A:WP.EXE C:\WP50 (Enter)

Repeat the command for each of the required and recommended files copying from their respective disks. If you are using an EGA, VGA, or other high performance monitor, you may have to copy the special screen drivers and resource files (*.WPD and *.FRS) appropriate for your monitor. These are located on the Fonts/ Graphics disk, as shown in Table 1.2. Select those files appropriate for your monitor.

Step #2: Editing or Creating an AUTOEXEC.BAT file to include the PATH Command

Since you will be installing the WordPerfect program files in a separate directory from your data directory, you will have to establish a "PATH" to the WP50 directory. This will permit you to start the WordPerfect 5.0 program from any directory on the hard disk. Here's how it works. Normally, to start WordPerfect, you would have to make the directory in which the WordPerfect program files reside the "current directory"; that is, the directory in which the computer expects to process files. This is done by typing the simple command:

   CD \WP50 (Enter)

Which means "Change the current" directory to the directory called WP50. You would then type:

   WP (Enter)

to start the program (as explained below, under Starting WordPerfect).

What's the problem? No problem, except that WordPerfect expects to find your data in the directory called WP50. As explained above, however, it's desirable to keep your data elsewhere. You can issue a command from within WordPerfect to change the directory to your data directory each time you run the program, but there's an easier way that only has to be done once. That's where the PATH command comes in. Once you set a PATH back to the directory called WP50, you can make the data directory the current directory, and start WordPerfect, even though the program files reside elsewhere. In other words, the PATH command tells the computer, "if you can't find the files you're looking for here, check in the directory called [X]." The advantage of this approach is that your data files are immediately available, and you don't have to change directories from within WordPerfect.

The best way to create a PATH is to include the PATH command in your AUTOEXEC.BAT file, which runs each time you start your computer. If your PATH command is part of the AUTOEXEC.BAT file, your PATH back to the directory called WP50 is automatically set each time you turn on the computer. The following sections explain what to do if you already have an AUTOEXEC.BAT file with or without a PATH command. If your computer was set up for you by someone else, chances are it already has an AUTOEXEC.BAT file. If not, you might have to create one from scratch. Either way, it only takes a couple of minutes, and requires no programming knowledge.

To determine if you have an AUTOEXEC.BAT file, look in the root directory. The AUTOEXEC.BAT file must be located there. To check, start up your computer and make sure you are at the DOS prompt. Switch to the root directory by entering the command:

  CD \ (Enter)

Then instruct the computer to list the file on the screen with the command:

  TYPE AUTOEXEC.BAT (Enter)

If you already have an AUTOEXEC.BAT file, its contents will be listed on the screen. If the AUTOEXEC.BAT file does not exist, you will get the warning:

  `File not found`

indicating that the AUOTEXEC.BAT file does not exist yet. Use the appropriate sections below to modify or create an AUTOEXEC.BAT file.

Editing an existing AUTOEXEC.BAT file

If you have an AUTOEXEC.BAT file, scan the screen listing to see if it already contains a PATH command, as in:

path = c:\[directory names]

Note: there may be a number of different directories to which the computer is already PATHed. The key is the phrase "path=".

The following procedure uses a simple text editor supplied with DOS, called EDLIN, to add the WP50 directory to an existing PATH, or add the PATH command for the first time.

1. Make a backup copy of your existing AUTOEXEC.BAT file by copying it to a file with a new name with the command:

   COPY AUTOEXEC.BAT AUTOEXEC.ARC (Enter)

2. Type:

   EDLIN AUTOEXEC.BAT (Enter)

If you get the error message:

`Bad command or file name`

you do not have the EDLIN.COM file available. Place your original DOS disk in the A: drive and enter the command:

   A:EDLIN AUTOEXEC.BAT (Enter)

The words:

`End of input file`

appear on the screen. Underneath the message the EDLIN prompt— a single asterisk (*)—is presented, as shown in Figure 1.2

3. At the asterisk prompt enter the command L, which stands for List the contents of the file being edited. The screen will then display the contents of your AUTOEXEC.BAT file, with a number before each line. If you already have the PATH command, go to step #4; if you don't have one, go to step #7.

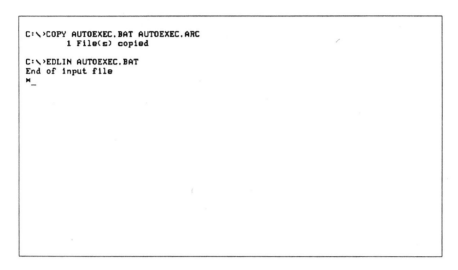

```
C:\>COPY AUTOEXEC.BAT AUTOEXEC.ARC
        1 File(s) copied

C:\>EDLIN AUTOEXEC.BAT
End of input file
*_
```

Figure 1.2 *EDLIN Prompt*

4. To display on screen the contents of the chosen line, enter the number of the line containing the PATH command and press (Enter). Underneath it, EDLIN will display the same line number, followed by an asterisk and the cursor, as shown in Figure 1.3. By pressing the (F3) key, you cause the text of the selected line to be copied to the blank line, where the cursor is positioned at the end. Insert a semicolon (;), followed by C:\WP50 (or whatever name you chose for your WordPerfect program directory). Press the (Enter) key to effect the change to the existing line.

5. Check by listing the file again with the List command used in step 3. If it's incorrect, repeat step 4. If it's correct, save the new file by entering the command E for Exit. This saves the new version of the AUTOEXEC.BAT file to disk.

6. Activate the new PATH command by typing:

    AUTOEXEC (Enter)

    Now proceed to the next section—you're ready to add or modify your CONFIG.SYS file, if necessary. Go to page 18 for instructions.

```
C:\>EDLIN AUTOEXEC.BAT
End of input file
*1
        1:*PATH=C:\;C:\DOS;C:\DBASE;C:\WINDOWS;C:\PM
        2: PROMPT $P$G
        3: MODE COM1:9600,N,8,1,P
        4: SET TEMP=C:\PM
        5: MENU
*1
        1:*PATH=C:\;C:\DOS;C:\DBASE;C:\WINDOWS;C:\PM
        1:*PATH=C:\;C:\DOS;C:\DBASE;C:\WINDOWS;C:\PM;C:\WP50
*E

C:\>_
```

Figure 1.3 *Editing Existing PATH Command*

7. To add a new PATH command to an AUTOEXEC.BAT file that doesn't already contain one, you must insert a new line at the top of the file. Enter the command

   i1 (Enter)

and you will be presented with a blank line numbered 1. Enter the total PATH command:

   PATH C:\;C:\DOS;C:\WP50 (Enter)

to include both the ROOT directory (C:\) and the DOS directory (C:\DOS) as well as \WP in the PATH. Include the DOS directory since it is where the DOS utilities such as CHKDSK and EDLIN should reside. (If they don't, you should move them there with the DOS COPY command). Include the root directory since it accumulates program files not properly stored elsewhere. Note: You can also include PATHS to your other program directories. For instance, if you had data directories for dBASE and Crosstalk, as well as WordPerfect, your PATH might look like:

   PATH=C:\;C:\DOS;C:\DBASE;C:\XTALK;C:\WP50(Enter)

(or whatever names you chose for the directories). The key point to remember is that EACH DIRECTORY MUST SHOW THE

DRIVE, FOLLOWED BY A COLON, A BACKSLASH, THE FULL
DIRECTORY NAME, AND A SEMICOLON. The last directory in
the path should not be followed by a semi-colon.

To exit the insert mode and complete the editing, press and hold
the (Ctrl) key and simultaneously press the (Break) key. The
EDLIN asterisk prompt will reappear.

8. Check by listing the file again with the List command used in step
3. If it's incorrect, repeat step 7. If it's correct, enter the command
E for Exit to save the new AUTOEXEC.BAT to disk and exit the
EDLIN editor.

9. Activate the new PATH command by typing:

    AUTOEXEC (Enter)

Now proceed to the next section—you're ready to add or modify
your CONFIG.SYS file, if necessary. Go to page 18 for instructions.

Creating an AUTOEXEC.BAT file

If you do not currently have an AUTOEXEC.BAT file, you should
create one that includes the PATH command as well as certain start
up commands such as PROMPT, DATE, and TIME. If you are using
a multifunction board that contains a clock, you'll probably want
to include the name of the clock setup program provided with your
multifunction board, so your computer will correctly date stamp
files as it creates them. Check the manual for your multifunction
board to obtain the name of the clock setup program.

Use the following steps to create an AUTOEXEC.BAT from scratch.

1. Make sure that the root directory is the current directory by
entering the command:

    **CD ** (Enter)

Then create the file by typing:

    COPY CON: AUTOEXEC.BAT (Enter)

    PATH C:\\;C:\\DOS;C:\\WP50   (add any other directo-
    ries, separated by a semi-
    colon). (Enter)

    PROMPT PG (Enter)

Name of clock program (Enter) [Only use if appropriate.]

DATE (Enter)   [Only if you don't have a clock program.]

TIME (Enter)   [Only if you don't have a clock program.]

2. To complete the AUTOEXEC.BAT file, press the (F6) key. ^Z appears on the screen. Now press (Enter). The screen will display notes:

   `1 file copied`

   indicating that the batch file was created.

3. Simply creating or changing the file doesn't affect the current session. You must run the new AUTOEXEC.BAT program. Type:

   AUTOEXEC (Enter)

   to execute the program and establish the new PATH. Now, each time you start your computer, the PATH is properly set. (As a bonus, the PROMPT PG command shows the name of your current directory as part of the DOS prompt, so you'll never be lost in your hard disk. If you don't have a clock, enter the date and time when prompted.)

   You're now ready to complete the final step before selecting your printer. This involves creating or modifying your CONFIG.SYS file, if necessary, as described below.

Step #3: Editing or creating a CONFIG.SYS File

In addition to the AUTOEXEC.BAT file, you must also have a CONFIG.SYS file. This file tells the computer how to allocate its memory resources to various functions. To run WordPerfect 5.0, your CONFIG.SYS file must contain the command FILES=20 (or a greater number).

If you have used the auto-installation routine described above, WordPerfect automatically created or modified your CONFIG.SYS file to include the Files=20 command. If so, skip the rest of this section and go on to the final step, installing a printer.

If you chose a manual installation, and already have an CONFIG.SYS file, check it to see if it has a Files=20 (or greater) line. If not, use the DOS text editor, EDLIN, to modify it. You might also have to create a CONFIG.SYS from scratch. This simple task takes only a few minutes. Instructions for all three situations are discussed below. First things first, though—let's find out if you do have a CONFIG.SYS file. Start up your computer and enter the command:

CD \ (Enter)

to make sure you're in the root directory. Then instruct the computer to list the CONFIG.SYS file on the screen with the command:

TYPE CONFIG.SYS (Enter)

If you already have an CONFIG.SYS file, it's contents are shown on the screen, as shown in the example in Figure 1.4.

If one of the lines listed in your CONFIG.SYS file is:

Files=20 (or some number above 20)

you can skip this section, and proceed to the printer installation section on page 27. If there is no such line listing, or "Files=" is present, but the number is less than 20, you must edit it. Proceed to page 20. If you receive the message:

File not found

you either mistyped CONFIG.SYS (try again), or the file doesn't exist. In that case, go to page 22 for instructions on creating a

```
C:\>EDLIN CONFIG.SYS
End of input file
*1
        1:*DEVICE = EMM.SYS AT D000 Z58
        2: lastdrive=n
        3: buffers = 30
        4: files  = 20
        5: fcbs=16,8
        6: device = msmouse.sys /c1
        7: DEVICE = \EXDSKBIO.DRV
        8: DEVICE = \DRIVER.SYS /D:2 /T:80 /S:9 /H:2 /C
        9: DEVICE=C:\QMSJS\JETSCRPT.SYS  -P1  -I1  -LZ
*_
```

Figure 1.4 *Sample CONFIG.SYS Listing*

CONFIG.SYS file.

Editing an existing CONFIG.SYS file

1. Before you start to edit the CONFIG.SYS file, be sure to make a backup copy of the current version by copying the file to a new name with the command:

   COPY CONFIG.SYS CONFIG.ARC (Enter)

   To start the EDLIN editor, enter the command:

   EDLIN CONFIG.SYS (Enter)

   If you get the error message:

   Bad command or file name

   you do not have the EDLIN.COM file available. Place your original DOS disk in the A: drive and enter the command:

   A:EDLIN CONFIG.SYS (Enter)

2. The words:

   End of input file

   appear on the screen. Underneath the message you will be presented with the EDLIN prompt, a single asterisk (*).

```
C:\>COPY CONFIG.SYS CONFIG.ARC
        1 File(s) copied

C:\>EDLIN CONFIG.SYS
End of input file
*_
```

Figure 1.5 *EDLIN Prompt*

3. At the asterisk prompt enter the command L , which stands for List the contents of the file being edited. The screen then displays the contents of your CONFIG.SYS file, with a number before each line. If you don't have a "Files=" command, continue with step 3, but skip step 4. If you do have a "Files=" command, but it's less than 20, go directly to step 4.

To add the Files=20 line, type the command

    i1 (Enter).

You are presented with a blank line numbered 1. Type:

    FILES=20 (Enter)

The computer then displays line 2. To end the editing session, simultaneously press the (Ctrl)+(Break) keys and you are presented again with the EDLIN asterisk prompt. Save the new CONFIG.SYS by entering the command E for Exit.

4. If your CONFIG.SYS file already contains the line "Files=", but the number following the (=) sign is less than 20, you need to increase it. Enter the number preceding the "Files=" line and press (Enter). EDLIN repeats the line number underneath the display, followed by an asterisk and the cursor. By pressing the (F3) key, the text of the selected line will be copied to the blank line where the cursor is positioned. The cursor will move to the end of the line, as illustrated in Figure 1.6.

Use the (BackSpace) key to erase the current number, enter 20 and press (Enter). The EDLIN asterisk prompt reappears. To save the new CONFIG.SYS, enter the command E for Exit.

5. Before you continue, you must reboot your system to activate the CONFIG.SYS file. Make sure your DOS disk is no longer in your A drive if you put it there to use EDLIN. Now simultaneously press the (Ctrl) and (Alt) keys, then, holding them down, press the (Del) key. Your system will restart, taking instructions from the modified CONFIG.SYS file.

Now turn to pages 25 and 27, for instructions in starting the program and installing your printer. You're almost done!

```
C:\>edlin config.sys
End of input file
*1
        1:*DEVICE = EMM.SYS AT D000 258
        2: buffers = 30
        3: files   = 15
*3
        3:*files   = 15
        3:*files   = 20
*e

C:\>_
```

Figure 1.6 *Editing "Files = 20" Command*

Creating a new CONFIG.SYS file

If you do not currently have a CONFIG.SYS file, you must create one. While you're at it, even though it's not required by WordPerfect 5.0, you should also create a BUFFERS=15 command to allocate more memory to the disk Input/Output buffers. It is easiest to create the new CONFIG.SYS file using the COPY CON command, as follows:

1. Make sure that you are located in the root directory by entering the command:

    CD \ (Enter)

    Then type:

    COPY CON: CONFIG.SYS (Enter)

    FILES=20 (Enter)

    BUFFERS=15 (Enter)

2. To complete the CONFIG.SYS file, press the (F6) key. ^Z appears on the screen. Now press (Enter). The screen will display:

    1 file copied

indicating that the batch file was created.

3. Before you continue to the final step, installing your printer (page 27), you must reboot your system to activate the new CONFIG.SYS file. Make sure your DOS disk is no longer in your A drive if you put it there to use EDLIN. Now simultaneously press the (Ctrl) and (Alt) keys, then, holding them down, press the (Del) key. Your system will restart, taking instructions from the modified CONFIG.SYS file.

FLOPPY DISK INSTALLATION

While we strongly recommend the use of a hard disk for WordPerfect 5.0, it is possible to run it on a floppy disk-based system. Your system needs at least two floppy disk drives, or you will be constantly swapping floppy disks. WordPerfect provides no automated installation routine for floppy disk-based systems, so you will have to do all the work yourself.

Preparing the Disks

The process for installing the system on floppy disk is actually very easy, despite the daunting number of disks. The first step is to format one blank disk for each of the original WordPerfect disks, except the Printer disks. Label each of the new disks corresponding to one of the original WordPerfect disks.

The new disk labeled WordPerfect 1 (or WordPerfect 1 / WordPerfect 2 if you are using 3 1/2" disks) must have the DOS system files transferred to it. This is easily accomplished by placing the new disk in drive A and entering the command:

FORMAT A: /S (Enter)

The remaining blank disks can be formatted with the command:

FORMAT A: (Enter)

These new disks will become your *working* disks. The disks provided by WordPerfect will be referred to as the *original* disks.

You must now create a CONFIG.SYS file on the working copy of the WordPerfect 1 (or WordPerfect 1 / WordPerfect 2) disk that you just formatted. Place the working copy into Drive B: and your regular DOS system disk in Drive A:. Check the CONFIG.SYS file on your system disk for the presence of the command FILES=20. To do this enter the command:

TYPE A:CONFIG.SYS (Enter)

If the error message "File Not Found" appears or the listing does not contain the FILES=20 command or the numerical value is less than 20, you must follow procedure A below; otherwise skip to procedure B.

Procedure A

Type:

COPY A:CONFIG.SYS+CON B:CONFIG.SYS (Enter)

The system responds with the prompt **CON**. Type:

FILES=20 (Enter)

Press (F6) and the system will respond with ^Z. Press (Enter) and the system will respond with:

`1 File Copied`

If you want to copy the new CONFIG.SYS file back to your system disk, you can do so by entering the command:

COPY B:CONFIG.SYS A: (Enter)

You are now ready to begin copying the WordPerfect files to your new working disk.

Procedure B

Enter the command:

COPY A:CONFIG.SYS B: (Enter)

You are now ready to begin copying the WordPerfect files to your new working disk.

Copying the Files

Place the original WordPerfect 1 in drive A: (if you are using 3 1/2 inch floppy disks, it is marked WordPerfect 1 / WordPerfect 2) and the working disk in drive B: (it may already be there). Enter the command:

COPY A:WP.EXE B: (Enter)

The WordPerfect 1 disk is now complete. Place the next pair from the remaining disks into the drives, with the original in drive A: and the working disk in drive B:. Enter the command:

COPY A:*.* B: (Enter)

Repeat this copying process for each of the remaining disk pairs. This concludes the floppy disk installation procedure.

STARTING WORDPERFECT

Hard Disk System

Since you created a PATH to the WordPerfect program directory as part of the installation procedure, you can start WordPerfect from any subdirectory simply by typing:

WP (Enter)

at the DOS prompt. As we explained earlier, you should set up a separate directory for your WordPerfect data, either as a subdirectory of the WP50 directory or as a separate directory off the root directory. To create a separate directory called WP50DATA for your documents, type:

CD \ (Enter)

to ensure that the root directory is the current directory. Then type:

MD \WP50DATA (Enter)

In either case, you can start WordPerfect by first changing the default directory to your data directory with a command like:

CD \WP50DATA (Enter)

Be sure to substitute the name of your data directory. Finally you can start WordPerfect with the command:

WP (Enter)

You are now ready to proceed to the printer selection process below.

HINT: If you plan to keep all your documents in the directory called WP50DATA (or any other of your choosing), create a batch file to facilitate switching directories and starting WordPerfect (A batch file executes a sequence of steps with just one command from the keyboard.) Here's how:

1. Type:

> **CD**
>
> **COPY CON:WP.BAT** (Enter)
> **CD\WP50DATA** [or whatever name you gave your data directory] (Enter)
>
> **WP** (Enter)
>
> **CD ** (Enter)

2. Press (F6) and the computer displays:

> **^Z**
>
> Press (Enter) and the computer notes:

> **1 file copied**

3. The next time you enter WP, the computer makes your data directory the current directory and calls up WordPerfect. Since the system is PATHed to the directory containing the WordPerfect program files, it will have no trouble finding the necessary startup files. Once WordPerfect is loaded, your data files are immediately available, without having to change directories. When you exit WordPerfect, the batch file returns you to the root directory.

Floppy Disk System

Place the working copy of the WordPerfect 1 (or WordPerfect 1 / WordPerfect 2) disk in drive A: and one of the original Printer disks in drive B:. The printer disk is required for the initial printer installation described below and is not necessary for subsequent operation. In general, you insert your data disk in drive B:. Enter the command:

B: (Enter)

to change the default drive to the B: drive. Then start WordPerfect with the command:

A:WP (Enter)

Replace the WordPerfect 1 disk with the WordPerfect 2 disk when instructed to do so by the system. If you are using a 3 1/2" disk-based system, both sets of files are contained on the single disk and you do not need to change disks. You are now ready to proceed to the initial printer selection process below.

INSTALLING A PRINTER

Before you can create any hard copy with WordPerfect, you must select your initial printer even if you do not have one connected to your computer at this time. You can change this selection later, but you must select something at this time. The process for selecting printers is simple. The following process is "minimal" printer installation. If you have a LaserJet Series II with font cartridges and/or soft fonts, turn to Appendix B for a thorough discussion of installing the printer. See Appendix C for an explanation of how to change fonts.

1. Press and hold the (Shift) key and press the (F7) key.

2. Type:

S

to choose Select Printer.

3. Type:

A

to select Additional Printers. If you have copied all the printer disks to your hard disk, you will be presented with a list of the available printers. If you are using a floppy disk-based system or you did not copy all the printer disks to your hard disk (there's really no need to), you are presented with the message:

`Printer Files Not Found`

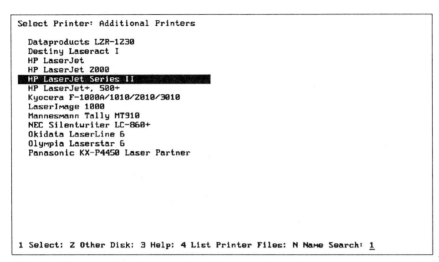

Figure 1.7 *List of Printers from Disk 1*

and you must place the Printer 1 disk in your A: or B: drive. Type **O** to select Other Disk, and enter the name of the drive (A: or B:) into which you placed the Printer 1 disk. You will now be presented with the list of printers, partially shown in Figure 1.7.

4. Press the (Down Cursor) key until your selected printer's name is highlighted. If you cannot find your printer, enter **O** for Other Disk, insert the Printer 2 disk in drive A: or B: and enter the drive name again as described above. Again, press the (Down Cursor) key until your selected printer's name is highlighted. If you still can't find the name of your printer, repeat the above procedure for the remaining printer disks. If you still can't find your printer, call WordPerfect Corp for assistance.

5. When you have highlighted the name of your printer, press the (Enter) key to select the printer. WordPerfect will display the message "Printer file name" followed by the default printer file name. You can press (Enter) to accept the default file name or enter a new name of your own choosing. WordPerfect will copy the necessary printer files from the Printer disk to either your hard disk

or the WordPerfect 2 disk. After copying the files, WordPerfect begins to update the available font file and shows a message containing useful information about your printer. It will also display a timer count down. When it is complete, press (F7) to exit to the Printer Setting Menu.

The Printer Setting Menu is described in detail in the printer installation chapter. At this time the only critical element is to ensure that the Port setting is correct. WordPerfect assumes that you want data sent from the computer to the printer via your main parallel port (called LPT1:). If this is not the case, enter **P** to select Port and select the correct port from the list at the bottom of the screen. If you select a serial port (COM1 through COM4), you also have to supply the communications data (baud rate, parity, etc, listed on your pre-installation checklist). Check your printer's manual if you are not certain what communication data it uses.

When you are satisfied with the printer settings, press (F7) to exit the Printer Setting Menu. The last step in installing a printer is to actually select it. WordPerfect allows you to define many printers as you have just done, so you can select from among them as required in the future. To select a printer, you must highlight the name of the desired printer using the up and down cursor keys and then enter **S** for Select. After you select a printer, WordPerfect will return you to the print menu. If you return to the selection menu, you will note that the printer you chose is now marked with an asterisk. Since you have only defined one printer at this time, the selection process seems sort of redundant, but it is still required. After selecting your printer, press (F7) to exit the Print Menu. You can now either continue with the Navigation section of this book or exit WordPerfect and take a break.

EXITING WORDPERFECT

When you are finished with a WordPerfect session, press (F7) to exit. The system asks you if you wish to save the current document. Enter Y, type a name and press (Enter) if you want to save it to disk, or N, if you want to abandon it. The system asks you if you are sure you want to exit WordPerfect. Enter Y to confirm your exiting, or N to return to a blank document.

CAUTION: You must exit WordPerfect by the proper method. Simply turning the computer off causes problems, and may cause you to lose data. If you do "crash out," the next time you run WordPerfect, the logo screen will ask:

Are there other copies of WordPerfect running (Y/N)

Type N, and WordPerfect will continue.

2

Navigating in
WordPerfect 5.0

THE SCREEN

Status Indicator

When you start WordPerfect, your screen displays the program's logo, which contains the program name and version number. The screen then appears to be blank. Why such a sparse screen, when many word processor screens are festooned with rulers and menus? WordPerfect's philosophy is that an uncluttered mind works better with an uncluttered screen. Rulers and menus are merely distractions, and the blank screen allows you to focus on your writing. Which is what word processing is all about.

Actually, the screen isn't *totally* blank—in the bottom right hand corner, you can see the Status Line, which gives you the following information (see Figure 2.1).

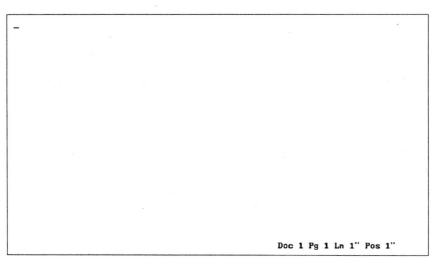

Figure 2.1 *WordPerfect Status Line*

Doc: WordPerfect allows you to work on two documents at once, and to cut and paste pieces from one into the other. This valuable feature is discussed in the next chapter. The **Doc** indicator tells you whether you are looking at Document 1 or 2.

Pg: WordPerfect "knows" how many lines of type to put on a page, depending on the type font and paper size you're using. Pages are separated by a dotted line, as shown in Figure 2.2. (The number following **Pg** indicates the assigned page number of the current page).

Ln: This indicator shows the vertical position of the cursor on the current page. For example, if you set up WordPerfect in inches, a "Ln 9.16" means that the cursor is 9.16 inches from the top of the page.

Pos: The **Pos**(ition) indicator shows the horizontal location of the cursor. A horizontal position of 5.1" means that the cursor is 5.1 inches from the left edge of the page.

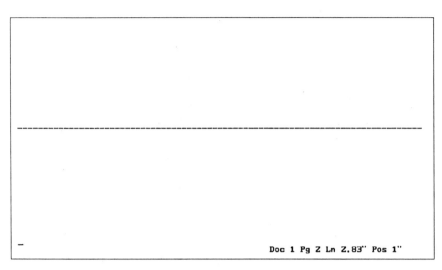

Figure 2.2 *Page break (dotted line)*

After you save a file (See Chapter 4), and then work on it later, the name of the file also appears in the left hand corner, as shown in Figure 2.3.

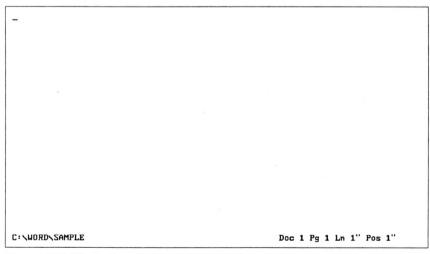

Figure 2.3 *File indicator*

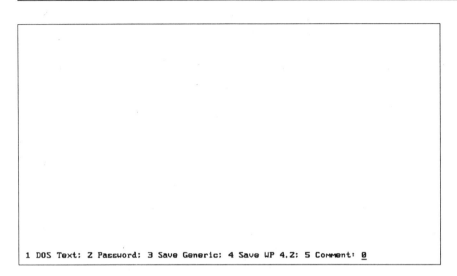

1 DOS Text: 2 Password: 3 Save Generic: 4 Save WP 4.2: 5 Comment: 0

Figure 2.4 *Bottom menu for Text In/Out Features* (Ctrl-F5)

When you select a feature that presents several options, such as Format-Page and Type Font-Select (See Chapters 3 and 5), WordPerfect displays two types of menus. (The menus are called up with the function keys (F1) through (F10), or through combinations of the function keys with the (Ctrl), (Shift), or (Alt) keys. These are discussed in Chapter 3). Menus allowing you to select from among five or fewer options are usually displayed along the bottom of the screen, underneath your text, as shown in Figure 2.4. Those with more than five options fill the whole screen, lying "on top" of your text, as shown in Figure 2.5. When WordPerfect does display a "full screen" menu, it only temporarily occupies the screen; as soon as you are finished with a menu, it clears and your text reappears.

Now that you know how WordPerfect displays information on the screen, let's consider how the program uses the keyboard to move the cursor around the page and through the document.

```
Format: Page

    1 - Center Page (top to bottom)     No

    2 - Force Odd/Even Page

    3 - Headers

    4 - Footers

    5 - Margins - Top               1"
               Bottom               1"

    6 - New Page Number             1
        (example: 3 or iii)

    7 - Page Numbering              No page numbering

    8 - Paper Size                  8.5" x 11"
            Type                    Standard

    9 - Suppress (this page only)

Selection: 0
```

Figure 2.5 *Sample of full page menu for Page Format* (Shift-F8)+2

THE KEYBOARD

The cursor is the blinking dash on the screen, probably in the upper left hand corner if you just started WordPerfect and haven't entered anything through the keyboard yet. The cursor shows where a character will be placed on the screen when you press a key on the keyboard. It automatically moves one space to the right each time you press a key. You can also move it along without entering any characters by pressing the (Space Bar)—the large key at the bottom of the keyboard.

Try typing several sentences. When you get to the right margin, the cursor jumps down to the left-most edge of the next line. This is called "wrapping," and eliminates the need to press a carriage return, as you would with an electric typewriter (or fling the metal bar on the carriage as you would with a manual typewriter). WordPerfect may or may not try to break up and hyphenate the last word on the line, depending on how you personalize the program (as explained in

Chapter 4). Notice that the cursor will move across space created by the (Space Bar) when you press the cursor keys. When you encounter "virgin territory," however, where the (SpaceBar) has never roamed, where you have never entered text, or placed a "hard (carriage) return" (by pressing the (Enter) key), the cursor will not move, no matter how many times you press the cursor key. This is because WordPerfect "sees" spaces as characters and hard returns as hidden codes, even though they appear on the screen as blanks. In Chapter 5, we show you how to display all the hidden codes WordPerfect actually stores as part of your document, which is a useful way of altering the screen.

Once you enter some text, you can use the cursor keys to move the cursor to any character appearing on the screen.Unfortunately, not all microcomputer keyboards position the keys in the same locations, so the placement of your cursor key is dependent on the type of computer you have. We use the standard IBM PC keyboard (there are three common IBM keyboards, and several that are less widely used) in the following discussion.

IBM PC/XT

On an IBM keyboard, the four cursor keys, which have arrows pointing up, down, left, and right, are located on the right side. The "classic" 88 key keyboard combines the cursor keys and the numeric keypad, which contains keys for the numbers zero through nine. Normally, the keys function in cursor movement mode; that is, when you press them, the cursor moves in the direction of the arrow along the characters you've typed, or the spaces you've created by pressing the (Enter) key (See below). If you press the (Num Lock) key, however, the numeric keypad is activated, so pressing 8 places an "8" on the screen, rather than moving the cursor up one space.

As a convenience, when (Num Lock) is activated, the **Pos** indicator on the status line blinks. Press the (Num Lock) key and see for yourself what happens. Press (Num Lock) again and control returns to the cursor keys.

IBM AT

The original IBM AT keyboard is identical to the "classic" PC/XT, with the exception of a green light that glows when Num Lock is activated. The **Pos** indicator still blinks when (Num Lock) is activated.

IBM Enhanced AT and PS/2

The "enhanced" AT-style keyboard, also standard with the PS/2 line, has an additional set of cursor keys independent of the numeric keypad. These always move the cursor, regardless of whether the (Num Lock) key is pressed. (Num Lock) also causes **Pos** to blink. Because the dedicated cursor keys are always available, IBM switched the action of the (Num Lock) on the PS/2 line so that it is automatically activated when the computer is turned on.

IBM PC Desktop and Laptop Compatibles

If you have an IBM PC compatible, check your manual for information regarding the use of the cursor and (Num Lock) keys. Laptops may also vary, depending on the keyboard layout.

Special Cursor Movements

As you've probably discovered by now, each time you press the cursor key, the cursor moves one character or space up, down, left, or right, depending on its position. If you hold the cursor key down, the cursor zooms along without stopping. This is not always the most efficient way to get the cursor to where you want it, and WordPerfect offers a number of interesting alternatives for moving the cursor by more than one space at a time. The following "express" cursor options are arranged by increasing size of the cursor movements, starting with cursor movements by words and ending with movements by document.

Move by Word

If you place the cursor anywhere within a word and press:

(Ctrl + Right Cursor)

the cursor jumps to the first character of next word. Press:

(Ctrl + Left Cursor)

and the cursor moves backwards to the first character of the previous word. If you hold down either the right or left cursor keys while also pressing (Ctrl), the cursor moves repeatedly word by word until you release the key or there are no more words in the document.

Move by Line

The (Home) key, located in the upper left corner of the numeric keypad, is a powerful way to navigate around the document (On the enhanced AT/PS/2 keyboards there's also a dedicated (Home) key located above the dedicated cursor keys.) Press:

(Home) + (Home) + (Left Cursor)

and the cursor moves to the beginning of the current line. Press:

(Home) + (Home) + (Right Cursor)

or

(End)

and the cursor moves to the end of the current line. (Note: The (End) key is located at the lower left hand corner of the numeric keypad.)

Move by Screen

Sometimes it is convenient to move by "screenfuls," 25 lines at a time. For example, when you're reading a document on screen, it is convenient to be able to read a screen, then display the next screen. Note: this is different from moving by document pages with (PgUp) and (PgDn) keys, which moves by printed pages, as described below. To move down one screen at a time, press:

(+) key

> ## or (Home) + (Down Cursor)

The (+) key is located next to the numeric keypad. Note that the plus sign accessed by pressing (shift) + (=) does not achieve the desired action.

To move back up a screen, press:

> **(-) key**
>
> or
>
> **(Home) + (Up Cursor)**

The minus key is located above the (+) key, next to the right of the numeric keypad.

Holding down the plus or minus keys repeatedly moves the screen until you release the key, or the cursor reaches the top of the document or the last screen with text.

Move by Page

To move down one page, press:

> **(PgDn)**

To move up one page, press:

> **(PgUp)**

On the classic PC/XT keyboard, the (PgDn) and (PgUp) keys are located on the numeric keypad, sharing space with the 3 and 9 keys, respectively. They are normally active unless (Num Lock) is pressed. On the enhanced AT/PS/2 keyboards, the (PgDn) and (PgUp) keys are dedicated and are located above the dedicated cursor keys. If you press and hold the (PgDn) or (PgUp) keys, the cursor moves down by pages until you reach the end of the document, or up by pages until you reach the beginning of the document.

Move by Document

To move to the very last character of a document, press:

> **(Home) + (Home) + (Down Cursor)**

To move to the very beginning of a document, press:

(Home) + (Home) + (Up Cursor)

These two cursor movements are very useful for traversing a large document. Perhaps you want to get a quick page count, or move to the end of the document to do some editing. The (Home) + (Home) + (Down Cursor) combination makes it a breeze. Alternately, if you're working on the ending of a document, and need to zip back up to the beginning of a document to check something, (Home) + (Home) + (Up Cursor) is like an express elevator.

At this point you should be familiar with the WordPerfect display, and know the primary cursor movements. The best way to get the keystrokes engrained is practice. So before going any farther, you might want to type several pages. Then experiment with all of the "express" options just described. Don't worry about making or correcting mistakes—we cover that in the next section, which explains how to use the various editing keys.

EDITING KEYS

As you enter or proofread your text, you'll undoubtedly want to make changes in characters, words, or sentences. WordPerfect uses several of the standard keyboard keys to make the task easy. These are described below. (Note that while WordPerfect provides many ways to do the same word processing tasks, it is not necessary to learn them all. Pick out the ones that are easiest for you to remember and use, and develop a repertoire of basic skills. The goal is to quickly develop familiarity with the smallest subset of features that will accomplish your task. As you need to learn new ones, you can easily pick them up and add them to your knowledge base.)

Deletion Keys

WordPerfect allows you to delete in a number of ways. Use the one most convenient for your text.

Delete by Character

Move the cursor underneath the character you want to delete. Press the (Del) key, (located below the numeric keypad) once and the character is deleted. Try it. If you hold the (Del) key down, all characters to the right are "sucked in." Eventually you could delete an entire page or even a 200 page document. But that would be highly inefficient and time consuming. As we'll see in Chapter 6, WordPerfect provides powerful functions for altering and deleting large blocks of text.

An alternative way of deleting characters is to use the (Backspace) key, which is marked with a heavy left arrow and located in the upper right hand corner of the keyboard, above the (Enter) key. Each time you press (Backspace), one character to the *left* of the cursor is deleted. As in the case of the (Del) key, if you repeatedly hold down the (Backspace) key, WordPerfect continually deletes characters until the cursor "bumps" up against the beginning of the document.

Delete by Word

WordPerfect allows you to delete by words as well as characters. Try this. Place the cursor anywhere in the word you wish to delete. Then press:

(Ctrl - Backspace)

Shizam! The word and the space following it are gone. If you place the cursor in the space before the word, however, WordPerfect deletes the word to the *left* of the cursor. If you hold down the (Ctrl-Backspace) key combination, WordPerfect continually deletes words to the right of the cursor until you release the keys or there are no more words left to delete. Note: WordPerfect defines a "word" as any contiguous string of characters or numbers, including hyphenated strings; any breaks in the string indicates that the word has ended.

Two alternate ways of deleting words are also available. To delete a word to the left of the cursor, place the cursor in THE SPACE JUST AFTER THE WORD and press and release

(Home)

then press and release:

(Backspace)

The alternative for deleting a word to the right of the cursor is to place the cursor UNDER THE FIRST LETTER OF THE WORD TO BE DELETED, press and release:

(Home)

then press and release:

(Del)

The word to the right of the cursor is deleted.

Delete to End of Line

To delete from the cursor position to the end of the line, press:

(Ctrl - End)

The text from the cursor to the end of the line is removed from the screen.

Delete by Page

To delete the remainder of a page below the cursor, press:

(Ctrl - PgDn)

Since this command has dangerous consequences, WordPerfect asks you to confirm your choice by asking:

`Delete remainder of page (Y/N) No`

If you enter N or press enter (to accept the default of No), WordPerfect cancels the command. If you enter Y for Yes, everything beneath the cursor on to the page break is deleted.

CAUTION: Delete remainder of page means delete from the current cursor position to the end of the *printed page*, which means that you might delete material not shown on the screen, because the screen only shows a portion of the printed page. For example, if you are displaying the first 25 lines of a 54 line page on the screen, and select Delete to end of page, you will delete all 54 lines, including the 29 lines that you can't see. Therefore use this option with extreme care.

Note: Even if you decide that you really didn't want to delete the page, all is not lost; WordPerfect has an undelete feature, described in the next chapter, which enables you to undo your last three deletions.

Inserting Characters

WordPerfect defaults to "insert mode." In other words, if you place the cursor in the middle of a word, then enter text, WordPerfect inserts whatever characters you type at the cursor location, spreading the text as necessary to accommodate them. You've probably discovered this already as you've experimented with the keyboard.

The alternative is "Typeover" mode, in which your keystrokes overwrite existing text. To switch into Typeover mode, press the (Ins) key. The word "Typeover" appears in the lower left hand corner of the screen to remind you of the current mode. To return to Insert mode, press the (Ins) key again. This dual action in which one key switches between two functions is called "toggling"; you "toggle" the key between the two modes.

You can use either Insert or Typeover as your predominate mode, although most people prefer Insert mode, because it's generally more efficient to insert text and then delete unwanted text. Besides, Typeover is sometimes hard to control—you might find yourself overwriting and recreating text. Nevertheless, the choice is yours.

At this point, stop and experiment with the various key movements described above. Again, when several commands achieve the same results, you don't have to learn them all. The goal is to quickly assemble a collection of usable skills that meet your needs. In the following chapter, you'll learn about the commands issued through the special function keys, which lie at the heart of WordPerfect's power.

3

The Function Keys: WordPerfect 5.0's Command Center

ABOUT THE FUNCTION KEYS

So far you've used the keyboard to move the cursor, enter text, and delete text. The real power behind WordPerfect, however, resides in the special function keys, (F1) through (F10). On "classic" PC/XT-style keyboards, the function keys are arranged in two columns located on the left side. On enhanced AT-style keyboards and PS/2 keyboards, the functions keys, also labeled F1 through F12, are arranged in a single row across the top. (F11) and (F12) duplicate certain functions of keys (F1) through (F10)—more on that later.

You probably noticed two different templates packaged along with your diskettes. The one with the cutout is designed for the classic keyboard, while the single strip (folded in half in the packaging) is for the enhanced AT-style keyboards.

As you can see from looking at the templates, each key has four functions, designated by red, green, blue, and black print. The significance of the colors is as follows:

RED means press and hold the (Ctrl) key, press the function key once, then release both keys.

GREEN means press and hold the (Shift) key, press the function key once, then release both keys.

BLUE means press and hold the (Alt) key, press the function key once, then release both keys.

BLACK means press the function key alone.

In this way, ten function keys yield 40 functions. To help you remember the color coding, WordPerfect supplies color decals in the plastic pouch that contains the keyboard templates. The decals have two color dots, which have been strategically placed so that they don't obstruct the name of the key. Place them as follows:

The *RED* dot on the (Ctrl) key(s)

The *GREEN* dot on both (Shift) keys

The *BLUE* dot on the (Alt) key(s).

In this chapter, the features of each function key are described. Some of them are revisited in Chapters 5 through 8, as they are critical to everyday document creation and editing. Others are dealt with only in this chapter, as they are self-explanatory. Finally, some of the functions are for advanced use only, and are briefly described in Appendix A.

The following pages have been set up like a reference manual, organized by function key. As a reminder, next to each feature the color appears in parentheses, with

(R) = RED

(G) = GREEN

(B) = BLUE

(Bl) = BLACK

A usage comment is also given for each function, indicating whether it is universally used or generally reserved for advanced operations.

Finally, this chapter is organized by the function keys, rather than the functions themselves. Appendix E provides a table based on the functions (e.g. *Center, Right Align,* etc), and should be used when you need to track down the keystrokes for a specific command.

Key

Functions	Executed by	Usage
1. Shell (R)	(Ctrl-F1)	Depends on personal style
2. Setup (G)	(Shift-F1)	Generally used once
3. Thesaurus (B)	(Alt-F1)	Depends on personal style
4. Cancel (Bl)	(F1) alone	Everyday

SHELL

The Shell command allows you to go out to DOS and execute simple commands without leaving WordPerfect. This can be extremely useful. Let's say that you are backing up to a floppy disk, and the disk becomes full. Instead of quitting your WordPerfect session, you can execute the *Shell* command and return to DOS, format a disk, then return to WordPerfect.

After you press (Ctrl-F1), the bottom of the screen displays a menu with two choices:

1 Go to DOS: 0

If you change your mind, press 0. If you want to continue, press 1 or G. (You can select a function from any WordPerfect menu either by pressing the number corresponding to the option, or by pressing the highlighted letter within the option name. Pressing 0 always exits you to the previous menu if one exists, and then back into your text). The screen then shows the DOS prompt. Above the prompt, as a reminder that you're still in WordPerfect, the screen displays:

Enter 'Exit' to return to WordPerfect.

As soon as you type "Exit" and press (Enter), you will return to WordPerfect *at the exact same place you left off.*

CAUTION: If you use the *Shell* command with some RAM-resident programs, or if you use the *Shell* command from WordPerfect, go to DOS, start another program, say 1-2-3 and use *it's* shell command,

your computer may become "confused" and not know which program to return to when you enter Exit at the DOS prompt. In that case,
you may have no choice but to bail out by pressing (Ctrl)+(Alt)+(Del).
This restarts the computer, but also causes you to lose whatever you
had been working on and hadn't yet saved to disk.

SETUP

The *Setup* command, which you generally use once, allows you to
personalize the program by choosing among other things, whether
the status line displays units in inches, WordPerfect characters, or
other measures; how fast the cursor moves; and whether or not your
documents are backed up automatically. Chapter 4 covers each *Setup*
option in detail.

THESAURUS

WordPerfect is shipped with an electronic *Thesaurus* containing more
than 100,000 words. You can invoke it at any time and it provides
synonyms for whatever word is at the cursor. Some people use the
Thesaurus constantly, while others have no need for it at all. Try it for
a while and see if it's useful for you. If not, delete it from your disk,
as it consumes 360,000 bytes that you may need for something else.
Use of the *Thesaurus* will be described in Chapter 9.

CANCEL

This function is used to cancel other commands. For example, if you
invoke the *Thesaurus*, or begin a search and replace operation(See F2
key), and then decide you don't want to do either, you can press the
(F1) key to cancel whatever operation is in process. Note: if you are
several layers down in a complex series of menus, you may have to
press the (F1) key more than once to return to the "surface."

Another aspect of *Cancel* is to undo a deletion. If you make a
deletion, whether it's a word or a 100 pages (in one fell swoop), you
can retrieve the text by pressing (F1). This highlights the deleted text,
and WordPerfect displays the following two options:

Undelete 1 **R**estore; **2** **P**revious deletion: **0**

Restore brings the most recently deleted text back into the document at the position of the cursor.

Previous deletion shows your next most recent deletion. If you select the option again by selecting option #2, WordPerfect shows your third most previous deletion. If the text you want was zapped four deletions ago, you're out of luck. Remember, WordPerfect considers all deletions between cursor movements as a single deletion. For example, pressing the (Del) key four times without otherwise moving the cursor counts as one deletion. In contrast, deleting a space, then moving the cursor to the next character and deleting it counts as two deletions because the cursor was moved. Therefore, even though there are three levels of undelete, as you zoom along in the course of your normal typing, fixing typos and closing spaces, you may quickly lose your three chances to undo a mistake.

 Key

Functions	Executed by	Usage
1. Spell (R)	(Ctrl-F2)	Everyday
2. (Backward) Search (G)	(Shift-F2)	Everyday
3. Replace (B)	(Alt-F2)	Everyday
4. (Forward) Search (Bl)	(F2) alone	Everyday

SPELL

WordPerfect's spell checker, which contains more than 100,000 words, is second to none. It is easily invoked to check a word, a page, or a whole document. *Spell* is covered in detail in Chapter 9.

(BACKWARD) SEARCH

You can *Search* through a document to find a specific word, number or phrase. This is extremely useful for finding a specific line or paragraph. The Backward *Search* allows you to search from the current cursor position back to the beginning of the document. Searching techniques are discussed extensively in Chapter 8.

REPLACE

Whereas the *Search* function enables you to locate a word or phrase, the *Replace* function allows you to find a word or phrase, and replace it with another. For instance, let's say that you wrote a report and used the word "individuals" throughout. Later, you decided to soften the language and wanted to use "people" instead. The *Replace* function locates each instance of "individuals" and replaces it with "people." This is discussed further in Chapter 8

FORWARD SEARCH

This command allows you to search for a word, number, or phrase, starting from the current cursor location and moving to the end of the document. Its use is also discussed in Chapter 8.

 **Key**

Functions	Executed by	Usage
1. Screen (R)	(Ctrl-F3)	Occasional
2. Switch (G)	(Shift-F3)	Common
3. Reveal Codes (B)	(Alt-F3)	Everyday
4. Help (Bl)	(F3) alone	Depends on personal style

SCREEN

The screen function offers three options:

        0 Rewrite; 1 **W**indow **2 L**ine Draw: **0**

Rewrite is used if you have turned off the auto-rewrite feature (See Chapter 4, Personalizing WordPerfect). For purposes of speed, some people prefer *not* to have WordPerfect automatically reformat text as they indent, change margins, etc. If automatic screen rewrite is turned off, the screen reformats only as you scroll down the page. In some instances, when auto-rewrite has been turned off, the screen gets confusing, and it is necessary to use the *Rewrite* option to put everything into its proper format. WordPerfect automatically reformats (rewrites) the text before saving or printing.

Window allows you to see two documents at the same time on the screen, and switch back and forth between them using the *Switch* function, see below. This is useful when you need to compare two documents (see Figure 3.1), or when you plan to cut pieces of one document and paste them into the other.

Line draw enables you to draw lines and boxes of various widths, for incorporation into your document (see Figure 3.2). You can print shapes created with *Line draw* if your printer has the necessary line drawing capabilities. On many printers, the line draw characters are considered a special font and may have to be added to the printer with an optional cartridge or soft font (see Appendix C).

SWITCH

The *Switch* function is a close relative of the *Window* feature described above. As mentioned, WordPerfect allows you to create two documents at once, and you can cut a section from one document and paste it into the other. Whereas the *Window* feature shows a portion of both documents on the same screen, *Switch* allows you to create two documents, each with its own full screen. You can only see one document at a time unless you have opened a window as described above. *Switch* allows you change between the two documents. When you are looking at Document #1, pressing *Switch* once flips you into Document #2; pressing it again returns you to Document #1. The

```
1. Backup

     Wordperfect 5.0 can automatically back up your files as you

go along, so that in the event of hardware problem or power-outage

you won't lose any data.  This is called a Timed Backup.  Another

backup option assigns a new file name each time you save it, so
C:\WP1ZZ\CH4-B.1ZZ                              Doc 1 Pg 3 Ln 1" Pos 1"
```
```
     and it is necessary to use the Rewrite option to put everything

     into its proper format.


     Window allows you to see two documents at the same time on the

     screen, and switch back and forth between them, as shown in

     Figure 3.1.  This can be very useful when you need to compare
C:\WP1ZZ\CH3-B.1ZZ                              Doc 2 Pg 10 Ln 8.5" Pos 1.5"
```

Figure 3.1 *Example of window for two documents*

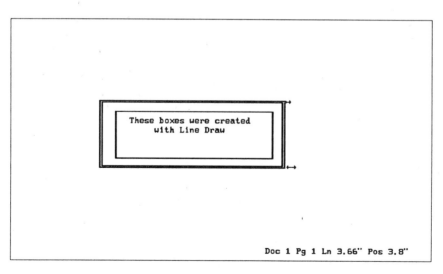

Figure 3.2 *Example of Line Draw* (Ctrl-F3)

number after **Doc** on the status line tells you which of the two documents you are currently viewing.

REVEAL CODES

This is one of the most powerful—and for some, the most intimidating—features of WordPerfect. It shows you what formatting codes WordPerfect stores in your document when you use bold, or underline, or format your text in any way. Whereas your screen shows only the effect of applying bolding, underlining, and other commands, WordPerfect is actually inserting complex codes that, if shown on the screen, would make your text illegible. Figure 3.3 shows the difference between what you see and what WordPerfect sees. The ability to view hidden codes is extremely important for editing formatted text; in fact, in some cases it's the only way to untangle the formatting commands you've issued. Chapter 8 explains how to use *Reveal Codes* as an editing tool.

HELP

WordPerfect provides help screens covering most functions. You can access the desired information three ways after pressing (F3) alone. First, you can press any alphabetic character key, and WordPerfect displays a list of features and corresponding keys that begin with that letter. For example, pressing (F3), then the "d" key, displays a list of features beginning with Date/Time (see Figure 3.4). When the listing continues on a second page, the bottom of the screen instructs you to type 1 to continue (see Figure 3.4).

The second way to display a help screen is to press (F3), then press the function key or key combination for which you desire information. For example, pressing (F3), then pressing (Alt-F3), for reveal codes, displays the help screen shown in Figure 3.5.

Sometimes, the help screen offers a number of options. For example, when you seek help with the Format function (Shift-F8), WordPerfect offers you a number of choices, as shown in Figure 3.6. If you choose, say option 1, for text line formatting options, still another level of choices is presented (see Figure 3.7). The next screen offers you an even finer breakdown of choices. Finally a help screen is presented for each item on the list. Figure 3.8 shows the help screen

```
 _

3. REVEAL CODES

This is one of the most powerful--and for some, the most

intimidating--features of WordPerfect.  It shows you what printer

codes WordPerfect stores in your document when you use bold, or

underline, or format your text in any way.  Whereas your screen
C:\WP1ZZ\CH3-B.1ZZ                              Doc Z Pg 1Z Ln 1.33" Pos 1"
[                                                                         ]
as indicated by the number after "[BOLD]Doc." [bold]In Chapter 6, you'll[SPg]
learn about techniques for using the [UND]Switch[und] feature.[HRt]
[BOLD][HRt]
3. REVEAL CODES [bold] [BOLD][HRt]
[bold]This is one of the most powerful[-][-]and for some, the most[SRt]
intimidating[-][-]features of WordPerfect.  It shows you what printer[SRt]
codes WordPerfect stores in your document when you use bold, or[SRt]
underline, or format your text in any way.  Whereas your screen[SRt]
shows only the effect of applying bolding, underlining, and other[SRt]
commands. WordPerfect is actually inserting complex codes that[SRt]

Press Reveal Codes to restore screen
```

Figure 3.3 *Example of Reveal Codes* (Alt-F3)

```
Key            Feature                              Key Name

Shft-F5        Date/Time - Insert or Define         Date/Outline
Ctrl-F8        Double Underline Text                Font,Z
Shft-F8        Decimal/Align Character              Format,4
Shft-F8        Decimal Tabs, Define                 Format,1
F5             Default Directory                    List Files
Ctrl-F10       Define Macros                        Macro Define
Shft-F5        Define Paragraph/Outline Numbering   Date/Outline,6
Shft-F7        Define Printer                       Print,S
Alt -F5        Define ToC,Lists,ToA,Index           Mark Text,5
F5             Delete File                          List Files
Backspace      Delete Left                          Backspace
Del            Delete Right                         Del
Ctrl-End       Delete to End of Line                EOL
Ctrl-PgDn      Delete to End of Page                EOP
Home Bk/Del    Delete to Word Boundary              Home Bksp/Del
Ctrl-F4        Delete Text                          Move
Ctrl-Backsp    Delete Word                          Delete Word
Ctrl-V         Diacriticals                         Compose
Ctrl-FZ        Dictionary                           Spell
Ctrl-V         Digraphs                             Compose

                Type 1 for more help: 0
```

Figure 3.4 *Help screen, invoked by press* (F3) *and letter "d"*

```
Reveal Codes

    Divides the screen and shows normal text on top and text with hidden
    codes on the bottom.  While in Reveal Codes you can edit or use any of
    WordPerfect's features.  Your editing is aided by being able to see the
    codes which affect formatting, etc.

    Codes are bolded so they can be distinguished from text.  Some codes show
    more information when the cursor is positioned directly on the code.

    To exit the Reveal Codes screen, press Reveal Codes._
```

Figure 3.5 *Reveal Codes help invoked by pressing* (F3) *then* (Alt-F3)

for one of the final choices, *Hyphenation.*

Finally, to display a copy of the function key template, press (F3) twice (see Figure 3.9).

To exit the help program, press (Enter) or the (Spacebar).

```
Format

    Contains features which change the current document's format.  Options on
    the Line, Page and Other menus change the setting from the cursor
    position forward.  Document Format options change a setting for the
    entire document.  To change the default settings permanently, use the
    Setup key.

    1 - Line

    2 - Page

    3 - Document

    4 - Other


            Type a menu option for more help: 0
```

Figure 3.6 *Help screen with options for additional help screens*

```
Format: Line

    These options should be selected at the first of the line, before any
    characters.

    1 - Hyphenation

    2 - Hyphenation Zone

    3 - Justification

    4 - Line Height

    5 - Line Numbering

    6 - Line Spacing

    7 - Margins - Left and Right

    8 - Tab Set

    9 - Widow/Orphan Protection

                    Type a menu option for more help: 0
```

Figure 3.7 *Sub-options for help screen selection*

```
Hyphenation

    Improves the visual appearance of the printed page by keeping the right
    margin more evenly aligned.

    Off:  WordPerfect is preset with Hyphenation Off.

    Manual:  Allows you to confirm the hyphenation of each word.  Position the
        hyphen with the arrow keys.  If you do not want to hyphenate the
        word, press Cancel.

    Auto:  WordPerfect hyphenates words for you.  If it cannot hyphenate
        according to its rules, it places you in manual hyphenation for that
        word only.

Note:  To turn off hyphenation during spell-checking or any scrolling command,
    press Exit when the first hyphenation message appears._
```

Figure 3.8 *Help screen for option selected from sub option list*

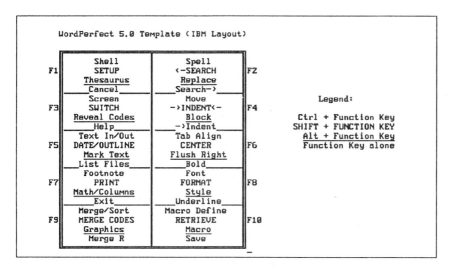

Figure 3.9 *Help screen for function key layout, IBM PC/XT keyboard*

 **Key**

Functions	Executed by	Usage
1. Move (R)	(Ctrl-F4)	Everyday
2. Indent (L/R) (G)	(Shift-F4)	Everyday
3. Block (B)	(Alt-F4)	Everyday
4. Indent (Bl)	(F4) alone	Everyday

MOVE

The Move feature can save you a great deal of time moving around and deleting sentences, paragraphs, and pages. When you select *Move*, you are offered four options:

Move **1** Sentence **2** Paragraph **3** Page **4** Retrieve: **0**

The first three specify how much text you want to manipulate. The fourth, *Retrieve*, retrieves a previously cut block of text. Once you identify the quantity of text to be manipulated, a second menu appears offering you the choices of

    1 **M**ove 2 **C**opy 3 **D**elete 4 **A**ppend: **0**

Option #1 allows you to quickly move a sentence, paragraph, page, or previously blocked text (see below under *Block*) to another location, while option 2 allows you to copy a sentence, paragraph, or page, or previously blocked text to another location, without altering the original text. Option 3 deletes a sentence, paragraph, or page. The quantity of text is determined by the location of the cursor. WordPerfect defines:

a sentence as continuous text up to the next terminal punctuation mark (period, exclamation mark, or question mark), plus the space following the mark.

a paragraph as continuous text up to the next hard (carriage) return.

a page as continuous text up the next page break.

The fourth option in the series, *Append* allows you to attach a sentence, paragraph, page, or previously blocked text to the end of a file on disk. All of the functions associated with the move key are discussed in Chapter 8, which covers editing text.

INDENT (L/R)

This function creates an equal indent from the left and right margins. The left margin is indented to wherever the next tab has been set, and the right margin is automatically moved in toward the left by an equal amount. Text is indented until you press (Enter), which issues a hard (carriage) return. *Indent* is useful for quotations and other text that needs to be set off from the rest of the text and centered. If you insert an indent command in front of an existing paragraph, all text up to the next hard (carriage) return will be indented.

BLOCK

The *Block* function is one of the most important power tools that WordPerfect provides. It enables you treat a block of text as if it were a single character. For example, you can "block off" a whole paragraph and press the bold key, in which case the entire paragraph is made bold. The same holds for underline. You can also delete a block of text, move a block of text and place it elsewhere (i.e., cut and paste), or perform special functions, such as upper- or lowercase everything within the block.

To create a block, simply put the cursor on the first character to be included (a block can be one character or hundreds of pages), press (Alt-F4), and then move the cursor over or down to where you want the block to end. The text in the block will be highlighted. Then press a function key to deal with the contents of the block *en masse*. This important WordPerfect capability is discussed in Chapter 8.

INDENT

Unlike the *Indent (L/R)*, which "squeezes" the text from both the left and right margins, this *Indent* causes the text to left align at the next tab and remain there until you press (Enter), which inserts a hard return. If you edit the text or insert additional text in an indented paragraph, WordPerfect automatically re-wraps the text so that it conforms to the indented margin. This feature is extremely useful for creating indented paragraphs without having to reset the left margin. Again, if you insert the indent command in front of an existing paragraph, the text will be indented up to the next hard (carriage) return.

 **Key**

Functions	Executed by	Usage
1. Text In/Out (R)	(Ctrl-F5)	Depends on personal needs
2. Date/Outline (G)	(Shift-F5)	Depends on personal needs
3. Mark Text (B)	(Alt-F5)	Advanced
4. List Files (Bl)	(F5) alone	Everyday

TEXT IN/OUT

This function contains a potpourri of features, some of which seem to be odd bedfellows. You may have frequent use for some of the features, and will probably never touch the others.

When you press (Ctrl) - (F5), the following menu is displayed.

1 DOS **T**ext; **2 P**assword; **3** Save **G**eneric; **4** Save **W**P 4.2; **5 C**omment:**0**

DOS Text refers to various ways of saving a file in ASCII format, so programs other than WordPerfect can read it. When you save in ASCII format, you lose all the WordPerfect formatting, such as bold, underline, tabs, etc. *DOS Text* also presents a number of options for retrieving an ASCII file. Since these are beyond the scope of this book, check your WordPerfect reference manual should you have a need to use them.

Password allows you to "encrypt" a document so no one can view, retrieve, or print it without entering the correct password. When you select the password option, you will be presented with the following menu:

Password 1 Add/Change; **2 R**emove: **0**

Add/Change appends a password to the current document, or changes the password in a current document. The password becomes part of the document, although no one can see it. When you select this option, WordPerfect prompts you to:

Enter Password:

For security purposes, your keystrokes are not be echoed back to the screen, so be careful. As a caution, WordPerfect asks you to re-enter the password to confirm your choice. If the password is different from your original input, WordPerfect displays:

ERROR: incorrect password

and asks you to begin again and enter the password. The password is then added to the document on screen. You must still save it to a file on disk before password protection becomes effective.

When you go to retrieve a file with a password (See below, List Files and the F10 key), WordPerfect will prompt you to:

Enter Password

If you enter the wrong password, it displays the message:

ERROR: File is locked

and you have to start the retrieval process again.

CAUTION: If you forget a password, there is no way to gain access to the file. Use passwords that mean something to you.

Remove is the only way you can get a password out of a document's file structure. To select *Remove*, however, you must have access to the file; you can't use the option unless the file has been "unlocked" and is on the screen. Again, you must resave the unlocked file to disk, overwriting the locked version, to deactivate the password.

Save Generic stores your file without WordPerfect codes while maintaining the format. For instance, centered text remains centered, but with spaces inserted instead of WordPerfect's centering codes. This may be useful if you are transferring WordPerfect files to another word processing program.

Save WP 4.2 allows you to save your WordPerfect 5.0 files in WordPerfect 4.2 format. This will continue to be a valuable feature until the rest of the world makes the great leap onto the cutting edge of word processor technology. Remember, you can always read a 4.2 file with Version 5.0, but Version 4.2 cannot read a Version 5.0 file. Note: when you save a Version 5.0 in Version 4.2 format, most of the new 5.0 features are converted to their Version 4.2 equivalent; however, some cannot be converted and will be lost.

Comment is a means of putting notes to yourself or others within a document. The notes, offset in a double rule, can be seen on the screen, but won't print, unless you convert them to text. A comment can be up to 600 characters (approximately 150 words). The rectangle will automatically adjust itself to the size of the comment. You can place comments anywhere in the document, and you can create as many as you like.

Comments can be extremely valuable when more than one person is working on a document, and you wish to pass along

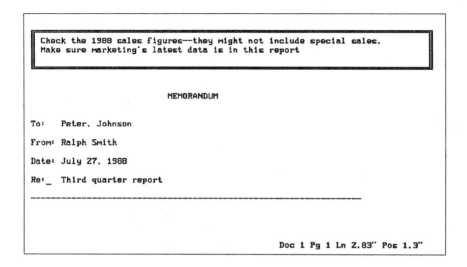

Figure 3.10 *Sample comment screen*

messages or remind someone that a certain task needs to be done. For
example, you might want to remind yourself or someone to "Check
the 1988 sales figures—they might not include special sales..." You
can also use the comment box as a header to describe the draft number
or other archival aspects of a draft. Figure 3.10 shows how a comment
appears in a document.

When you select *Comment,* the following options are displayed:

Comment: 1 Create; **2 E**dit; **3** Convert to **T**ext: **0**

Create displays a double rule box into which you can type your
comment. Press (F7) when you are done entering your comment.

Edit enables you to alter the contents of a comment. If you have
more than one comment in your document, the edit function selects
the comment immediately **ABOVE** the cursor. When you are finished
editing, press (F7).

Convert to text changes the comment text to document text. Once
a comment is converted to text, it appears where the upper left hand
corner of the comment box was originally located. Regular text can
be converted to a comment by using the following procedure:

1. Block the text to be converted by placing the cursor at the beginning of the text. Pressing (Alt-F3) and then highlight the desired block with the cursor keys.

2. Press *Text In/Out* (Ctrl-F5) and WordPerfect will prompt you with:

> **Create a comment? (Y/N) No**

3. Type Y and the text will be converted to a comment.

DATE/OUTLINE

Like the *Text In/Out* function, the *Date/Outline* function contains a number of functions that bear little relationship to each other. When you press (Shift-F5), you are presented with the following menu:

1. Date **T**ext; **2** Date **C**ode; **3** Date **F**ormat; **4** **O**utline; **5** **P**araNum: **6** **D**efine: 0

Date Text inserts the current date (and time, if desired). If your system clock (which remembers the date) is correct, or if you don't have a clock but you entered today's date correctly when you started your computer, the correct date appears at the cursor. Note that the *Date Text* option is a one-shot affair; once the date is in place, it will not change. If you need to always show the current date, select the next option, *Date Code.*

Date Code puts a code in the text, calling for the current system date so that the date in the document will be updated as the system date changes. If you have a to-do list, for example, you might want it to always display the current date. Or, you might want to include the date code in a standard memo format. When you retrieve the memo format and enter the text of the memo, it automatically prints with the current date. This "dynamic" approach contrasts with the static one used in the previous option.

Date Format allows you to display the date and time in a variety of formats, such as:

07/26/87,

July 26, 1987, or

Tue July 26, 1988 9:32am.

```
Date Format

     Character    Meaning
        1         Day of the Month
        2         Month (number)
        3         Month (word)
        4         Year (all four digits)
        5         Year (last two digits)
        6         Day of the Week (word)
        7         Hour (24-hour clock)
        8         Hour (12-hour clock)
        9         Minute
        0         am / pm
        %         Used before a number, will:
                     Pad numbers less than 10 with a leading zero
                     Output only 3 letters for the month or day of the week


     Examples:   3 1, 4       = December 25, 1984
                 %6 %3 1, 4   = Tue Dec 25, 1984
                 %2/%1/5 (6)  = 01/01/85 (Tuesday)
                 8:90         = 10:55am


Date format: 3 1, 4
```

Figure 3.11 *Date format options*

```
07/27/88  18:40              Directory C:\WP122\*.*
Document size:   51580   Free:   333824   Used:  573232        Files:  39

. <CURRENT>   <DIR>                   .. <PARENT>   <DIR>
ALTD    .WPM      93  07/21/88 21:20  ALTE    .WPM      84  07/27/88 16:32
ALTF    .WPM     256  07/19/88 17:03  ALTL    .WPM      78  07/24/88 21:50
ALTO    .WPM      90  07/26/88 09:01  ALTQ    .WPM      74  07/17/88 17:32
ALTS    .WPM      87  07/21/88 21:20  ALTT    .WPM     110  07/27/88 14:35
ALTW    .WPM      94  07/26/88 15:52  APPA-A  .      7455  07/24/88 12:22
CAT     .        648  07/27/88 13:41  CATALOG .       427  07/27/88 13:46
CH1-I   .122   57047  07/27/88 17:32  CH1HUH  .     50247  07/27/88 17:36
CH2-D   .122   23951  07/27/88 17:42  CH3     .ARC  23685  07/27/88 00:23
CH3-B   .122   51384  07/27/88 12:43  CH4-B   .122  25094  07/27/88 14:44
CH5NOTES.        463  07/27/88 12:44  CH6-AA  .122  33975  07/25/88 23:34
CHAP1   .        325  07/27/88 18:02  CHAP1-I .122  56497  07/25/88 23:34
CHCOMP  .      65879  07/27/88 17:02
EDIT    .        922  07/27/88 00:16  EDITCHAP.     1165  07/26/88 20:07
FHEAD   .       1341  07/26/88 19:47  FONT-B  .122  17470  07/26/88 12:59
FRNT-A  .122    5793  07/27/88 17:34  INTRO-C .122  15426  07/27/88 17:52
KEY     .        197  07/26/88 19:21  MONITOR .      179  07/27/88 16:34
OUTLINE .122    3856  07/17/88 17:35  PGR-SPEL.     1276  07/27/88 14:20
SAMPMEM .        891  07/27/88 18:38  SECTIONS.      726  07/27/88 17:54

1 Retrieve; 2 Delete; 3 Move/Rename; 4 Print; 5 Text In;
6 Look; 7 Other Directory; 8 Copy; 9 Word Search; N Name Search: 6
```

Figure 3.12 *File manager*

The program defaults to month, spelled out, day, and year. Other options are shown in Figure 3.11. As you can see from Figure 3.11, the various options correspond to a number, and the numbers are entered at the bottom of the screen after the words

Date format:

Note: Once you change the date format in *any* document, the date displays remains that way even in other documents, until you change it again.

Outline uses a traditional style outline to help you organize your thoughts. It starts with Roman numeral I and subordinates to Capital "A," etc, for eight levels, each indented. The mechanics of the outliner are briefly described in Appendix A.

Para Num places numbers, according to a user-defined format, in front of paragraphs. This feature is dynamic; if you have numbered a series of paragraphs and insert a new one in the middle of the series, all subsequent numbers are advanced.

Define is used to assign the numbering style of the outliner and the paragraph numbering feature. You can enter virtually any numbering system you wish, made up of Arabic and Roman numerals, and alter the display with respect to parentheses and other features.

MARK TEXT

This function contains a number of highly advanced features beyond the scope of this book, including ones for automatically referencing page numbers and footnotes, linking a series of chapters into a master document, and creating an index or table of contents. Refer to your manual for details about using these features.

LIST FILES

The *List Files* functions display WordPerfect's file manager, which is a very convenient way to retrieve, delete, rename, print, view, or copy a file. It also enables you to search files to determine which ones contain a certain word or phrase.

When you press (F5), WordPerfect first displays the current directory in the lower left hand corner of the screen. You can either change the directory temporarily by editing the directory name, or for the duration of the session by pressing the (=) key, typing in a new directory name, and pressing (Enter).

When you press (Enter) after the directory name, the file manager is displayed (see Figure 3.12). Use the cursor keys to move the highlighted bar over the file you wish to act upon. Then select an option. The various options of the file manager are discussed at length in Chapter 11.

 Key

Functions	Executed by	Usage
1. Tab Align (R)	(Ctrl-F6)	Depends on personal style
2. Center (G)	(Shift-F6)	Everyday
3. Flush Right (B)	(Alt-F6)	Depends on personal style
4. Bold (Bl)	(F6) alone	Everyday

TAB ALIGN

This feature is used to align decimal points, commas, or other characters. It is useful when you are typing columns of numbers that you wish to align by decimal point, rather than align by left or right edges.

CENTER

This fundamental function allows you to instantly center text (a character, a word, a phrase, or a whole block) between the left and right margins.

FLUSH RIGHT

The *Flush Right* command aligns a character, a word, a phrase, or a whole block with the right margin.

BOLD

Bold can act upon a character, a word, a phrase, or a whole block of text. When you press (F6), all characters are bolded until you press (F6) again.

 **Key**

Functions	Executed by	Usage
1. Footnote (R)	(Ctrl-F7)	Depends on personal style
2. Print (G)	(Shift-F7)	Everyday
3. Math/Columns (B)	(Alt-F7)	Depends on personal style
4. Exit (Bl)	(F7) alone	Everyday

FOOTNOTE

WordPerfect offers extensive footnoting and endnoting capabilities. Footnotes are automatically placed on the same page as their references, while Endnotes are placed at the end of the text. Among other options, you can create, edit, and renumber footnotes and endnotes, and, in addition, you can control the spacing between and within notes, the style of the notes, and how many lines of a note are printed together. Footnotes and endnotes are discussed in depth in Chapter 7.

PRINT

WordPerfect gives you excellent control over the printing process. When you invoke the *Print* function, the main print menu is displayed, providing options for printing the full document or the page of the document in which the cursor is currently positioned. Several other options are also available, and are discussed at length in Chapter 10.

MATH COLUMNS

The *Math/Columns* function contains features for performing simple columnar tabulations, as well as creating columns of text for special reports, newsletters, and tabloids. The *Column* feature is discussed in Chapter 6. The *Math* features are beyond the scope of this book. Refer to the manual if you wish to try them.

EXIT

The *Exit* function is the ONLY "legal" way to exit WordPerfect. If you are working on a document and press (F7), WordPerfect displays the following message in the lower left-hand corner:

Save document: (Y/N) Yes

If you want to save the document you're working on, press (Enter). If you've never saved the document before, WordPerfect prompts you for the document name:

Document to be saved:

Type the name you wish to assign the file. You can use a maximum of eight characters or numbers in the main name, plus three alphanumeric characters in the extension, which is separated from the main name by a period. There are several scenarios that might happen at this point, depending on whether or not you are working on two documents:

1. If you are working in Document #1, and you don't have a second document (or vice versa), when you press (Enter) after typing the file name, WordPerfect asks you if you want to exit the program. Type Y, and you are returned to the DOS prompt.

2. If you are working on two documents on the screen and Press (F7), and then save your file, WordPerfect asks if you want to Exit the current document. If you type Y, WordPerfect transfer you to the second document.

If you type N in either case, WordPerfect clears the screen and you can begin a new document.

 Key

Functions	Executed by	Usage
1. Font (R)	(Ctrl-F8)	Depends on hardware
2. Format (G)	(Shift-F8)	Everyday
3. Styles (B)	(Alt-F8)	Depends on personal needs
4. Underline (Bl)	(F8) alone	Everyday

FONT

The *Font* option allows you to change the type fonts of words, headlines, characters, or any other text. The ability to choose fonts is entirely dependent on your printer. Appendix C provides a complete explanation of how to change fonts within a document.

FORMAT

All of WordPerfect's page formatting options branch from the *Format* function. When you select the *Format* option, you are given the choice of four major format groupings. Within those groupings there are a number of options, as shown below. Commonly used options (followed by a plus + sign) are explained in Chapter 5. Options that represent advanced features (followed by a minus - sign), are not discussed in this book. Consult the WordPerfect manual if you wish to learn more about the advanced features.

Line Format
Hyphenation (+)
Justification (+)
Line Height (-)
Line Numbering (+)
Line Spacing (+)
Margins Left/Right (+)
Tab Set (+)
Widow/Orphan Protection (+)

Page Format
Center Page (top to bottom) (+)
Force Odd/Even Page (-)
Headers and Footers (+)
Margins Top/Bottom (+)
New Page Number (+)
Page Numbering (+)
Paper Size/Type (+)
Suppress (page numbering, headers & footers, etc) (+)

Document Format
Display Pitch (-)
Initial Codes/Font (+)
Redline Method (-)
Summary (of document) (-)

Other
Advance (-)
Conditional End of Page (-)
Decimal characters (-)
Language (-)
Overstrike (-)
Printer Functions (-)
Underline Spaces/Tabs (-)

STYLE

WordPerfect allows you to create style sheets that contain commonly used formats, including text, that can be stored in a "style sheet library." For example, you might want to create a style sheet for memos, containing all the standard headings ("To," "From," etc), or a style sheet for a report, containing certain header or footer codes as well as column settings. Refer to the WordPerfect manual for guidelines in creating style sheets.

UNDERLINE

Like *Bold, Underline* can act upon a character, a word, a phrase, or a whole block of text. When you press (F8), all characters typed will be underlined until you press (F8) again.

 **Key**

Functions	Executed by	Usage
1. Merge/Sort (R)	(Ctrl-F9)	Depends on needs
2. Merge Codes (G)	(Shift-F9)	Depends on needs

3. Graphics (B)   (Alt-F9)   Depends on needs
4. Merge R (Bl)   (F9) alone   Depends on needs

MERGE/SORT

The *Merge/Sort* function is a combination of two semi-related sets of features. The *Merge* features are used to combine two documents on the screen or as ouput created by the printer. For example, you can merge a letter with a list of names and addresses to create a "personalized" letter (you know, the kind you get in junk mail that appear to be individually typed with your name.)

The *Sort* function allows you to sort lines of text, paragraphs, or addresses within a merge file. You can also control the sort order.

Both *Merge* and *Sort* are briefly described in Appendix A.

MERGE CODES

For use with sophisticated merges, the *Merge Code* option is used to insert a variety of merge codes into the document.

GRAPHICS

WordPerfect 5.0 has unique graphic capabilities that enable it to incorporate graphic elements from other programs and to "flow" text around those elements. (See Appendix A.)

MERGE R

This is a short-hand key for entering the Merge R code, used to separate individual items in an address or other list. It is used extensively in preparing files for merging.

 **Key**

Functions	Executed by	Usage
1. Macro Def (R)	(Ctrl-F10)	Common
2. Retrieve (G)	(Shift-F10)	Everyday
3. Macro (B)	(Alt-F10)	Common
4. Save (Bl)	(F10) alone	Everyday

MACRO DEF

Macros are special files that execute a series of keystrokes. Their power lies in the fact that with one keystroke combination (most macros are executed by pressing the Alt key plus an alphabetic key), you can trigger a number of commands that would otherwise be time consuming to do individually.

For example, a macro for double spacing might be designed to invoke the *Format* function, select the *Line* options, select the *Line Spacing* option, set the spacing to 2, then return to the current document. You could name and execute this macro by pressing (Alt-D). Another macro, executed by pressing (Alt-S), might be designed to do the same, but set the spacing to 1. By pressing (Alt-D) and (Alt-S), you could easily shift back between double and single spacing without digging through the format menu options each time.

Macros are briefly described in Appendix A, but you should read the manual supplied with WordPerfect for more details. Also, for a set of more than 450 ready-to-run macros on a disk, see *WordPerfect Power Pack*, by Randall, Thompson, and Bennett, available from Brady Books.

RETRIEVE

The *Retrieve* function allows you to load a file into the current document. If you know the name of the file, *Retrieve* is a convenient way to load a file; if you don't remember the exact name, you're better off using the *List Files* option (F5). You can also use *Retrieve* to combine two files on the screen, or to bring in "boilerplate" paragraphs at a desired location in a document.

MACRO

As explained under the *Macro Def* function, you can execute macros by using an assigned (Alt) + alphabetic key combination. If this were the only way to execute a macro, the number of feasible macros would be limited by the number of letters in the alphabet:26. WordPerfect also allows you to assign a macro a common name of your choosing. To execute such a macro, press (ALT-F10) and type the macro name, followed by (Enter).

SAVE

This function allows you to easily save the current document to disk and continue editing. When you press the (F10) key, if a file name is not yet assigned to the document, WordPerfect prompts you in the lower left corner of the screen with:

Document to be saved:

Enter the file name (up to eight characters in the main body of the file name, and three characters in the extension, which is separated from the main name by a period), then press (Enter) to save the file to disk. If you have already saved the file before, WordPerfect prompts you with the previously assigned file name in the form:

Document to be saved: [plus previously assigned
                         file name]

Press (Enter) to save the document with its current name. If you wish to save it under a different file name, edit the current name, or type a new one, followed by (Enter). Unlike the *Exit* function, the *Save* function does not ask if you would like to leave WordPerfect; rather, it leaves you in the current document.

Key

(Only available on the Enhanced AT and PS/2 type keyboards).

Functions	Executed by	Usage
1. Reveal Codes (Bl)	(F11)	Everyday

REVEAL CODES

Functionally equivalent to pressing (Alt-F3). The advantage is that if you have an enhanced keyboard, you can initiate this function with a single keystroke.

 Key

(Only available on the Enhanced AT and PS/2 type keyboards).

Functions	Executed by	Usage
1. Block (Bl)	(F12)	Everyday

BLOCK

Functionally equivalent to pressing (Alt-F4). The advantage is that if you have an enhanced keyboard, you can initiate this function with a single keystroke.

4

Personalizing WordPerfect:
Using the Setup Options

HAVE IT YOUR WAY

You can customize many aspects of WordPerfect according to your preferences and needs. This is done through the *Setup* function, which is accessed by pressing (Shift-F1). This presents you with the main *Setup* menu shown in Figure 4.1.

You can change as few or as many of the options as you wish, and once you've selected an option, you can go back and change it any time. The main *Setup* menu has eight options. When you select an option, WordPerfect usually displays a submenu or a screen with several additional choices. Occasionally WordPerfect also displays sub-sub menus. You can return to the previous submenu and then back to the main *Setup* menu by repeatedly pressing the (F7) key or (Spacebar). If you press the (Esc) key, you work your way back up through the cascade of menus; however, your changes might not be saved. Finally, if you press (F7) or the (Spacebar) while at the main *Setup* menu, you return to the current document.

```
Setup
     1 - Backup

     2 - Cursor Speed               50 cps

     3 - Display

     4 - Fast Save (unformatted)    No

     5 - Initial Settings

     6 - Keyboard Layout

     7 - Location of Auxiliary Files

     8 - Units of Measure




Selection: 0
```

Figure 4.1 *Main Setup Menu*

Each of the seven main menu options and their various sub-options are discussed in detail below.

BACKUP

Wordperfect 5.0 can automatically back up your files as you go along, so that in the event of a hardware problem or power-outage you won't lose any data. This is called a *Timed Backup*. Another backup option, *Original Backup*, assigns an archival file name to the previously saved file each time you save it again with the same name. This allows you to save the current version of a document and still preserve the previous version. You can use neither backup option, either backup option, or both. To access the *Backup* options submenu, select option #1 or B for *Backup*. You are presented with the menu shown in Figure 4.2.

```
Setup: Backup

    Timed backup files are deleted when you exit WP normally.  If you
    have a power or machine failure, you will find the backup file in the
    backup directory indicated in Setup: Location of Auxiliary Files.

        Backup Directory

    1 - Timed Document Backup              Yes
        Minutes Between Backups            3


    Original backup will save the original document with a .BK! extension
    whenever you replace it during a Save or Exit.

    2 - Original Document Backup           No






Selection: 0
```

Figure 4.2 *Backup Menu*

Timed Backup

The *Timed Backup* option instructs WordPerfect to make a periodic temporary backup file of the current document on the screen. It is important to understand that this is only a *temporary backup*, and it is only useful if you terminate the WordPerfect session abnormally due to a power blackout or accidental crash. When you leave WordPerfect normally, the temporary timed backups are *automatically deleted*. If you do terminate the session abnormally, the backup files named WP{WP}.BK1 and WP{WP}.BK2, which correspond to Document 1 and 2 in the current session, are not deleted. The .BK1 and .BK2 files can be found in the directory specified by the *Setup* setting for Location of Auxiliary files (see below). You can copy the backup files to your data directory, retrieve them, and then save them with the proper name, thereby recovering from a potentially catastrophic data loss.

If you restart the system, having terminated abnormally, the system asks:

Are other copies of WordPerfect currently running (Y/N)

Enter N, and then proceed. When the first timed backup occurs, WordPerfect displays, at the bottom of your screen:

Old Backup File Exists 1.Rename; 2. Delete

You can either select to rename it at this time or delete the old backup.

You can turn the *Timed Backup* option on and off by selecting 1 at the backup options menu, then entering Y or N at the first option, which asks if you want a timed backup. If you enter Y, the cursor moves down to the next line, which allows you to enter the desired time (in minutes) between backups. We suggest you make the time interval as short as you can tolerate—the backup process causes the system to pause while the backup is being made, and if you have a sluggish hard disk, you might find the process annoying. If you set the backup for once every 30 minutes, though, you're defeating the purpose of the protective mechanism—30 minutes worth of document is a *lot* to recreate from memory. The authors use a three minute interval and find it satisfactory. (Even speedy writers can't generate all that much text in three minutes.)

Finally, note that the *Timed Backup* option does not provide any protection against failure to save your changes, or accidentally saving a bad copy of a document over a good original. If you want to protect original documents, go on to the next section. Otherwise, press (F7) to return to the *Setup* menu.

Original Backup

The *Original Backup* option protects against your editing a previously stored document, and overwriting it with a version that is either incorrect or undesirable for some reason. This option automatically creates a backup copy of the original document with the same main name and the .BK! extension. This allows you to recover the previous version of a document if you decide you don't like the changes after all. The main liability of this option is that it tends to proliferate files and take up disk space. If you use it, you may want to periodically edit your backup files, deleting those that are no longer necessary.

To select the *Original Backup* option, select 2, then type Y, followed by (Enter). Press (Enter) again to return to the *Setup* main menu. You can always change your mind and de-activate either backup option any time.

CURSOR SPEED

WordPerfect allows you to control the speed at which characters are repeated when you hold down a particular key. This is measured in terms of Characters Per Second (CPS). You can set the speed for a value between from 10 CPS to 50 CPS. The goal is to set the value as high as you can reasonably control. Try a setting of 30 CPS (3 times faster than Normal) for a while and move up to 40 or 50 CPS if you find it helpful.

The *Cursor Speed* option in WordPerfect 5.0 is compatible with the Repeat Performance software distributed by WordPerfect, but may be incompatible with other cursor control programs. If you already own Repeat Performance, you may want to continue to use it since it has more control options and can be used with your other software as well as WordPerfect. In order to continue to use Repeat Performance, however, you must set the Cursor Control to *Normal*. If you're using another cursor control program, you must turn off WordPerfect 5.0's cursor control. This is accomplished at the time you start WordPerfect, by using the /NC option. You should start WordPerfect by entering:

WP /NC (Enter)

This disables the cursor control system and allows your cursor control program to work within WordPerfect 5.0.

DISPLAY

While WordPerfect automatically detects and sets itself up for most widely available monitor and adapter types, (monochrome text,

```
Setup: Display

    1 - Automatically Format and Rewrite     No

    2 - Colors/Fonts/Attributes

    3 - Display Document Comments             Yes

    4 - Filename on the Status Line           Yes

    5 - Graphics Screen Type                  Hercules 720x348 mono

    6 - Hard Return Display Character

    7 - Menu Letter Display                   BOLD

    8 - Side-by-side Columns Display          No

    9 - View Document in Black & White        No




Selection: 0
```

Figure 4.3 *Display Menu*

monochrome graphics, CGA, EGA, VGA and so on), you may want to
install another display, or change the current display. You may also
wish to change many of the display options. Figure 4.3 shows the
main Display menu.

Automatic Format and Rewrite

This option allows you to select between two screen rewrite options. When set to Yes, WordPerfect automatically rewrites the full
screen each time you make an editing change. If you select No to
turn it off, WordPerfect only rewrites lines affected by an editing
change as you scroll through the document. This can save considerable amounts of formatting time as you edit, but may make it
harder for you to visualize the results of your editing.

Colors/Fonts/Attributes

The *Color/Font* and *Attribute* menus vary depending on the type of
monitor you have installed. In general, you are presented with a
series of choices as to how you want the special fonts and colors
displayed on your monitor. You can then view a sample of the
selected display and either accept or alter any of the individual font

display characteristics. Note that if you change the monitor under option #5, below, you can select a different set of display options. The display options are stored for each type of monitor separately, and can be copied or moved between them. In addition, you can choose to store different display options for each of the two document screens.

To demonstrate the display options, this chapter assumes as a model the use of a Hercules Monochrome Graphics Plus monitor adapter, a popular monochrome adapter with both graphics and extended font capabilities. When WordPerfect was first installed, it detected the presence of the "Herc" card and set the default monitor to the Hercules monochrome display pattern (see Figure 4.3 above). It also set the default display font to the normal text font supported by the Hercules adapter. See Figure 4.4.

Note that an asterisk marks the *Normal Font Only* option, identifying that the option has been selected. If you select option #1 for screen attributes, you are presented with the display shown in Figure 4.5.

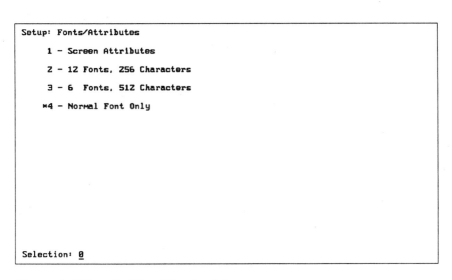

Figure 4.4 *Hercules Font Selection Menu*

```
Setup: Attributes

Attribute                Blink  Bold  Blocked  Underline  Normal  Sample
Normal                     N     N      N         N         Y     Sample
Blocked                    N     N      Y         N         N     Sample
Underline                  N     N      N         Y         N     Sample
Strikeout                  N     N      N         N         Y     Sample
Bold                       N     Y      N         N         Y     Sample
Double Underline           N     N      N         N         Y     Sample
Redline                    N     N      N         N         Y     Sample
Shadow                     N     N      N         N         Y     Sample
Italics                    N     N      N         N         Y     Sample
Small Caps                 N     N      N         N         Y     Sample
Outline                    N     N      N         N         Y     Sample
Subscript                  N     N      N         N         Y     Sample
Superscript                N     N      N         N         Y     Sample
Fine Print                 N     N      N         N         Y     Sample
Small Print                N     N      N         N         Y     Sample
Large Print                N     N      N         N         Y     Sample
Very Large Print           N     N      N         N         Y     Sample
Extra Large Print          N     N      N         N         Y     Sample
Bold & Underline           N     Y      N         Y         N     Sample
Other Combinations         N     N      N         N         Y     Sample

Switch to switch; Move to copy settings        Doc 1
```

Figure 4.5 *Hercules Font Display Sample — Normal Text Font Only*

You can edit the individual font attributes or leave them as they are. We recommend the latter. Press the (F7) key to leave the sample and return to the *Fonts/Attributes* menu. Now Select option #2 for the 12 Font, 256 Character display. Again display the sample screen attributes by selecting option #1.

You will immediately notice that the shadow and the outline fonts are now correctly represented on the screen. Further investigation reveals that many of the other font variations are also represented in a more true-to-life format. This is because the Hercules Mono-Graphic Plus adapter supports many more fonts than normal text. You can choose between the two types of displays on the basis of your own taste.

In a similar fashion, you are presented with a series of font selections and a methodology for viewing samples and selecting among them. The specific number and variety of choices vary depending on your installed monitor and adapter.

Display Document Comments

When you insert comments—notes to yourself or other readers—into a document using the *Text In/Out* option (see Chapter 3, p 60), you can choose to have them displayed on the screen or not. If you select No, you are only able to detect the presence of a comment by its code when in Reveal Codes mode (Alt-F3)—see Chapter 3, p 53. In any case, comments are never printed.

Filename on Status Line

This option determines whether the name of the document is displayed in the lower left corner of the screen as you edit it. You must have saved or retrieved the document for WordPerfect to know what the file name is.

Graphics Screen Type

When installed, WordPerfect automatically senses the type of monitor and adapter connected to the computer. If you change your monitor or add a second monitor, you must select this option to select the new monitor driver from the list of supported monitors. If you are using a monitor not listed, you must obtain a WordPerfect driver from the manufacturer (the file must have a .WPD extension). Otherwise call WordPerfect to determine which existing driver to select for your monitor.

Hard Return Display Character

You can select any of the available WordPerfect characters to represent a hard (carriage) return on the screen. This can help you edit files that contain extensive formatting commands.

Menu Letter Display

Many of the WordPerfect 5.0 menus use mnemonic letters in addition to the number to allow you to make selections. When you first install WordPerfect, these letters are highlighted as **bold**. For example, in the *Text In/Out* option, the "P" in the Password option is bolded. You can use any of the font variations that your monitor can display to highlight these characters.

Side-by-side Column Display

When this option is set on (the default), side-by-side columns are displayed as such on the screen. You can speed up scrolling and editing, by displaying each column on a separate page. This is done by setting this option to No. If you select the No option, the pages are still printed as side-by-side columns.

View Document in Black & White

When this option is set to Yes, WordPerfect shows documents in View Document (preview) mode, as black on white, even on color monitors. When set to No, color monitors display documents in color. Black on white displays generally have a higher resolution so the text is clearer and easier to read.

Fast Save

The *Fast Save* option saves a document to disk without first formatting it for printing. While this can cut out some time in saving documents, you cannot use the resulting files for any of the print-from-disk procedures. You can, of course, reload the document and print it from within WordPerfect. In general, unless you are repeatedly saving various editions of a very large document that you know you won't need to print from file, you are probably best off leaving this option at the default No.

INITIAL SETTINGS

The *Initial Settings* menu, (see Figure 4.6) allows you to establish several of WordPerfect's operational features and the opening values for such items as tabs, margins, and page number position for each new document you start. It is broken down into six sub-sections.

Beep Options

This feature allows you to select the events that cause WordPerfect to beep. See Figure 4.7.

```
Setup: Initial Settings
     1 - Beep Options
     2 - Date Format                    3 1, 4
     3 - Document Summary
     4 - Initial Codes
     5 - Repeat Value                   8
     6 - Table of Authorities




Selection: 0
```

Figure 4.6 *Initial Setting Menu*

```
Setup: Beep options
     1 - Beep on Error            No
     2 - Beep on Hyphenation      Yes
     3 - Beep on Search Failure   No







Selection: 0
```

Figure 4.7 *Beep Options*

```
Date Format

    Character    Meaning
        1        Day of the Month
        2        Month (number)
        3        Month (word)
        4        Year (all four digits)
        5        Year (last two digits)
        6        Day of the Week (word)
        7        Hour (24-hour clock)
        8        Hour (12-hour clock)
        9        Minute
        0        am / pm
        %        Used before a number, will:
                    Pad numbers less than 10 with a leading zero
                    Output only 3 letters for the month or day of the week


    Examples:    3 1, 4       = December 25, 1984
                 %6 %3 1, 4   = Tue Dec 25, 1984
                 %2/%1/5 (6)  = 01/01/85 (Tuesday)
                 8:90         = 10:55am


Date format: 3 1, 4
```

Figure 4.8 *Date Format Options*

Date Format

The Date format option allows you to define the default appearance of the date functions in documents. (See Figure 4.8.) The date functions are controlled by (Shift-F5). (See Chapter 3.)

Document Summary

The two options under this submenu control the Document Summary. (See Figure 4.9.)

A document summary is a pre-formatted comment placed at the beginning of the document. The summary contains information about the date of creation, revision number, and other useful attributes. To create a document summary, and have WordPerfect prompt you to enter the data when you save or exit the file, enter Yes for option #1. To instruct WordPerfect to search the document for the subject, enter the key words that you want WordPerfect to search for in the document. WordPerfect then searches the document for the key phrase and copies the subsequent phrase to the document summary box. In this fashion, WordPerfect automates the process of adding the topic to the summary. In general, you should accept the default, "RE," so that whatever you place after the

```
Setup: Document Summary

     1 - Create on Save/Exit        No

     2 - Subject Search Text        RE:













Selection: 0
```

Figure 4.9 *Document Summary Options*

word RE at the beginning of your text appears in the summary box. If you turn off the document summary feature, you can still create a summary from the format document menu (Shift-F8) + 3 + 5. WordPerfect, however, will not prompt you for data input when you exit.

Initial Codes

The initial codes feature allows you to set up any of the common formatting codes as you would in a regular editing session. The difference is that the codes which you enter here are used as the default codes for every new document you create. For example, if you always want to set the left margin to 1.5 inches and the top to 2 inches, set them up here. Thereafter, those margins are the defaults for each documemt you start.

While you may select initial codes according to your own needs and styles, the authors recommend that you use "justification off" as an initial code. With non-proportional type fonts, justification of the right margin may sometimes create "rivers" between words as the program attempts to even out the spacing of words on a line. Other times, it may jam words too close together. Either way, the resulting text may be hard to read and aesthetically unpleasing.

With proportional fonts, justification can properly manipulate the character and word spacing, creating a pleasing "typeset" feel. If you're not sure whether a font is "mono-spaced" or proportional, check your printer manual.

To turn off justification as an initial code, after selecting item 4 from the *Initial Settings* menu, press (Shift- F8) for the *Format* menu, select option #1 for line, then select 3 for *Justification*. Type N, followed by (Enter) and the press (F7) to exit. The screen shows [Just Off] under the ruler bar. Each time you start WordPerfect, the program assumes you want justification turned off. If you switch to a proportional font and wish to turn justification back on for a specific document, use the *Format, Line,* options, select 3 for Justification, and press Y.

Note: All of the other formatting options, such as margins, tabs, and page number positions are entered as initial codes in the same fashion.

Repeat Value

When you press the (Esc) key before pressing a character, the words "Repeat value = 8" are displayed in the lower left hand corner of the screen. If you then type a character, the character is repeated eight times (Note: The words "Repeat value =" are not displayed if (Esc) is used to exit from a menu.) The Repeat function works with any character, the (Spacebar), the (Tab) key, and several commands.

The *Initial Settings* option allows you to reset the Repeat Value to something other than 8. The default value of 8 is generally sufficient, and you shouldn't need to change it unless you have a specific need for another value. For example, if you are always inserting the same character 10 times or repeating a command 10 times, you may want to change the default to 10.

Table of Authorities

This submenu sets the format and style of the Table of Authorities, used in legal word processing. You need only concern yourself with this option if you're using the *Table of Authorities* option and want to change the default format.

KEYBOARD LAYOUT

The *Keyboard Layout* option allows you to reassign the function of the keys when using WordPerfect. WordPerfect supplies several alternative keyboard formats on the Conversion disk with the extension .WPK. If you are interested in using an alternative keyboard layout, you should copy the .WPK files to your WordPerfect directory on you hard disk, and then use this option to select or edit one of them. Warning: This is only a project to be undertaken by the strong of heart.

LOCATION OF THE AUXILIARY FILES

This submenu, shown in Figure 4.10, allows you to define alternative locations for the various support files. You can use this in concert with your directory plan discussed in Chapter 1 to maximize the efficiency of storage of your files. This option is most useful for advanced installations, and if you are uncertain about creating additional directories, *do nothing*; WordPerfect first looks in the current directory, and if it doesn't find the files, it looks in the main program directory.

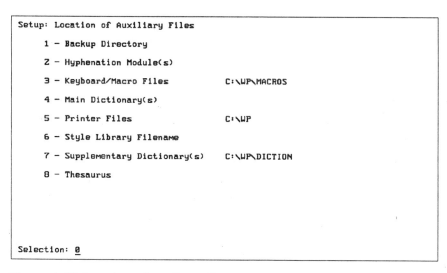

```
Setup: Location of Auxiliary Files

    1 - Backup Directory

    2 - Hyphenation Module(s)

    3 - Keyboard/Macro Files          C:\WP\MACROS

    4 - Main Dictionary(s)

    5 - Printer Files                 C:\WP

    6 - Style Library Filename

    7 - Supplementary Dictionary(s)   C:\WP\DICTION

    8 - Thesaurus




Selection: 0
```

Figure 4.10 *Location of Auxilary Files*

UNITS OF MEASURE

This option permits you to change the fundamental unit of measure used to describe the position of margins, tabs, page sizes and so on. The default unit is inches, which works quite well. Some users involved with publishing may find working in Points more efficient, while some die-hard WordPerfect 4.2 users may find the transition to 5.0 easier when working in lines and columns.

You can actually split the decision, by using inches for your format menus and displays, such as margins and page size, etc, while displaying the current position on the status line in the more familiar WordPerfect units (lines and columns). When you first select the *Units of Measure* option, you have two choices. Select 1 to change the numeric input, and 2 to change the Status Line Display (see Figure 4.11).

```
Setup: Units of Measure

     1 - Display and Entry of Numbers          "
             for Margins, Tabs, etc.

     2 - Status Line Display                    "


Legend:

     " = inches
     i = inches
     c = centimeters
     p = points
     u = WordPerfect 4.2 Units (Lines/Columns)






Selection: 0
```

Figure 4.11 *Units of Measure*

At this point, you've customized WordPerfect to your personal taste. As your needs and preferences change, you can always go back into *Setup* and make the appropriate changes.

5

Creating Documents With WordPerfect

ONWARD

If you've been reading this book sequentially, you've built up a base of knowledge about how to navigate within WordPerfect and how to use the function keys. If you're just tuning in and have no prior experience with WordPerfect, you might want to quickly review Chapters 2 and 3.

In this chapter, you learn how to format documents; that is, how to set up the basic attributes that determine how a printed page will look. As you read along, you're strongly advised to input text and manipulate it according to the step-by-step instructions. The best thing to do is input your own text, which helps you increase familiarity with the keyboard.

THE MAIN FORMAT MENU

WordPerfect allows you to alter a number of different aspects of a document. When you select the *Format* option, (Shift-F8), WordPerfect displays the main *Format* menu, which lists all of it's formatting commands under four main categories: *Line, Page, Document,* and *Other.* (See Figure 5.1) *Line* options, as the name implies, are concerned with aspects of individual lines of characters and words, and include margins, tabs, spacing, etc. *Page* options refer to format issues affect whole pages, such as page number position, headers, and footers. *Document* options refer to format changes that effect every page of a document, from beginning to end. None of the *Other* options are within the scope of this book—refer to your WordPerfect manual for information on their use.

IMPORTANT NOTE: For several of the options to work, they must be executed while the cursor is at the very top of the document, placed before text or formatting codes such as bold, underline, etc. If you have done anything to a document before entering the desired formatting codes, the best way to ensure proper placement at the top is to press:

(Home) + (Home) + (Home) + (Up Cursor)

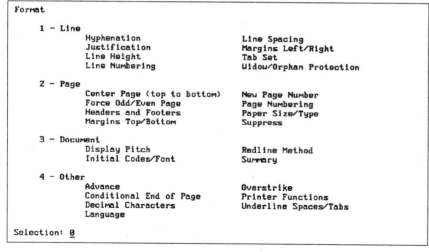

```
Format

    1 - Line
               Hyphenation                   Line Spacing
               Justification                 Margins Left/Right
               Line Height                   Tab Set
               Line Numbering                Widow/Orphan Protection

    2 - Page
               Center Page (top to bottom)   New Page Number
               Force Odd/Even Page           Page Numbering
               Headers and Footers           Paper Size/Type
               Margins Top/Bottom            Suppress

    3 - Document
               Display Pitch                 Redline Method
               Initial Codes/Font            Summary

    4 - Other
               Advance                       Overstrike
               Conditional End of Page       Printer Functions
               Decimal Characters            Underline Spaces/Tabs
               Language

Selection: 0
```

Figure 5.1 *Format Options*

This combination places the cursor at the very beginning of the document, ahead of all existing codes.

LINE OPTIONS

When you select number 1 from the *Format* options menu shown in Figure 5.1, WordPerfect displays the *Line* format options menu shown in Figure 5.2. Most of these options are fundamental to formatting a document, so we'll consider each one in the order in which it appears in the menu. As you read about each option, you're encouraged to experiment for yourself and see the effect it has on your document.

Hyphenation

WordPerfect gives you several choices for hyphenating text. Remember, WordPerfect automatically "wraps" to the next line when you approach the right margin. It must therefore make a decision whether to hyphenate and break words apart or kick them intact down to the next line.

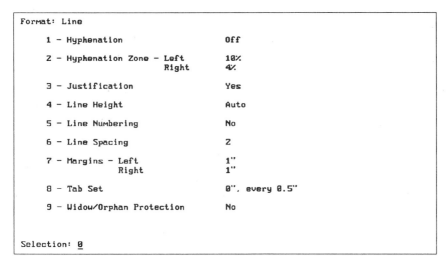

```
Format: Line

    1 - Hyphenation                  Off

    2 - Hyphenation Zone - Left      10%
                          Right      4%

    3 - Justification                Yes

    4 - Line Height                  Auto

    5 - Line Numbering               No

    6 - Line Spacing                 2

    7 - Margins - Left               1"
                  Right              1"

    8 - Tab Set                      0", every 0.5"

    9 - Widow/Orphan Protection      No


Selection: 0
```

Figure 5.2 *Line Format Options*

Although WordPerfect has a set of hyphenation rules, it is preset with hyphenation turned Off. In the Off mode, a word that is too big to fill the space between the cursor and the right margin is pushed to the next line. (The determination of when WordPerfect pushes a word down depends on the "hyphenation zone" setting, described below).

If you want to turn hyphenation on, select option 1, and the following menu appears on the bottom of the screen:

1 Off; **2** Manual; **3** Auto: **0**

Manual hyphenation means that WordPerfect takes a best guess at where to break the word and then beeps to ask you whether it is alright. If the placement is correct, press the (Esc) key. If you do not approve of the hyphenation break, you can either change it by moving the cursor to the proper place and pressing (Esc), or press (F1) to cancel the hyphenation, in which case the word in question is forced to the next line.

Try the following. Change hyphenation to manual by selecting option 2, then exit to the main screen and type in the following:

This is a test of the two hyphenation options. In my experimentation, I plan to compare both options.

If you have set WordPerfect for standard 8 1/2 by 11 inch paper with one inch left and right margins (the default) and are using Courier 10 pitch type face, the word experimentation should be hyphen-ated. If you are using another size paper or a diferent font, you may need to juggle to the sample phrase to force the hyphenation.

Continuing with the example, notice how WordPerfect beeped and paused after breaking the word at "experimenta—"; press (Esc), and WordPerfect allows you to continue. Finish the line, and press (Enter) to go to a new line. Try entering the same sentence, this time using the cursor keys to adjust the placement of the hyphen. Press (Esc) when the hyphen is located where you want it within the word "experimentation." Finish typing the line and move to a new line by pressing (Enter). Type the same sentence yet a third time, and press (F1) when WordPerfect asks you to confirm the hyphenation in "experimentation"—watch how WordPerfect cancels the hy-phenation and pushes "experimentation" to the next line.

Auto hyphenation works as follows. If the word break fits WordPerfect's hyphenation rules, WordPerfect makes the hyphenation and continues without asking you to confirm. If it encounters a situation that does not fit within its hyphenation rules, it switches to manual mode (for that word only), asking you to confirm or alter the word break.

To see how this works, clear the screen by entering:

   (F7) + N + N

Switch hypehnation to *Auto* and repeat the test you just did with the *Manual* mode. Notice how WordPerfect hyphenated before "tion" and allowed you to keep typing on the next line. Now let's confuse WordPerfect: move the cursor to a new line, and when you get to the word "experimentation," type the word as "experimentbcbc." This nonsense jumble defies all WordPerfect's hyphenation rules, so the program takes a guess, hyphenating the word at "experimentbc—bc" and asks you to confirm, as if you were in *Manual* hyphenation mode. WordPerfect continues, in *Auto* hyphenation mode, until it encounters another word it can't handle.

Why not always use Auto hyphenation? And why does WordPerfect default to hyphenation OFF? The answer to both of these questions is that hyphenation has its trade-offs. When hyphenation is ON, WordPerfect tries to get as many words as it can near the right margin. This means more hyphenated words, which are harder to read. Further, in *Manual* mode, many people find it annoying to stop and confirm hyphenation breaks. Remember, WordPerfect occasionally asks you for a confirmation, even when in *Auto* hyphenation mode. With hyphenation off, you are never slowed down, but you get a more "ragged" right edge. Many people find this an acceptable trade-off, and leave the hyphenation feature OFF. If the ragged edge bothers you, or you plan to justify your documents, (see Justification), you should turn on hyphenation to *Manual* or *Auto*.

Hyphenation Zone

This is something that you probably won't need to adjust; if you plan to leave hyphenation off, you can move on to the next option.

If you're planning on using *Manual* or *Auto* hyphenation, though, you ought to understand the principle involved.

The hyphenation zone (called the "hot zone" in earlier versions of WordPerfect) refers to an amount of space to the left and right of the right margin. It determines whether a word will be hyphenated or wrapped. The left hyphenation zone is preset to 10 percent of the current line length, or about 0.65 inches on an 8 1/2 by 11 inch piece of paper. The right hyphenation zone is set to four percent of the current line length, which is about 0.25 inches to the right of the right margin. If a word begins after it crosses into the left hyphenation zone and terminates before the right hyphenation zone, it is wrapped to the next line, unhyphenated. If, however, a word begins before the left hyphenation zone and continues beyond the right hyphenation zone, it is hyphenated.

You can adjust the hyphenation zone as a percentage of the length of the line, less margins. By making the hyphenation zone smaller, WordPerfect hyphenates more words; conversely, larger hyphenation zones mean less hyphenation. Suggestion: leave the zones at their default settings unless you find a good reason to change them.

Justification

This option refers to whether text is aligned at the right margin as well as the left margin, or whether the text is "ragged right," with lines of varying length. Justified text has a more formal, "typeset"— like feel. Books (like this one) are typically set in justified type, although "rag" right is perfectly acceptable for many types of publications (see Figure 5.3 for comparison).

Justified text poses several problems. First, depending on the line length, you may find wide spaces or "rivers" between words. Very short lines may look especially bad. The problem is accentuated with "mono-spaced" type fonts, i.e. type fonts in which the spacing for each letter is the same. Most type fonts on today's printer's are monospaced, unless they're specifically designated as "propor-tional," meaning that the spacing of letters is proportional to their width. With a mono-spaced font, an "l" and "m" occupy the same amount of space; with a proportional font, an "l" takes up less space than an "m." (see Figure 5.4). Proportional fonts are far better

```
Where a calculator on the ENIAC is equipped with 18,000
vacuum tubes and weighs 30 tons, computers in the
future may have only 1000 vacuum tubes and perhpas
weigh only 1 1/2 tons.

(Popular Mechanics, March 1949, p 258.)


Where a calculator on the ENIAC is equipped with 18,000
vacuum tubes and weighs 30 tons, computers in the future
may have only 1000 vacuum tubes and perhpas weigh only
1 1/2 tons.

(Popular Mechanics, March 1949, p 258.)
```

Figure 5.3 *Ragged Right (top) vs Justified (bottom)*

suited to justified text, and if you don't have access to one, you should probably stick to an unjustified right margin (See Figure 5.5).

The second problem with justification is that it tends to create more hyphenation. When a paragraph contains multiple hyphenations,

```
The phonograph...is not of any commercial value.
— Thomas A. Edison


The phonograph...is not of any commercial value.
— Thomas A. Edison
```

Figure 5.4 *Monospaced Font (Courier, 10 pitch), vs Proportional Font*
(Times Roman 10 pitch)

```
When a calculator on the ENIAC is equipped with 18,000
vacuum tubes and weight 30 tons, computers in the
future may have only 1000 vacuum tubes and perhaps
weigh only 1 1/2 tons.
(Popular Mechanics, March 1949, p. 258)
```

When a calculator on the ENIAC is equipped with 18,000 vacuum tubes and weight 30 tons, computers in the future may have only 1000 vacuum tubes and perhaps weigh only 1 1/2 tons.
(Popular Mechanics, March 1949, p. 258)

Figure 5.5 *Monospaced paragraph (top) vs proportionally-spaced paragraph (bottom). Notice how extra wide spacing between the first words of the top line in the monospaced paragraph. In contrast, the proportionally-spaced paragraph is much more evenly and tightly spaced*

the hyphens can create a visual effect called a "ladder," which is considered poor graphic form.

Finally, if you ever plan to import one of your documents into a desktop publishing program for fancy production, justification may cause all sorts of problems.

In short, turn justification off if you haven't already done so through the setup procedure described on page 86 of Chapter 4. If you turn off justification as part of your setup options, you won't have to do so for each document you create. Instead, you'll have to turn justification ON for those occasions where it might be appropriate.

Line Height

Line height is the top to bottom space of a line of characters. WordPerfect does a splendid job of adjusting line height according to the type font you are printing. Suggestion: don't mess with it. The default is set for *Auto*, and you should just leave it there.

Line Numbering

In some situations, it's desirable to have line numbers print in front of each line (see Figure 5.6). When proofing a contract or technical document, for example, it may be easier to refer to line numbers. To print out numbers, select the *Line Numbering* option from the menu and enter Y for yes. The menu shown in Figure 5.7 will be displayed.

```
 1         Use the following steps to create an AUTOEXEC.BAT from
 2         scratch.
 3
 4              1.  Make sure that the root directory is the current
 5                  directory by entering the command:
 6                       CD \  (Enter)
 7                    Then create the file by typing:
 8                       COPY CON: AUTOEXEC.BAT (Enter)
 9                       PATH C:\;C:\DOS;C:\WP50  (add any other
10                       directories, separated by a semi-colon).
11                  (Enter)
12                       PROMPT $P$G  (Enter)
13                       Name of clock program (Enter)  [Only use
14                       if appropriate.]
15                       DATE (Enter)   [Only if you don't have a
16                       clock program.]
17                       TIME (Enter)   [Only if you don't have a
18                                      clock program.]
19
20              2.  To complete the AUTOEXEC.BAT file, press the (F6)
21                  key.  ^Z will appear on the screen. Now press
22                  (Enter) and the screen will display:
23                            1 file copied
24                       indicating that the batch file was
25                       created.
26
27              3.  Simply creating or changing the file doesn't affect
```

Figure 5.6 *Example of Printout with Numbered Lines*

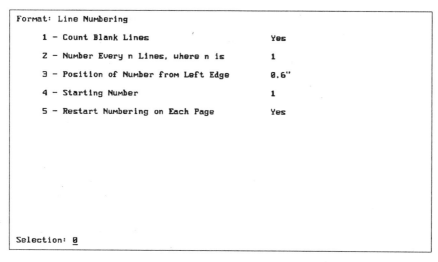

Figure 5.7 *Line Numbering Menu*

The menu choices are as follows:

Count Blank Lines. If you don't want blank lines to be numbered, change the default Yes to No by typing N.

Number Every n Lines, where n is. If you want every line to be numbered, leave the default at 1. If you want every other line numbered, change the 1 to 2. Changing the 1 to a 3 would result in every third line being numbered, etc.

Position of Number from Left Edge. This lets you control how far in from the left edge of the paper the numbers are printed.

Starting Number. Your line numbering will begin with whatever number is entered for this option. If you want the line numbering to begin with 1, leave the default setting as is.

Restart Numbering on Each Page. You can either have WordPerfect begin the numbering on each page (by leaving the default at YES, or number the lines consecutively, regardless of page breaks (type N for NO).

Finally, be aware that WordPerfect does <u>not</u> show the line numbers on screen—you can only see them when you print or preview a document (see Chapter 8).

Line Spacing

Use this option to control the amount of spacing between lines. The default setting is 1, for single spacing. Enter 1.5 for one-and-a-half spacing, 2 for double spacing, etc.

Note that only text *after* a line spacing setting reflects the new value. If you change from single to double spacing at the beginning of line 10 of a document, only text from that point forward will be double-spaced; text on lines 1 through 9 will be single-spaced (or whatever spacing setting had been previously selected). Thus, if you want an entire document to be double, triple, or some other value than single, make sure that you enter a value for *Line Spacing* while the cursor is on the top line, upper left hand corner. If you have a two-line title or headline and want it to be single spaced, start the new spacing command underneath the title.

You can change spacing as many times as you like throughout the course of the document. A single spaced, indented paragraph is often useful for offsetting quotes in a double spaced document. To do so, position the cursor beneath the last double spaced line before the quote, enter a value of 1 for *Line Spacing*, then press (Shift-F4) to indent the paragraph. When you finish the quote, press (Enter) to break the indent and enter a value of 2 for the *Line Spacing*.

Experiment with the *Line Spacing* option a bit. You'll soon find it's one of the most frequently-used options in your tool kit of WordPerfect functions.

Margins

This option controls the placement of the left and right margin. If you're used to WordPerfect 4.2, beware that in version 5.0 the left margin is calculated from the left edge of the paper, and the right margin is calculated from the right edge. A margin setting of Left 1" and Right 1" means one inch in from both sides of the page. In Version 4.2, both margins were calculated from left edge. Bear this difference in mind, or you are in for a surprise.

Margins settings, like *Line Spacing,* only affect text beneath the changed setting. If you change the margins midway down a page, the new settings will not be reflected in the text on the top part of the page. Also, as with *Line Spacing,* you can change margins as many times as you want in a document—margin settings will remain in effect until new margin values are added.

To change the margins for an entire document, make sure that the cursor is in the upper left hand corner of the top line of the first page. Remember, only text *after* a margin setting will have the desired placement on the page.

Try setting a few different margins before going on to the next topic.

Tab Set

The tab ruler is a key to formatting WordPerfect documents. When you select *Tab Set,* the ruler is displayed at the bottom of the page of the current document (see Figure 5.8). The default setting is one left-aligned tab every half inch (or five WordPerfect character units), depending on how you have set up your program—see Chapter 4).

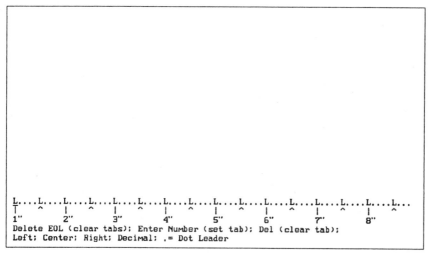

Figure 5.8 *Tab Setting Ruler*

As you can see from Figure 5.8, each tab is marked with an "L" above the ruler. In addition to left-aligned tabs, WordPerfect supports, center, right-aligned, and decimal-aligned tabs with or without dot leaders. You can combine any or all of these into a single tab ruler. The tab settings can be altered as follows.

- **Delete all tabs** from the cursor position to the end of the line by pressing (Ctrl-End). You can use the (Ctrl-End) function from any point along the ruler.

- **Delete individual tabs** by moving the cursor to a specific tab, then pressing the (Del) key.

- **Enter (L)eft tabs** by moving the cursor to each tab position you want to create, and typing L or by typing the number for the tab position (e.g. 2.3). The numbers will appear underneath the tab ruler, on the right side as you type them. When you press (Enter), a left tab is placed at the desired position. A left tab is the most common form of tab; text is pushed to the right of each tab position. When you enter L's, you're really just customizing the conventional effect of the tab key. When you're done entering tabs, press (F7) twice to return to your document.

- **Enter (C)enter tabs** by moving the cursor to the desired positions and typing a C. Whereas text moves to the right of a Left tab, it moves evenly to the left and right of a center tab. In other words, it's like using WordPerfect's centering function (Shift-F6). Center tabs are useful for aligning text in lists and reports. When you finish entering tabs, exit by pressing (F7) twice.

- **Enter Right tabs** by placing an R at the desired tab stop. Text aligns to the right, as it would with the Flush Right function (Alt-F6). Press (F7) two times when you've entered all your tabs.

- **Enter Decimal tabs** by typing D at desired tab stops. A decimal tab aligns text to the left of a decimal point. This is useful for aligning columns of numbers. As with all tab sets, press (F7) twice to return to your document.

- **Enter Dot Leaders** by pressing the period (.) key at any tab setting (Left, Center, Right, or Decimal). The tab set position will be highlighted. To create a line of dot leaders, highlight a series of tabs. Then press (F7) two times to return to the document.

Each time you press (Tab) while creating a document, a dot leader is placed between the tab stops. This is useful for creating telephone lists, price lists, and other lists in which separate columns of data are made easier to read when connected with leaders (See Figure 5.9).

IMPORTANT NOTE: Only text *after* a tab setting will be affected by changes you've made to the tab ruler. Also, make sure that you make your tab changes at the beginning of a line; otherwise, you may not get the expected results. If you insert a new tab setting into a document, all subsequent text with tabs will be affected until you restore the original tab setting.

```
Product                                            Price
─────────────────────────────────────────────────────────

Computers

Model 100. . . . . . . . . . . . . . . . . . . . .$1,250
Model 200. . . . . . . . . . . . . . . . . . . . .$1,850
Model 300. . . . . . . . . . . . . . . . . . . . .$2,250
Model 400. . . . . . . . . . . . . . . . . . . . .$2,750
Model 500. . . . . . . . . . . . . . . . . . . . .$3,250
Model 600. . . . . . . . . . . . . . . . . . . . .$4,450


Accessories

Model A20. . . . . . . . . . . . . . . . . . . .$   150
Model A22. . . . . . . . . . . . . . . . . . . .$   220
Model A23. . . . . . . . . . . . . . . . . . . .$   275
Model B20. . . . . . . . . . . . . . . . . . . .$   340
Model B25. . . . . . . . . . . . . . . . . . . .$   420
Model C20. . . . . . . . . . . . . . . . . . . .$    69
Model C30. . . . . . . . . . . . . . . . . . . .$   120
Model A40. . . . . . . . . . . . . . . . . . . .$   199
```

Figure 5.9 *Example of Dot Leaders*

Widow/Orphan Protection

"Widows" and "orphans" are common typesetting terms. A widow occurs when the first line of a paragraph prints out on the last line of a page. An orphan is just the opposite—it happens when the last line of a paragraph prints out on the first line of a page.

Widows and orphans can both be avoided by selecting *Widow/Orphan Protection* and typing Y for Yes.

You might as well leave the protection on for all your documents, by inserting it into your initial codes during setup. (See Chapter 4, page 89.) The only reason you may not want to use the feature is that WordPerfect handles widow and orphan protection by adjusting the number of lines per page, and although unlikely, you may sometime have a particular need to maintain a constant line count for each page.

Your Turn

Before going on to the *Page* options, take some time to experiment with the *Line* options, if you haven't done so already. Play with your text until you're familiar with the various line functions. Notice the effects of altering the justification, margins, line spacings, and other formatting options. When you're finished, with your experimentation, press:

(F7) + N + N

to clear the documents from the screen without exiting from WordPerfect. When you're ready, move on to the *Page* options described below.

```
Format: Page

    1 - Center Page (top to bottom)     No

    2 - Force Odd/Even Page

    3 - Headers

    4 - Footers

    5 - Margins - Top               1"
                  Bottom            1"

    6 - New Page Number             1
          (example: 3 or iii)

    7 - Page Numbering              No page numbering

    8 - Paper Size                  8.5" x 11"
          Type                      Standard

    9 - Suppress (this page only)

Selection: 0
```

Figure 5.10 *Page Format Options Menu*

PAGE OPTIONS

Option number 2 of the *Format* options menu (Shift-F8) displays the *Page* formatting option menu (see Figure 5.10). The *Page* formatting options control the attributes of individual pages.

Each option is discussed below. As with the *Line* options section, you will get the most out of the book by trying out various options as you read about them.

Center Page (top to bottom)

As the name implies, this option centers texts vertically on a page. It is useful for centering letters, creating title pages, and creating tables. Note: to make sure that you center all text vertically, press:

(Home) + (Home) + (Up Cursor)

before selecting the *Center Page* option. WordPerfect defaults to No for this option; when you select option 1 of the *Page* format option menu, *Center Page* automatically changes to Yes. Selecting Yes, however, just centers the current page. At the next page, the *Center Page* option is again turned off again. In other words, you have to select *Center Page* for each page in your document.

Force Odd/Even Pages

This format option allows you to force a page to begin with an odd or even number. When you select this option, WordPerfect displays the following choices:

1 **O**dd; 2 **E**ven: **0**

The first choice forces an odd page, the second forces an even one. The main use for this feature is with multiple chapter documents where each chapter starts on a right page, which by convention is always an odd numbered page.

Headers and Footers

A header is a line of type that appears at the top of a page; a footer is a line of type on the bottom of a page (see Figure 5.11).

A header or footer might contain the title of a manuscript, chapter name, and/or its author, the date, a draft number, or anything else that is appropriate. Headers and footers have been combined in this section, because they are identical in use, except for their placement on the page.

WordPerfect allows you to create two headers andfooters per page (see Figure 5.12).

When you select the *Header* option, WordPerfect prompts you with:

1 Header **A**; 2 Header **B**: **0**

where "A" refer to the first of two possible headers, and "B" refers to the second.

Footer is the same, except that the menu displays Footer A and Footer B. When you select Header A/B or Footer A/B, you will be presented with the following options:

1 **D**iscontinue; 2 Every **P**age; 3 **O**dd Pages; 4 **E**ven Pages; 5 **E**dit: **0**

Discontinue means stop printing a previously defined header or footer.

Every page places both the A and B header or footer on each page.

```
    Example of Header A
                          INTRODUCTION:
                  THE ORIGIN OF SOFTWARE SPECIES
                  (With apologies to Charles Darwin)


    A New Breed of Software
         Every  major  software  maker  puts  its  products  through  a
    continual evolution to provide new features and improve existing
    ones;  as  in  the  biological  world,  constant  change  in  the
    microcomputing marketplace is the key to survival.  Sometimes the
    change is small, involving minor cosmetic surgery, the fixing of
    minor bugs, or the addition of a few features.  This is usually
    accompanied by a fractional change in the version or release number
    of  the  program,  say  from  1.0  to  1.1.   Other  times,  the  changes
    represent a quantum leap and in effect create a whole new product,
    in which case the version jumps from 1.0 to 2.0, 2.0 to 3.0, and
    so on.
         Word Perfect is no exception; version 5.0 represents a major
    departure from version 4.2, adding scores of new features that make
    it one of the most powerful word processor available. Actually,
    with  its  laser  printer  control  and  new  formatting  commands,
    WordPerfect 5.0 lies somewhere in the software kingdom between a
    word processor and a desktop publishing program.   The resulting




    Example of Footer A
```

Figure 5.11 *Example of Single Header and Footer*

```
Example of Header A
Example of Header B
                          INTRODUCTION:
                    THE ORIGIN OF SOFTWARE SPECIES
                    (With apologies to Charles Darwin)


A New Breed of Software
     Every  major  software  maker  puts  its  products  through  a
continual  evolution  to  provide  new  features  and  improve  existing
ones;  as  in  the  biological  world,  constant  change  in  the
microcomputing marketplace is the key to survival.  Sometimes the
change  is  small,  involving  minor  cosmetic  surgery,  the  fixing  of
minor  bugs,  or  the  addition  of  a  few  features.  This  is  usually
accompanied by a fractional change in the version or release number
of  the  program,  say  from  1.0  to  1.1.   Other  times,  the  changes
represent  a  quantum  leap  and  in  effect  create  a  whole  new  product,
in  which  case  the  version  jumps  from  1.0  to  2.0,  2.0  to  3.0,  and
so on.
     Word  Perfect  is  no  exception;  version  5.0  represents  a  major
departure  from  version  4.2,  adding  scores  of  new  features  that make
it  one  of  the  most  powerful  word  processor  available.  Actually,
with  its  laser  printer  control  and  new  formatting  commands,
WordPerfect 5.0 lies somewhere in the software kingdom between a
word  processor  and  a  desktop  publishing  program.   The  resulting




Example of Footer A
Example of Footer B
```

Figure 5.12 *Example of Two Headers and Footers*

Odd & Even pages place the A header or footer on odd pages, and the B header or footer on even pages, or vice versa.

Edit allows you to change the text of a header or footer.

Creating a Header A or Footer A

When you select options 2 through 4, WordPerfect displays a blank screen. Enter the text you want to appear in the header or footer of the selected pages. When creating a header or footer, you can use many of WordPerfect's formatting functions. For example:

Center (Shift-F6) centers the text of the header or footer.

Flush Right (Alt-F6) aligns the header or footer text with the right margin.

Bold (F6) bolds text

Underline (F8) underlines text

Date (Shift-F5) can be used to insert today's date, (option #1) or to insert a date code (option #2) so that the header or footer always displays the current date.

In addition, you can enter a unique page numbering code, ^B (Ctrl-B). Whenever WordPerfect encounters ^B, it increments the page number. While WordPerfect provides extensive standard page numbering options (See Below, #7), the ^B command allows you to customize the placement of the page number—wherever ^B appears, the page number appears. You can also add other text around a ^B command. For example, if you want to link the chapter or section number of a report with the page number, you might include:

    1-^B

in your header or footer line. This labels pages 1-1, 1-2, 1-3, etc. For the next section, you can change the header to include

    2-^B:

so that pages are numbered 2-1, 2-2, 2-3, etc.

Alternately, you could use a colon (:) instead of a dash, or spell out Page, as in:

    1:^B or

Page ^B

The former produces pages numbered 1:1, 1:2, 1:3, etc, while the latter prints pages numbered Page 1, Page 2, Page 3, and so on.

When you finish creating the text for your header or footer, press (F7) to return to your document.

Creating a Header B or Footer B

Header or Footer B is created in the same way as a Header or Footer A. You must, however, ensure that they don't overlap with a Header or Footer A. You can do this either by left aligning Header or Footer A and right aligning Header or Footer B on the same line, or by spacing them on different lines.

For example, if Header A occupies one line, when you you create Header B and are presented with a blank screen, press (Enter) so that Header B starts on the *second* line. This way, the text for Header A appears on the top line, and the text for Header B prints underneath it. To check the placement, you can use the *Print Preview* option (Shift-F7) + 6 to see how the page will actually look when printed.

Editing a Header or Footer

If you want to edit a footer or header later on, place your cursor at the top of the document, select Header/Footer A or B, whichever is appropriate, then select 5 for edit. Your text appears on a blank screen. Change the copy as you like, then press (F7) to exit to the *Page* format options menu. Press (F7) to return to your document.

IMPORTANT NOTES

1. Like most of the formatting options, all headers and footers should be created when the cursor is at the top of the document, before your text; otherwise they may not print where you expect them.

2. Headers and footers cannot be seen on the screen, except for print preview (Shift-F7) + 6.

3. If you create a header or footer that appears in, say, the left hand

corner of the page, then select a page numbering position in the same location the header or footer takes precedence. If you want the page number to appear as part of a header or footer, use the code ^B within the header or footer text. Do not use standard page numbering as described below.

Try creating a header or footer of your own before you go on to the next section.

Margins (Top and Bottom)

Use this option to control how much space appears above and below the text. Select 5, and the cursor moves to the Top margin option. Enter the top margin value in inches or units of your choice, as measured from the top of the page. When you press (Enter), the cursor will move to the Bottom margin option. Enter the bottom margin value, in inches or other units, as measured from the BOTTOM of the page. Press (Enter) again, and the cursor will return to the selection line at the bottom of the screen. Press (F7) twice to return to your document. Note that the Margin (Top/Bottom) option sets the amount of space above and below the text for the rest of the document, unless you change the setting on a subsequent page.

New Page Number

Normally, WordPerfect begins counting pages with the first page shown on the screen, as indicated by the Pg indicator on your Status Line. For example, you may want to separate chapters of a document into separate files but use continuous page numbers. If Chapter 2 began on page 47, you would move the cursor to the top of the document and insert a *New Page Number* code by pressing:

   (Shift-F8) + 2 + 6

and then entering the desired starting page number (i.e. "47").

Another use for the *New Page Number* command would be when you have a title page, a table of contents, or a blank page before the actual text begins. In that case, you might want the first page of the text to be numbered page 1. Move the cursor to the top of the first text page, select the New Page Number option, type:

> 1 + (Enter) + (F7)

Now, here's where things can get a bit confusing. If you get back to the first page of your document, the **Pg** indicator says page 1, and it increases until you reach the first page of the text, at which point it returns to 1. Won't that look weird when the document prints out? No, because WordPerfect won't *print* a page number unless a *Page Numbering* command has been issued. You can either wait until the first text page to place the *Page Numbering* command, or you can place the *Page Numbering* command at the top of the document; but use the *Suppress* option to keep the page number from printing on the beginning pages.

Before describing the *Page Numbering* and *Select* options, one other aspect of the *New Page Number* option needs to be discussed. If you enter a new page number in Arabic form (e.g. 1, 2, 3, etc) numbers print out in Arabic style. If you enter a new page number in Roman style (i, ii, iii, etc), the page numbers print out in Roman style.

For example, let's say that before the first page of text, you have a title page and table of contents, and a few pages of acknowledgements and notes. You wish to number the acknowledgements and notes with Roman letters. Go to the top of the first page to be numbered in Roman style, select the *New Page Number* option, and type:

> 1 + (Enter) + (F7)

Next, go to the top of the first page of text, and select the *New Page Number* option again, and type:

> 1 + (Enter) + (F7)

After you set the *Page Numbering* position as described below, the front matter of your document will be printed with Roman page numbers, and the text will be printed with Arabic page numbers. Again, on the screen things will seem a bit strange. When the cursor is in the title page, the status line indicates page 1. Page down, and the table of contents is shown as page 2. But when you get to the first page of the front matter, the **Pg** indicator of the Status Line says 1 in Arabic form. This is because the **Pg** indicator can only display page numbers in Arabic form, even though you specifically entered a new page number in Roman form. The numbering continues from page i until you reach your first page of text, at which point it returns to 1, because you entered a *New Page Number* command there. Just keep track of where you've entered *New Page Number* commands, and you won't have any problems.

Page Numbering

As mentioned above, in order to print a page number, you must enter a page number position. When you select option #7 from the *Page* options, WordPerfect displays a number of page number positions, as shown in Figure 5.13.

Enter the number corresponding to the desired page number position, and the display will return to the *Page* format menu. Press (F7) to return to the document. All pages print with the page number in the selected position, until you enter a new *Page Numbering* command.

Like many of the formatting options, a *Page Numbering* setting placed directly AFTER a code such as Bold will produce a bold page number. The easiest way to avoid such problems is to ensure that

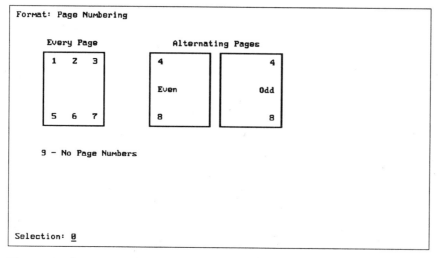

Figure 5.13 *Page Number Position Options*

the page number command appears at the very top of the page or document by pressing the (Home) key three times followed by the (Up Cursor) before using *Page Number* feature.

Paper Size/Type

The *Paper Size* option allows WordPerfect to correctly determine the number of lines to be placed on a page. When you select the option, you will be presented with the *Page Size* menu, shown in Figure 5.14.

Select the size of the paper you're using, or O for Other, in which case you'll be prompted to enter a width and length. The *Paper Type* menu (Figure 5.15) will then be displayed.

This option refers to the type of form you set up with your printer definition. If you have only done the basic installation described in Chapter 1, then select *Standard*—that is always present. If you have set up your printer according to the procedure described in Appendix B, setting up a LaserJet Series II, you can use other paper types, also as explained in Appendix B.

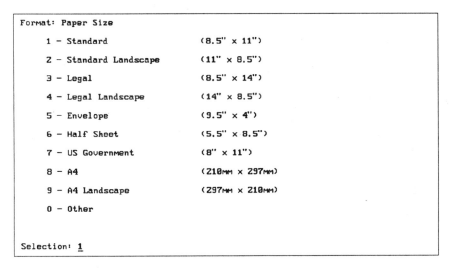

```
Format: Paper Size

    1 - Standard               (8.5" x 11")

    2 - Standard Landscape     (11" x 8.5")

    3 - Legal                  (8.5" x 14")

    4 - Legal Landscape        (14" x 8.5")

    5 - Envelope               (9.5" x 4')

    6 - Half Sheet             (5.5" x 8.5")

    7 - US Government          (8" x 11")

    8 - A4                     (210mm x 297mm)

    9 - A4 Landscape           (297mm x 210mm)

    0 - Other


Selection: 1
```

Figure 5.14 *Page Size Options*

```
Format: Paper Type
     1 - Standard

     2 - Bond

     3 - Letterhead

     4 - Labels

     5 - Envelope

     6 - Transparency

     7 - Cardstock

     8 - Other




Selection: 1
```

Figure 5.15 *Page Type Options*

Suppress

There are occasions where you don't want a page number, a header, or a footer to appear on a page. This might be a divider page, a title page, or an intentional blank page. Move the cursor to the page for which you want to suppress various printing attributes, and select option #9 from the *Page* format menu. WordPerfect displays the list of options shown in Figure 5.16.

To turn off everything select option #1—you don't have to enter Y or N; simply selecting the option activates it. Notice that when you select option #1, all of the suppress header and footer options (4 through 8) automatically turn to YES. If you select option #2, which works the same way (no Y or N is necessary), the suppress header and footer options change to YES, but the suppress page numbering options, 3 and 4, remain NO.

One bit of counter-intuitive logic needs to cleared up. Option 3, *Print Page Number at Bottom Center*, works in just the opposite fashion as the Suppress page numbering and suppress headers/ footers (Options 4 through 9). When you say YES to options 4 through 9, you are telling WordPerfect to suppress the functions

```
Format: Suppress (this page only)

    1 - Suppress All Page Numbering, Headers and Footers

    2 - Suppress Headers and Footers

    3 - Print Page Number at Bottom Center   No

    4 - Suppress Page Numbering              No

    5 - Suppress Header A                    No

    6 - Suppress Header B                    No

    7 - Suppress Footer A                    No

    8 - Suppress Footer B                    No




Selection: 0
```

Figure 5.16 *Suppress Options Menu*

associated with those numbers. But when you say YES to option #3, you instruct WordPerfect to go ahead and print the page number in position 6, bottom center (In other words, YES means *don't* suppress). NO means don't print (i.e., go ahead and suppress).

The reason WordPerfect provided this option is that many people like to set up a format in which all of the body of a document prints with pages on the right or left bottom of the page, but the title page and chapter head page prints with the page number in the bottom center. Option #3 of the Suppress menu eliminates the need to put in different *Page Numbering* positions for the title page and the text.

Finally, if you make a mistake and decide you really don't want to suppress everything for the current page, you have to select those items you want "unsuppressed," and enter an N. If you press (Enter), you will return to the Page format options menu. If you press (F7), you return to the document.

Your Turn

At this point, you've been through all of the *Page* formatting options, and should be able to control the format and look of each page. As with the *Line* format options, experimentation is the best way to learn how to use *Page* format options. Before going on, try each option if you haven't done so already.

DOCUMENT FORMAT OPTIONS

Option 3 of the Format options menu (Shift-F8), displays the *Document* format options menu (Figure 5.17), which allows you to select "global" options for an entire document. Of the options presented, only the second, *Initial Codes* and the third, *Initial Font*, are within the scope of this book. Refer to your WordPerfect reference manual for information about the other options.

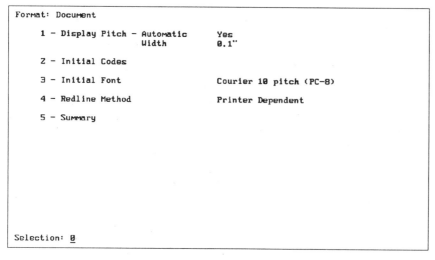

```
Format: Document

      1 - Display Pitch - Automatic      Yes
                          Width          0.1"

      2 - Initial Codes

      3 - Initial Font                   Courier 10 pitch (PC-8)

      4 - Redline Method                 Printer Dependent

      5 - Summary




Selection: 0
```

Figure 5.17 *Document Options Menu*

Initial Codes

If you installed WordPerfect yourself, you probably recall setup option 5, which offered you the opportunity to create *Initial Codes,* such as justification off, a particular margin setting, etc. The *Setup, Initial Codes* options apply to any document you create or retrieve. The *Document, Initial Codes* option allows you to change initial codes for the *current document*—i.e., the one on the screen. In other words, it's an opportunity to override the settings you entered during the Setup.

Note that you can easily override the initial settings of the installation by simply selecting each item, and entering a new value for the current document. For example, let's say you entered a particular margin setting, tab setting, and a particular page number position during the installation. For the current document, you could go into the *Line* options menu and change the margins and tabs, then call up the *Page* options menu and change the page numbering position. The advantage of the *Document, Initial Codes* option is that you can use it to make all desired changes in one shot.

When you select the *Document, Initial Codes* option, the screen divides as shown in Figure 5.18. Any codes entered from the *Setup, Initial Codes* option will be displayed beneath the form ruler. You can either delete those codes or add new ones. To enter new initial codes, call up the desired function, as if you were formatting a document.

For example, if you want to make the left and right margins different from those you set up during the installation, call up the *Line* options menu by pressing:

(Shift-F8) + 1

Select *margins* (option #7), type in the desired left margins (say, 1.5"), press (Enter), type in the desired value for the right margin (say 1.25"), press (Enter), and then press (F7). The margin settings will appear in code form, as shown in Figure 5.18.

You can include most of the format options that you've read about so far in the same way. Note that the *Setup, Initial Codes* are present, since they are the program's default codes. Use the cursor to

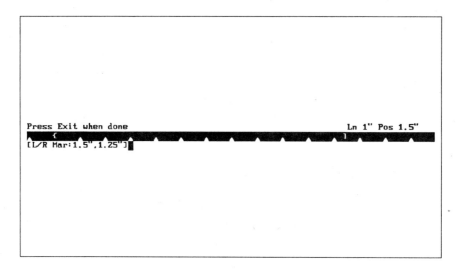

Figure 5.18 *Document Options Menu*

highlight any codes that you don't want in the current document
and press the (Del) key to get rid of them. Then enter your new
codes for the current document. When you finish entering *Initial
Codes*, press (F7) and the Document format option menu will be displayed. Press (Enter) and the general *Format* option will be displayed. Alternately, press (F7) and you will return to the document.

When you save this document, the *Document,Initial Codes* will be
saved. Therefore, the next time you print or retrieve the document,
the new settings will override the *Setup, Initial Codes* you entered
during installation, as well as any WordPerfect default settings. Remember, though, the codes entered through the *Document, Initial
Codes* option only apply to the document in which they were
entered. Once that document clears the screen, any new documents will be formatted by the *Initial Codes* established through the
Setup menu, and by any remaining WordPerfect default settings.

Initial Font

One of the great improvements WordPerfect 5.0 offers over previous versions is its ability to deal intelligently with many fonts. As

described in Appendix C, WordPerfect uses a "base font" as a starting point for all fonts in a document. Other fonts, (e.g., italics, bold, etc) are specified as variations of the base font. When you installed your printer, you selected an initial font to be used as the starting base font for all documents using that printer definition.

The *Initial Font* option allows you to override the initial font you assigned during the printer installation—for the current document. It is quite similar to selecting a different base font from the font menu (Ctrl-F8). You should use the initial font option when you want to make a change throughout a document and use the base font option when you are making a temporary font change that is not a simple variation of the current base font.

Your Turn

Create a set of initial codes using the *Document, Initial Codes* option. Try entering a margin command, a tab set command, and a page number position. Now enter some text. Save the document by pressing:

(F7) + Y + [filename] + N

then retrieve the document by pressing:

(Shift-F10) + [filename]

Notice how the margins, tab set, and page number position are the same as those you entered for the *Document, Initial Codes*.

OTHER

The last option in the Format menu (Shift-F8), is *Other*. Press 4, and the *Other* format options menu will appear on the screen. All of the *Other* options are for advanced use, and are beyond the scope of this book. If you want to learn more about them, consult the manual supplied with the program.

PUTTING IT ALL TOGETHER

At this point, you know quite a bit about WordPerfect—how to navigate, how to use the function keys, and how to format pages. If you experimented with the various features as you read along, you might have even created a document or two. If not, now is a good time to do so. Try the following exercise, in which you create a letter and a memo. The memo is particularly important, as it reviews many of the features and commands you've learned so far. It's worth putting a little bit of time into creating the memo, because you'll use it again in Chapter 9, when you learn how to edit a document.

Type a letter

1. Place the cursor where you want the date. If you're using a block format, the date will be flush with the left margin. Press:

   (Shift-F5) + 1

   and the date will appear (If you want to change the date format, refer to Chapter 3).

   If you want the date two thirds or so over, use the (Spacebar) key to move the cursor to the desired location. Press:

   (Shift-F5) + 1

   and the date will be displayed at the cursor location.

2. Press (Enter) as many times as necessary to place the addressee at the desired location. Then type in his or her name, title, company, city, state, and zip. Press (Enter) twice.

3. Type in "Dear so and so," Press (Enter) twice.

4. Enter the body of the letter. If you indent paragraphs, use the tab key. If you leave them in block form, just type. To separate paragraphs with an extra space, press (Enter) at the end of the paragraph.

5. Finish the letter with an appropriate closure.

6. Print your letter by turning on your printer, and pressing:

   (Shift-F7) + 1

7. If you wish, you can save the letter by pressing:

(F7) + Y + [file name] + N

Type a memo

This exercise is be most effective if you can type at least two pages of memo text. You might actually want to get an old memo and use it for copy. Better yet, compose a memo that you actually need to submit. That way, the exercise will yield an immediately useful document.

Finally, memo formats tend to be idiosyncratic, and the following is the one preferred by the authors. You can modify it as you see fit.

1. Set the page numbers to the bottom of every page by entering:

(Shift-F8) + 2 + 7 + 6 + (F7)

2. Create a footer by entering

(Shift-F8) + 2 + 4 + 1 + 2

Then enter a couple of words describing the subject of the memo in the footer text. Next, move the cursor flush right by pressing:

(Alt-F6)

and enter today's date by pressing:

(Shift-F5) + 1

Finally, return to the document by pressing:

(F7) + (F7)

The footer will contain the subject matter on the left, and the date on the right. The page number will appear in the middle, because you selected "bottom middle, every page" for page number placement in Step #1. You could have also embedded the page number in the footer by using the ^B page command. This would have been done as follows:

(Shift-F8) + 2 + 4 + 1 + 2

to create the footer. Next, enter a couple of words describing the subject of the memo and move the cursor to the center of the document by pressing

(Shift-F6)

Enter the embedded page number command by typing:

(Ctrl-B)

and move the cursor flush right by pressing:

(Alt-F6)

Next, enter today's date by pressing:

(Shift-F5) + 1

Finally, return to your document by pressing:

(F7) + (F7)

3. Suppress the footer and page number for the first page by entering:

(Shift-F8) + 2 + 9 + 1 + (F7)

4. Enter the tab ruler screen and delete existing tabs. Press:

(Shift-F8) + 1 + 8 + (Ctrl-End)

If you set your Units of Measure to inches during setup (or didn't change the WordPerfect defaults, which are already set to inches), type:

1.6 + (Enter)

This will place a tab at 1.6 inches. Return to your document by pressing (F7) twice.

5. Enter the heading, **MEMORANDUM** by pressing

(Shift-F5) + (Caps) key + (F6) + (F8)

Then type

memorandum (F6) + (F8) + (Caps) + (Enter) + (Enter) + (Enter)

Here's what you just did:

The (Shift-F6) combination moves the cursor to the center of the document, so all text on the following line will be centered.

The (Caps) key tells WordPerfect to make all following letters upper case.

The (F6) key tells WordPerfect to bold all following characters.

The (F8) key tells WordPerfect to underline all following characters.

When you entered "memorandum," it should have appeared on the screen centered, upper case, bold, and underlined.

Pressing the (Caps), (F6), and (F8) keys turned off the capitalization, bold, and underline functions. (This is called toggling-press a key once and it turns on a function, press it again and it turns the function off.)

The centering function automatically turns off when you pressed the first (Enter) after the word "memorandum."

6. Change the line spacing to double space by entering

      (Shift-F8) + 1 + 6 + 2 + (Enter) + (F7)

7. Start bold by pressing:

      (F6)

   then type:

      To:

   Turn off bold by pressing:

      (F6)

   Now press:

      (Tab)

   and type in the recipient's name + (Enter)

8. Turn on bold again by pressing:

      (F6)

   then type:

      From:

   and toggle bold off by pressing:

      (F6)

Press:

>   (Tab)

Type in your name or some other sender's name + (Enter)

9. Press:

    >   (F6)

    then type:

    >   **Date:**

    and press:

    >   (F6)

    again to put the word "Date" in bold and press:

    >   (Tab)

    Press:

    >   (Shift-F5) + 1 + (Enter)

    to insert today's date. (Refer to Chapter 3, page 63 if you want to change the way that the date is displayed.)

10. Press:

    >   (F6)

    then type:

    >   **Re:**

    Press:

    >   (F6)

    Press:

    >   (Tab)

    Type in the topic of the memo + (Enter).

11. Hold the dash key so that you create a line of dashes up to position 7.2 inches (if you haven't changed the default margins of Left = 1 inch, Right = 1 inch). This will separate the ID part of the memo. Press the (Enter) key twice to space down to the body of the text.

12. Turn single spacing back on by entering:

    (Shift-F8) + 1 + 6 + 1 + (Enter) + (F7)

13. Type the body of your memo. While doing so, try the following: indent a paragraph by an equal amount left and right by pressing (Shift-F4). Indent a couple of paragraphs from the left by using the (F4) key. Remember, the words will continue to indent as part of the same paragraph until you hit the (Enter) key. When you are ready to return to the full margin, press (Enter).

14. Print the memo by entering:

    (Shift-F7) + 1

15. Save the file (you'll need it for Chapter 9) by entering:

    (F7) + Y + [file name] + [N]

Congratulations! At this point, you've used many of the basic features that you'll need for everyday word processing. The next two chapters focus on two other important features of WordPerfect 5.0: column formatting (Chapter 6), and footnote/endnote creation (Chapter 7). Chapter 8 explores WordPerfect's powerful editing features. Naturally, you don't have to wait until you finish a document to edit it. In fact, most people learn to format, compose, and edit a document as they go along, so that the distinction between document creation and editing begins to blur and fade away. Document formatting/creation and editing have been separated in this book into individual chapters for the sake of instruction—it's a bit much to take it all in at once. Once you begin using the program, you'll find yourself using a variety of tools, ranging from initial formatting options to cut and paste features.

If you want to take a break and absorb the material in this chapter, this is a good time to do so. Otherwise, continue reading and experimenting—the more time you spend experimenting with WordPerfect 5.0 and using it to create actual documents, the more quickly you'll become a Word Perfectionist.

6

Column Formats

SETTING UP A MULTI-COLUMN FORMAT

WordPerfect allows you to easily arrange text in multiple columns. This is very useful for newsletters and lengthy reports, which might be hard to read or visually boring in a single column. The procedure for creating columns seems at first daunting, but once you've set up a column format you'll find it quite easy.

To create a multiple column document, two steps are required. First, you must define the columns. This is done by pressing

(Alt-F7)

which displays the *Column Definition* menu shown in Figure 6.1.

Here's how to define columns using the menu.

Select the column type

Two main types are available: *Newspaper* and *Parallel. Newspaper* columns are designed for newsletters and other communications in

```
Text Column Definition

    1 - Type                              Newspaper

    2 - Number of Columns                 2

    3 - Distance Between Columns

    4 - Margins

    Column    Left      Right    Column    Left       Right
    ‾‾‾‾‾‾    ‾‾‾‾      ‾‾‾‾‾    ‾‾‾‾‾‾    ‾‾‾‾       ‾‾‾‾‾
    1:        1"        4"       13:
    2:        4.5"      7.5"     14:
    3:                           15:
    4:                           16:
    5:                           17:
    6:                           18:
    7:                           19:
    8:                           20:
    9:                           21:
    10:                          22:
    11:                          23:
    12:                          24:

    Selection: 0
```

Figure 6.1 *Column Definition Menu*

which the information flows continuously down the page, from column to column. A sample of *Newspaper* column format is shown in Figure 6.2.

Parallel columns are designed for documents in which the information flows "horizontally," as in a price list or telephone directory (see Figure 6.3).

A second type of *Parallel* column is called *Parallel* with *Block Protect*. *Block Protect* keeps a set of columns from being split apart if an entry in one column extends beyond the current page. Let's say that you have four columns in a phone directory: name, department, title, and telephone number. One entry, which has two phone numbers, is the last one on a page. The page, however, only has room for the first phone number, and the second kicks over to the next page. Without *Block Protect*, the second page would have a phone number at the top, but no corresponding entries to the left. With the *Block Protect* option, the last entries across all four columns are moved as a group to the next page. That way, the second page begins with a complete set of entries.

A New Breed of Software

Every major software maker puts its products through a continual evolution to provide new features and improve existing ones; as in the biological world, constant change in the microcomputing marketplace is the key to survival.

Sometimes the change is small, involving minor cosmetic surgery, the fixing of minor bugs, or the addition of a few features. This is usually accompanied by a fractional change in the version or release number of the program, say from 1.0 to 1.1.

Other times, the changes represent a quantum leap and in effect create a whole new product, in which case the version jumps from 1.0 to 2.0, 2.0 to 3.0, and so on.

Word Perfect is no exception; version 5.0 represents a major departure from version 4.2, adding scores of new features that make it one of the most powerful word processor available. Actually, with its laser printer control and new formatting commands, WordPerfect 5.0 lies somewhere in the software kingdom between a word processor and a desktop publishing program. The resulting hybrid might therefore best be called a "document processor."

However you describe WordPerfect 5.0, one thing is certain; with its added power comes a steep learning curve. New users may find a seemingly overwhelming number of functions and concepts to learn. And those familiar with version 4.2 might be a little dismayed to find that a number of familiar key strokes have been changed. The good news is that despite WordPerfect 5.0's enormous power, a relatively easy-to-manage subset of the program's functions enable you to easily handle day-to-day use of the program for creating correspondence, memos, reports, manuscripts, and other basic documents.

A Shortcut

Simply WordPerfect is designed to guide you through the essential WordPerfect functions. Some of the special functions for which you may only have occasional use are also briefly described in the last chapter.

Rather than drag you through a tutorial in which you create a silly letter or memo, then manipulate it a hundred ways, the book strives to match the mental processes you'll probably go through from the moment you open the box to the first time you print a document.

As you read along, you can experiment with your own text and create documents relevant to your own pursuits. Here's the flow of logic:

-Installing the program
-Finding your way around
 the keyboard
-Learning the use of each
 function key
-Personalizing the program
-Creating and formatting text
-Editing text
-Checking your spelling
-Printing your document
-Saving and retrieving your
 document

Figure 6.2 *Sample Newspaper Columns*

TELEPHONE DIRECTORY

Name	Department	Title	Tel #
Alston	Factory	Foreman	X2343
			X4323
Barnet	Marketing	Manager	X2312
Carlson, R.	Marketing	VP	X2343
			X4321
Dennet, W.	Sales	VP	X3234
			X2321
Durston, V.	Stockroom	Manager	X3221
Ephraim, R.	Purchasing	Manager	X8763
Fedder, G.	Purchasing	Sr Buyer	X8732
			X1121
Grant, S.	Finance	VP	X9874
			X7633
Hilton, E.	Engineering	Manager	X4323
Hurley, R.	Shipping	Manager	X3432
			X9873
Iston, V.	Engineering	Supervisor	X6653
			X6654
Kramer, R.	Sales	Senior VP	X3423
Lister, W.	Factory	Dispatcher	X8767
			X9876
Mentin, J.	Factory	Scheduler	X4323
			X4324
Nimroy, Q.	Marketing	Forecaster	X1228
			X2543
Olston, E.	Receiving	Manager	X4444
Peters, T.	Maintenance	Manager	X7654
Quark, Q.	Finance	Senior VP	X4543
Reston. T.	Factory	Supervisor	X4564

Figure 6.3 *Sample Parallel Columns*

Enter the number of columns

You can enter up to 24 columns per page, depending on the size of the paper you're using. The default number of columns is 2. If you want two columns, evenly spaced, just press (Enter), and WordPerfect automatically sets up even Left and Right margins for the columns.

If you want more than 2 columns, type the desired number and press (Enter). WordPerfect calculates the left and right margins required for evenly spaced columns and indicates them on the screen. If these are acceptable, press (Enter), and WordPerfect returns to your document. If you want to manually adjust the spacing between columns, and the left and right margins for the individual columns, continue with the menu options below.

Decide the distance between columns

WordPerfect automatically determines the starting positions (left and right) for each column to create columns of equal width. You can specify whatever amount of space you want between columns; however, the greater the space, the smaller the column widths.

Set the margins

WordPerfect calculates the left and right margin positions for each column, assuming that you want columns of equal width. Should want to change the settings, select option #4; the cursor will move to the Column 1 position. You can then move the cursor to the left and right margin for each column, and enter whatever setting you desire.

When you press return after the last column setting, the cursor returns to the selection entry at the bottom of the screen. Press (Enter) or (F7) twice to return to the document. Once you complete all of the items in the *Column Definition* menu, WordPerfect places a hidden code in the document. You can view the code with the *Reveal Codes* function (Alt-F3). Press (Alt-F3) again to return to the document. (See Chapter 8 for more instruction about using *Reveal Codes*). That completes the column definition step. You can now proceed with the second step for using columns, which involves turning on the feature. The only tricky part of this two-step process is that you must place the columns on code (Alt-F7) AFTER the column definition code. If you try to turn on your columns above the code for column definition, WordPerfect displays the warning:

`ERROR: No text columns defined.`

You must then move the cursor down below the point at which you entered the column definition code. To do so, use *Reveal Codes* (Alt-F3) and scroll through the document to find the column definition code; position the cursor below it. Then press (Alt-F3) again to return to the document and insert the Column On code after the definition code by pressing (Alt-F7) +3.

NAVIGATING BETWEEN COLUMNS

Once you have turned columns on and entered your text, you must use some special cursor movements to maneuver among the columns. The best way to learn the navigation rules is to set up a dual column *Newspaper* format yourself and test the options.

Newspaper Columns

Cursor Movement Within Columns

If you have a two-column *Newspaper* format, think of it as two pages on the screen. When the cursor reaches the right margin of the first column, it returns to the left edge of the screen—even though the right edge might be only halfway across the page. This can be somewhat confusing at first, but becomes second nature with a little practice. As a help, when in column mode, WordPerfect adds another indicator to the Status Line, "**Col**," which displays the current column number. (See Figure 6.4.)

When you reach the bottom of the left column, the cursor "snakes" up to the top of the right column. When you finish the right column, the cursor automatically moves to the left column of the next page, and so on. Note that all of the cursor keys, as well as the

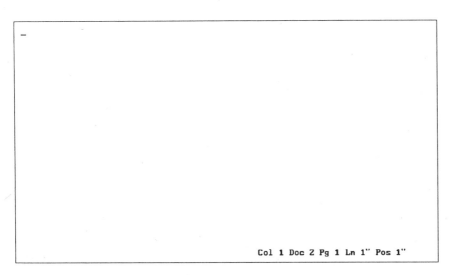

Figure 6.4 *Column Indicator on Status Line*

delete keys, function within each column as if the column were a
separate page.

Forcing the Start of a Newspaper Column

If you want to end a column and start another one, press:

(Ctrl-Enter)

and the cursor jumps to the beginning of the next column. If you
press (Ctrl-Enter) while the cursor is in the last column of the page,
the cursor moves to a new page, at the top of the left-hand column.
In this case, you'll see a double line on the screen, indicating that
a "hard new page" has been created. To undo the hard new page,
shift into *Reveal Codes* (Alt-F3), highlight the code [HPg] by moving
the cursor, press (Del), then press (Alt-F3) again to return to your
document.

Moving between columns

Once you've created the left and right columns, you can move the
cursor from the left to the right column by pressing:

(Ctrl-Home) + (Right Cursor)

To move from the right column to the left column, press:

(Ctrl-Home) + (Left Cursor)

If you have three or four columns, the same cursor movements apply for jumping between columns.

ENTERING ITEMS IN PARALLEL COLUMNS

When you turn columns on after defining *Parallel* columns, you need to press (Ctrl-Enter) after entering each item in a column. When you press (Ctrl-Enter), the cursor moves to the next column. When the cursor reaches the last column, it returns to the next line of the first column. In this way, WordPerfect allows you to enter "rows" of information.

If you need to enter more than one line of information in a particular column, press (Enter) instead of (Ctrl-Enter). You can enter as many lines per item in a column as you like; WordPerfect adjusts for the number of lines of a particular item and starts the next row at the appropriate place in the document.

If you selected *Parallel* columns with *Block Protect*, WordPerfect won't let you break up a multi-line item across two pages. Instead, it will bring all of the items in a particular row down to the next page.

TURNING OFF THE COLUMN SETTING

At some point, you may want to turn off the column setting and resume the normal text format. Call up the column menu by pressing:

(Alt-F7)

Select option #3, *Column On/Off* to turn the column feature off. At any point, you can turn the columns back on again using the same definition simply by re-selecting the *Column On* option after pressing (Alt-F7). You can also reset the column definition before turning the columns on, if you so desire. Make sure that the new definition follows the *Column Off* code of the first set of columns.

```
WordPerfect 5.0, one thing is
certain; with its added power
comes a steep learning curve.
New users may find a seemingly
overwhelming number of
functions and concepts to
learn.   And those familiar
with version 4.2 might be a
little dismayed to find that a


--------------------------------------------------------------------
                                number of familiar key strokes
                                have been changed.  The good
                                news is that despite
                                WordPerfect 5.0's enormous
                                power, a relatively easy-to-
                                manage subset of the program's
                                functions enable you to easily
                                handle day-to-day use of the
                                program for creating
                                correspondence, memos, reports,

C:\WP122\FIG6-2.122             Col 2 Doc 2 Pg 1 Ln 2.66" Pos 4.5"
```

Figure 6.5 *Column Per Page Display*

ALTERNATE COLUMN DISPLAY

In addition to displaying columns side-by-side, as they appear in print, WordPerfect allows you to display the columns on separate pages (see Figure 6.5). While the separate page display has the advantage of rewriting the screen and scrolling more quickly than the side-by-side display, you might find it more confusing. Besides, you have to use the *Print Preview*, (Shift-F7) + 6, to see what each page will look like when printed. The choice of which display to use is strictly one of personal preference.

To select the page-by-page display for columns, return to the system *Setup* function by pressing:

(Shift-F1) + 3 + 8

Enter N to display each column on a separate page. Each column is separated by a hard page break, displayed by a double dashed line. The Status Line indicator shows the column number as well as the regular page information.

Your Turn

If all this seems complicated, try it once. After you've formatted a few multi-column documents, you'll be an expert. For starts, keep it simple; even a basic two-column format can be an attractive and impressive document.

7

Footnotes and Endnotes

NOTES GALORE

WordPerfect offers a rich variety of features for creating and editing footnotes and endnotes. Footnotes appear on the bottom of the page on which their reference appears (see Figure 7.1). Endnotes, as the name implies, appear at the end of the document, or at a user-designated place, in the order in which they were written.

CREATING FOOTNOTES

To create a footnote, call up the main *Footnote/Endnote* menu, which is accessed by pressing (Ctrl-F7). The menu offers the following choices:

1 Footnote; **2** Endnote;   **3** Endnote **P**lacement: **0**

Select 1 for Footnote, and the *Footnote* menu will appear:

Footnote: 1 Create; 2 Edit; 3 New Number; 4 Options: 0

Problems and Solutions in the Media

Every day the newspapers and business publications recount
adventures in problem solving. To get the most out of such
stories, you should read them with an eye toward effective
solutions. As you watch how companies and individuals
grapple with their problems, use the D.A.R.E. method to
solve them yourself: Define, Anticipate, Risk, Evaluate.

Take a stroll with us through our local newsstand. Here,
check out this front page article explaining how IBM, in an
unprecedented combination Knight & Coach maneuver, gave one
its most advanced and secret chips to arch-rival DEC.[1] The
reason for this apparently insane act of generosity? IBM,
worried about the U.S. lagging too far beyond the Japanese,
determined that offshore competition posed more of a threat
than domestic competition. So it tipped the balance and
gave its American rival a break.

Could this ploy work in your business? Sure, if you're
plagued by foreign technology, why not share your brain-
storms with other hometown teams.[2] Perhaps the shoe and
textile industries, both sagging under the weight of cheaper
imports,[3] could especially benefit from this tactic.

---

[1] The New York Times, June 25, 1988.

[2] See also Business Week, July 1988, P 67.

[3] The Wall Street Journal, May 4, 1988.

Figure 7.1 *Sample Footnotes*

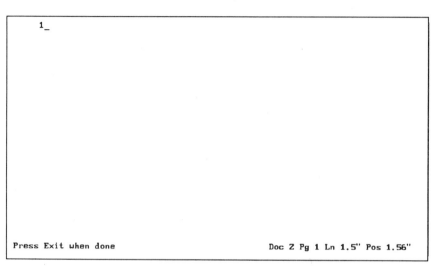

```
  1_




Press Exit when done                    Doc 2 Pg 1 Ln 1.5" Pos 1.56"
```

Figure 7.2 *Footnote Creation Screen*

Here's what each option means:

Create allows you to write a footnote. Make sure you position the cursor EXACTLY where you want the footnote number to appear before pressing the footnote key combination (Ctrl-F7). When you choose the *Create* option, the screen blanks, except for a number "1" in the upper left hand corner (see Figure 7.2). If this was your second footnote, the "1" would be replaced by a "2," and so on. All you have to do now is type—you can use all of the WordPerfect formatting and editing commands to create your footnote. When you're finished, press (F7) to return to the document.

The first thing you'll notice about your document is that you can't see the footnote; instead, the footnote number is embedded in your text, as in the following example:

In 1899, the Commissioner of the U.S. Office of Patents, Charles H. Duell, recommended to President McKinley that the patent office be dismantled, because, "Everything that can be invented has been invented."1

Notice that the footnote number (1) is located on the same line as the text, with no spacing. Don't worry—when the document

---

[1] Cerf, C., and Navasky, V. *The Experts Speak*. New York: Pantheon Books, 1984.

prints, it will be properly spaced and appear as a superscript. The footnote text will appear under a two inch line at the bottom of the page (the line can be eliminated or extended to the margins—See Options, below). You can see how the footnote number and text will print by using the *Print Preview* option (Shift-F7) + 6. Note: if your printer is capable of printing a variety of fonts, it automatically selects a smaller font for the footnote reference number.

As with the *Column Definition* function, WordPerfect places a special code in the text every time you create a footnote. You can see the code by pressing (Alt-F3), in which case the paragraph with the footnote appears as shown in Figure 7.3. The footnote code appears after the word "invented." Notice that the first 50 characters of the footnote are also shown, as a reminder of what the rest of the footnote contains.

Edit allows you to alter the contents of a footnote. When you select the *Edit* option, WordPerfect prompts you with the question:

Footnote number?

Enter the desired number and press (Enter); the text of the footnote appears as you typed it. When you're finished editing press (F7) to return to your document.

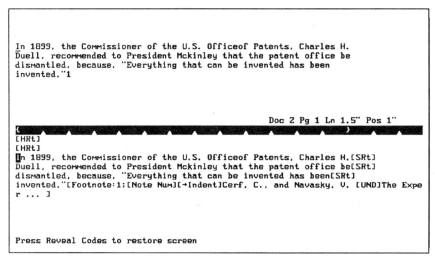

Figure 7.3 *Hidden Codes for Footnote. Shown in Reveal Codes* (Alt-F3)

New Number enables you to renumber the footnotes in a document. For example, you might want to start the numbering sequence from "1" each time you create a new chapter of a book or a new section of a report. All you have to do is position the cursor BEFORE the first footnote to be renumbered and AFTER the last footnote of the old sequence. Then select *New Number*. WordPerfect will prompt you with:

`Footnote number?`

Enter the new number, and press (Enter). Then press:

(Ctrl-F3) + (Enter)

to rewrite the screen. All footnotes AFTER the *New Number* command will be renumbered, starting with whatever value your entered when you selected *New Number.*

Options gives you the opportunity to customize the way footnotes are numbered, and the format in which they appear in your text. When you select *Options*, the menu shown in Figure 7.4 appears. Here's what each option means.

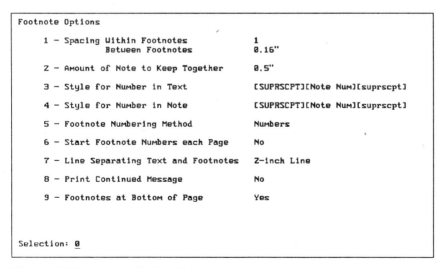

```
Footnote Options

    1 - Spacing Within Footnotes          1
                Between Footnotes          0.16"

    2 - Amount of Note to Keep Together    0.5"

    3 - Style for Number in Text           [SUPRSCPT][Note Num][suprscpt]

    4 - Style for Number in Note           [SUPRSCPT][Note Num][suprscpt]

    5 - Footnote Numbering Method          Numbers

    6 - Start Footnote Numbers each Page   No

    7 - Line Separating Text and Footnotes 2-inch Line

    8 - Print Continued Message            No

    9 - Footnotes at Bottom of Page        Yes



Selection: 0
```

Figure 7.4 *Footnotes Options Menu*

Spacing Within Footnotes/Between Footnotes.

When you select this option, the cursor first moves to "Within Footnotes." The default is "1," signifying single spaced. If you enter 1.5, the footnotes print at one-and-a-half space, and so on.

When you press (Enter), the cursor moves to the "Between Footnotes" selection. This refers to the amount of space between the footnotes. Note that in addition to the amount of space specified, WordPerfect adds a line below a footnote and a line above the subsequent footnote. Thus, the default setting of 0.16 inches actually prints out closer to a quarter of an inch between notes, depending on what font you're using.

Amount of Note to Keep Together.

WordPerfect has a rule for situations in which a footnote crosses from the bottom of one page to another: if it can keep at least half an inch on the first page, it divides the note and places the remainder on the second page. If there isn't room on the page for at least half an inch, it kicks the entire footnote, including reference number, over to the next page.

You can override this rule by entering a different amount for the portion of the note to be kept together on the first page. A number greater than the default half inch means more footnotes are moved to the next page; a smaller number means more fragmented footnotes crossing two pages. The choice is a matter of personal taste. Experiment and see for yourself.

Style of Number in Text.

This requires a more intimate knowledge of WordPerfect's printing capabilities. You are probably best off leaving the default as is—a superscript footnote number.

Style of Number in Note.

Ditto.

Footnote Numbering Method.

WordPerfect gives you the choice of numbering footnotes by numbers (1,2,3...), Letters (a,b,c,d, etc.), or characters. If you choose letters, the footnote references appear in lower case and double up after "z," making the next reference "aa," and triple up after "zz," and so on.

The *Characters* option is a little trickier. You can select up to five different characters (for example, $,#,!,+,*), which will be displayed on the menu after the words "Characters." WordPerfect cycles through the characters one by one, using each as a reference for a footnote. Once the fifth character (in our example, *) is used, it doubles up the first character ($$), then triples it ($$$) on the next pass, and so on. This can wind up bizarre looking and confusing, so unless you have a special application that only requires a few footnotes, you're probably best off sticking to numbers or letters.

Start Footnote Numbers Each Page.

WordPerfect gives you the opportunity to generate footnote numbers continuously throughout the document or to start renumbering footnotes on each page. The program defaults to N for this option, meaning that footnotes are consecutively generated until you issue a *New Number* command (see above). Type Y to restart the numbering on each page. (If you're going to use characters instead of numbers or letters, restarting the sequence on each page is definitely a better approach.)

Line Separating Text and Footnotes.

This option allows you to choose between:

    1 **N**o Line; **2** 2-inch Line; **3 M**argin to Margin: **0**

The program defaults to a two-inch line separating the text from the footnote. Select 1 to remove a separator line, and 3 to extend it across the page, between your margin settings. Whatever option you select is displayed in the menu.

Print Continued Message.

If a footnote gets split between two pages, you can instruct WordPerfect to add the words "Continued..." to the last line of the footnote that gets split. The message is also printed on the next page, at the beginning of the remainder of the footnote. Type Y to turn on the option.

Footnotes at Bottom of Page.

WordPerfect normally reserves enough space at the bottom of the page to insert all the footnotes referenced on that page. If the combined length of the text and the footnote are not sufficient to fill the page, WordPerfect can either print the footnote immediately after the text and leave the bottom of the page blank, or it can print the footnote at the bottom of the page and leave the space between the text and the footnote blank. As its name implies, setting this option to Yes accepts the latter, while setting it to no selects the former. (Hint: in a document where most pages have footnotes, the consistent placement of footnotes at the bottom of the page is probably more visually pleasing.)

When you have entered all your options, press (Enter) or (F7) and you will return to your document. Remember, footnote options only affect those footnotes that occur AFTER the options were selected. That means you must move the cursor to a point BEFORE the first footnote number. When you select any footnote option, WordPerfect enters a code **[Ftn Opt]**, which can be seen with the *Reveal Codes* feature. Press (Alt-F3) to go into *Reveal Codes* to view your options, then press (Alt-F3) to toggle back to the document.

If you're not sure where your code is, switch into *Reveal Codes* and cursor through the document. If you see your **[Ftn Opt]** after a footnote, highlight the code by moving the cursor over it, and press the (Del) key. Then move to a point before the first footnote reference and switch back to your document by pressing (Alt-F3) again. Select the desired footnote option again and all footnotes will conform to the style you choose.

One way to make sure the footnote option is in the correct place is to press:

(Home) + (Home) + (Home) + Up

and then enter your footnote option. This places the option code at the very beginning of the document, including any footnote codes. (Pressing the (Home) key twice plus up moves the cursor to the top of the document; adding the third (Home) instructs WordPerfect to place the cursor in front of any codes.)

Deleting Footnotes

To delete a footnote, find its reference on the screen and move your cursor underneath it. Then press the (Del) key. WordPerfect prompts you with:

`Delete [Footnote:X] (Y/N) No`

Where X is the footnote number in question. Press Y, and the footnote will be deleted. All footnotes beyond that point will be automatically renumbered.

Your Turn

If you haven't done so already, try creating a few footnotes, varying the style and numbering, as well as the other options. Again, practice makes...word perfect.

CREATING ENDNOTES

Endnotes, which are compiled into a running list that can be generated anywhere within a document, are created in a very similar way to footnotes. Where endnotes and footnotes part company is the way they are placed within the document—either at the end, or at a user-specified location (see below). To create, edit, or renumber an endnote, call up the main *Footnote/Endnote* menu by pressing (Ctrl-F7). The following choices will be displayed:

1 Footnote; **2 E**ndnote; **3** Endnote **P**lacement: **0**

Select 2 for Endnote. This will display the following menu:

Endnote:1 Create;**2 E**dit;**3 N**ew Number;**4 O**ptions: **0**

Choices 1, 2, and 3 are identical to those used for creating, editing, or renumbering footnotes. The fourth choice calls up an abbreviated version of the footnote *Options* menu (see Figure 7.5). The difference

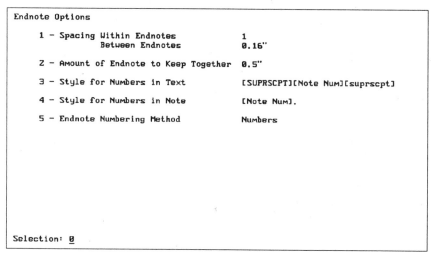
```
Endnote Options

    1 - Spacing Within Endnotes              1
             Between Endnotes                0.16"

    2 - Amount of Endnote to Keep Together   0.5"

    3 - Style for Numbers in Text            [SUPRSCPT][Note Num][suprscpt]

    4 - Style for Numbers in Note            [Note Num].

    5 - Endnote Numbering Method             Numbers




Selection: 0
```

Figure 7.5 *Endnotes Options Menu*

is that it is missing the options relating solely to footnotes (6 through 9, see Figure 7.4). The explanations for menu option items 1 through 5 are the same as those described above.

Placing Endnotes

While footnotes are generated page-by-page, endnotes are compiled into a single list. If you don't indicate where the list should be generated, it will be automatically created at the end of the document when you print. Like footnotes, endnotes cannot be seen on the screen, other than in *Reveal Codes,* which shows the note number and the first 50 characters. If you want to see what the page looks like without printing it, use the *Print Preview* option (Shift-F7) + 6.

So far the placement issue has been straightforward, and you are best advised to let endnotes be endnotes; that is, notes at the end of the document. If, however, you want to compile a list of all endnotes created up to a certain point, say at a section or chapter break, strap in and get ready for a wild jaunt through one of WordPerfect 5.0's more arcane functions: *Endnote Placement.*

```
stories, you should read them with an eye toward effective

solutions.  As you watch how companies and individuals grapple

with their problems, use the D.A.R.E. method to solve them

yourself: Define, Anticipate, Risk, Evaluate.

    Take a stroll with us through our local newsstand. Here,

check out this front page article explaining how IBM, in

anunprecedented combination Knight & Coach maneuver, gave one its

most advanced and secret chips to arch-rival DEC.1
┌─────────────────────────────────────────────────────────────────┐
│ Endnote Placement                                                 │
│ It is not known how much space endnotes will occupy here.         │
│ Generate to determine.                                            │
└─────────────────────────────────────────────────────────────────┘



===================================================================================
_ The reason for
                                          Doc 2 Pg 2 Ln 1" Pos 1"
```

Figure 7.6 *Endnote Placement Notice — Required Space Not Known*

To use the *Endnote Placement* option, first position the cursor exactly where you want the endnote(s) to be placed in your document, then call up the main *Footnote/Endnote* menu (Ctrl-F7), and select option #3. WordPerfect prompts you with:

Restart endnote renumbering (Y/N) Yes

If you answer Yes, WordPerfect starts the subsequent endnote with 1; if you answer No, WordPerfect continues numbering the endnotes consecutively. Either way, WordPerfect first indicates that the amount of space required for the endnotes created up to that point is not known. (See Figure 7.6). A double line, indicating a new page, appears underneath the message.

At this point, WordPerfect must calculate the amount of space required for the endnotes. If you're not overly concerned about the spacing, you can simply let WordPerfect handle the placement when it prints your document. If you want to preview the spacing, you can instruct WordPerfect to perform the calculation by pressing

(Alt-F5) + 6 + 5 + Y

The previous message will be replaced by a box with the words "Endnote Placement," indicating how much space the endnotes will

```
adventures in problem solving.  To get the most out of such

stories, you should read them with an eye toward effective

solutions.  As you watch how companies and individuals grapple

with their problems, use the D.A.R.E. method to solve them

yourself: Define, Anticipate, Risk, Evaluate.

    Take a stroll with us through our local newsstand. Here,

check out this front page article explaining how IBM, in

anunprecedented combination Knight & Coach maneuver, gave one its

most advanced and secret chips to arch-rival DEC.1
┌─────────────────────────────────────────────────────────────┐
│ Endnote Placement                                            │
└─────────────────────────────────────────────────────────────┘


=================================================================
   The reason for this apparently insane act of generosity?  IBM,
                                          Doc 2 Pg 1 Ln 4.33" Pos 1"
```

Figure 7.6 *Space Required by Endnoted — Compute Space with Ln Indicator*

occupy on the page (see Figure 7.7). The box doesn't actually show you how much space is required; rather, when you move the cursor above and below the box, note the status line and figure out from the **Ln** indicator exactly how much space the endnotes will use. When you print the document, all endnotes created up to the placement code appear on the page.

It is important to recognize that the process of Endnote renumbering will not begin until the page on which the endnotes will be printed.

Finally, if you want the endnotes to be placed on a separate page, first create a new (Hard) page by pressing (Ctrl-Enter). Then select the *Endnote Placement* option. *Endnote Placement* codes can be seen in *Reveal Codes* (Alt-F3), as:

[Endnote Placement][HPg]

[New End Num:1]

If you want to delete an Endnote Placement code, the job is best done from within *Reveal Codes*, (Alt-F3). Move the cursor to highlight **[Endnote Placement]**. Press the (Del) key. Then do the same for

[HPg] and [**New End Num:1**]. Press (Alt-F3) to return to your document. (See Chapter 8 for a complete discussion of *Reveal Codes*).

If this doesn't sound like fun, it's not. If you want notes at the end of a page, you're probably better off using footnotes. If you want endnotes at the end of a chapter or section, you'll most likely find it easier to split those sections into separate documents and let WordPerfect automatically generate the endnotes—at the end.

Deleting an Endnote

Endnotes are deleted the same way footnotes are deleted; move the cursor to the note reference number, and press the (Del) key. WordPerfect asks you to confirm your deletion. If you do delete an endnote, all endnotes beyond that point are automatically renumbered.

Your Turn

Create a series of endnotes, and print them out, by pressing (Shift + F7) + 1. If you're brave, experiment with the *Endnote Placement* option.

8

Editing Tools

YOUR EDITING TOOL KIT

There are many ways to edit a document, some of which you've already encountered earlier, such as *Reveal Codes* and the *Block* functions. In this chapter, we revisit those and other features and explore how to use them to alter your text. The chapter is divided into two basic sections: editing text, and editing formats/appearances. The former refers to word, sentence, and paragraph changes; the latter concerns modifying various format changes.

EDITING TEXT

The real power of a word processor is the ability to easily and instantly juggle words, sentences, paragraphs, and pages without resorting to scissors and tape, correction tape, or correction fluid. This involves six basic actions: 1) deleting text; 2) cutting and pasting text; 3) copying text; 4) inserting text; 5) searching for text; and 6) searching for and replacing text. This section explains how to use each action in editing a document.

As with other materials in this book, you'll learn the fastest if you experiment with them yourself. If you created a memo in Chapter 5, retrieve it with the following command sequence:

(Shift-F10) + Name You Gave to the File + (Enter)

(If you haven't created a memo, you're best off returning to Chapter 5 and doing so before proceeding—it's worth the effort.) As you read through this chapter, try modifying your text with the features described. Since you'll need your memo for various experiments, DON'T resave the memo under the same name after you've made modifications. That way you can call up the original version again and again, keeping it intact. If, during the course of your experimentation, your memo gets too mangled to be of use, press:

(F7) + N + N

which will clear the screen. Then recall the original memo, as you did above.

Block Functions

Deleting Text

You already know how to delete text with the (Del) key and the (Backspace) key. The block function is a much more efficient way to delete large chunks of text. Place the cursor at the beginning of words to be deleted. Press (Alt-F4) and move the cursor to the last word that you want to delete. Note that you can block "down" from the first to the last word, or "up" from the last word to the first word. As you "paint" the block, the words "*Block on*" flashes on and off in the lower left hand corner of the screen, and the **Pos** indicator of the status line as well as the text are highlighted. Once you've included all desired characters within the block, press the (Del) key. WordPerfect prompts you with:

`Delete Block? (Y/N) No`

If you enter a Y, the block is removed from the document. (If you didn't really want to delete the block, you can undo it by pressing the (F1) key. When you press the (F1) key, the block reappears, highlighted. Select **1** for Restore to bring the block back into the document. (WordPerfect stores your last three deletions; if you've deleted text after deleting the block, you may have to select **2** Previous Deletion.)

An alternative way of deleting a block of text is to save it to disk before you delete it from the document. To do so, press (F10) after the block is painted. The flashing "block on" will be replaced by the words

Block Name:

Enter the name you wish to assign the block and press (Enter). The block will be saved in a separate file under the name you entered.

After the saving function is complete, the block will be automatically turned off. If you want to highlight the same block and delete it, press (Alt-F4) to turn on the block function, then press (Ctrl-Home) twice followed by the (Del) key.

Cutting and Pasting Text

Electronic cutting and pasting is one of the most powerful word processing tools at your disposal. Try this. Pick a sentence or paragraph that you want to move to another location of the document. Move the cursor to the first character, and turn on the block function by pressing (Alt-F4). Move the cursor to the end of the text you want to cut and paste (this highlights the block) and press:

(Ctrl-F4) + 1 + 1

The block then disappears from your document. (Actually, it hasn't been deleted—it's stored in memory.) The screen displays:

Move cursor; press Enter to retrieve

Move the cursor to the *exact* location where you want the block of text placed and press (Enter). Voila! The text reappears in its new location.

You can use this mechanism to cut and paste as little or as much text as you like. It's generally faster to retype a word or two, rather than cut and paste them into their new location, but the choice is yours.

Electronic "trash bin"

One editing technique that you may find useful is to use your second document as a place to store bits and pieces of a text. Let's say that you're reading through a document and find some sentences or paragraphs that you know you can use, but they just don't work in their current location. Instead of deleting them, cut and paste them into your second document, by executing the following routine:

1. Position the cursor at the start of the text to be blocked.

2. Press (Alt-F4) and move the cursor to the end of the block.

3. Press (Ctrl-F4) + 1 + 1.

4. Press (Shift-F3) to switch to the second document. The Status Line indicator displays **Doc 2**.

5. Press (Enter). The text then reappears.

6. Press (Shift-F3) again. This returns you to document 1, as indicated by the **Doc** display of the Status Line.

You can transfer as much text from document 1 as you like into document 2, simply adding material. Later, when you find something in document 2 that you can re-integrate into document 1, you can cut it and paste it back again using the same process described above, but starting off in document 2. Each time you press (Shift-F3), the screen toggles between document 1 and 2. If you think you might use the material in document 2 later on, press (F10) to save and continue, or (F7) to save and exit.

Try it with your memo. Excise a sentence or two, then transfer it to document 2. Modify it, and cut and paste it back into document 1. Once you do this a few times, you are in command of a valuable editing tool.

Copying Text

Sometimes you might want to repeat a headline, a sentence, or a paragraph. For example, you might have a cautionary statement, a disclaimer, or some other text that gets repeated later in the text.

Instead of retyping it, you can block off the text, as above, but instead of pressing:

(Ctrl-F4) + 1 + 1

which cuts the block, press:

(Ctrl-F4) + 1 + 2

which leaves the original block in place. A copy of the block is tucked away in memory, to be inserted into the document when you place your cursor at the desired location and press (Enter). You can also use the copy function with dual documents, as described above, leaving copies of text in your second document for future use.

Try copying a paragraph from the top of your memo to the bottom. As you can see, it's a lot easier than retyping the material.

Inserting Text

Cutting and pasting is one way of inserting text into a particular location in a document. Another way is to retrieve previously saved paragraphs. There are two ways to do this.

1. Press (Shift-F10), type the name of the file containing the text, and press (Enter).

2. Press (F5), which lists all your files; use the cursor to highlight the file you want to insert, then press 1.

Either way, the file is placed in your document at the location of the cursor. The first method may be trickier, since it requires you to remember the file name. It also doesn't ask you to confirm the fact that you're about to insert text into the current document. This can be dangerous; if you enter the wrong file name, you might wind up injecting a 75 page document into your two page memo, in which case you have to block off the entire invading document and press the (Del) key.

The second method has several advantages. First, you get a list of all files, in case you forgot the exact file name. Second, you can view any file without retrieving it, by selecting option #6—no mistaking your two-paragraph long file from your 75-page long file (the number of bytes, also shown on the List Files screen, is a dead giveaway.) Finally, when you select option #1 to retrieve the file, WordPerfect prompts you with:

`Retrieve into current document (Y/N) No`

giving you a second chance to change your mind and avert potential problems.

As with many aspects of WordPerfect, the choice of which method you use is a matter of personal preference. However you retrieve the text, the technique is very useful for bringing in previously created "boilerplate" material. For instance, lets say you have a standard paragraph, a disclaimer, that appears in all your contracts. The first time you create the contract, block off the disclaimer with (Alt-F4), and press (F10). WordPerfect prompts you in the lower left hand corner of the screen to enter a block name. You might call it "DISCLAIM." (Keep file names as short as possible but still meaningful.) The next time you type a contract, when you reach the point where the disclaimer should be placed, insert "DISCLAIM using either of the two methods described above.

Try it yourself with your own memo. Pick a paragraph, save it as a block, then retrieve it into another location. As you can see, inserting previously saved work is a highly efficient way to get your typing done.

Search for Text

You will often find it helpful to search for a particular word or phrase during your editing. If you've proofread from hard copy and have some specific changes, it is sometimes faster to search for the specific word or phrase than to use the (PgDn) key and cursor keys to find the text in question.

Let's say that upon reflection, you decide to change the sentence reading, "In short, we find your product to be ill-conceived, cheaply produced, and totally unfit for the marketplace." In your hard copy, the sentence appeared on page 53, but you've deleted a number of paragraphs, so it will be tricky to find it with the GoTo command, (Ctrl-Home) + page #.

The solution? Search for key words in the sentence. The following procedure gives you step-by- step instructions for carrying out the search.

Conducting a Search

Press (F2), forward *Search*. When WordPerfect displays:

> `-> Srch:`

enter the words you want to find. You don't need to enter the whole sentence, just enough so WordPerfect can make a match with your text. Besides, if you entered the whole sentence, you might make a typographical mistake, and WordPerfect, in trying to make an exact match, would report:

> `* Not Found *`

The goal then, is to find the shortest possible chunk of the sentence that is be unique enough for WordPerfect to report a match. If you just type "In," WordPerfect stops at the first instance (of which there are probably plenty), and you will have to repeat the search until you find the sentence. "In short" is better (unless you abuse the phrase.) The word "ill-conceived" is also a good candidate, because it probably only occurs once in the document. From a standpoint of efficiency, "In short" would take you right to the beginning of the sentence, while "ill-conceived" would take you to the middle.

Whatever you choose, enter the search criteria words WITHOUT pressing (Enter). If you press (Enter), you add a hard return [HRt] (carriage return) code to your search criteria, which may cause WordPerfect to come up empty- handed. Instead press (F2) or (Esc), and the search begins. The cursor stops at the first instance it considers a match. If it is incorrect, press (F2) twice to continue. If WordPerfect can't find a match, or any additional matches beyond the last one found, it indicates:

> `* Not Found *`

Searching Rules

Several rules must be followed if *Search* is going to yield anything useful.

1. If you want to find a complete word, it must be separated by spaces. For example, if you are looking for "any," WordPerfect will stop at "many," "anyway," and "zany." You must therefore enter a space, using the (Spacebar) before and after "any" to make it a discrete, searchable word.

2. WordPerfect is somewhat "case-sensitive," meaning it distinguishes between lower and upper case letters under certain circumstances. If you search for the word "horse," it stops at "Horse," even though you entered a lowercase "h." On the other hand, if you enter "Horse" for your search, WordPerfect stops only for "Horse" with a capital "H."

Changing the Direction of the Search

You can search forward (from the current cursor location to the bottom of the document) by pressing (F2), or backwards (from the current cursor location to the top of the document) by pressing (Shift-F2). Sometimes WordPerfect might report "* Not Found *" even when a match exists, because you are searching in the wrong direction. In other words, you are beyond the text you were seeking, and continue searching away from it.

One solution is to press (Home) + (Home) + (Up Cursor) before beginning a forward search (this takes you to the top of the document), or if you are near the end of the document, (Home) + (Home) + (Down Cursor) before starting a backwards search. In part, its a matter of judgement; if you are reasonably sure you're near the text being sought, there may not be any need to go all the way back to the beginning or end of a long document. Take a chance that you're pointed in the right direction. The worst that can happen is that you'll have to repeat the search.

Finally, a short cut for changing directions is to press the (Up Cursor) or (Down Cursor) keys after pressing the (F2) key. This changes the search to the opposite direction, starting with the current location of the cursor. Try it yourself. Press (F2), then alternate pressing the (Up Cursor) and (Down Cursor) keys. Notice how the arrow in front of the word "Srch:," which indicates the direction of the search, changes from right (forward *Search*) to left (backwards *Search*) and vice versa.

Repositioning the Cursor After a Search

It is often helpful to reposition the cursor to your original location after completing a search. Sometimes, you only want to have a look at the text in question, rather than make alterations. In that case, you might want to return the cursor to its original position.

The express method is to press (Ctrl-Home) twice.

Extended Searches

If you want to search through the text in headers, footers, footnotes, or endnotes, as well as the regular document text, press (Home) before pressing (F2). This initiates an *Extended search*. All of the above rules apply to an *Extended Search*. When you find a word in a header, footer, or note, WordPerfect displays the contents in an edit screen. You can alter the text if you wish, and then press (Enter). In order to ensure that you will search ALL notes, etc., you must place the cursor at the very top of the document by pressing (Home) three times followed by the (Up Cursor) before starting the extended search.

Your Turn

Now that you know the basics of searching, press (Home) + (Home) + (Up Cursor) and try a forward search with your memo. Check out the differences in searching for lower and uppercase text. Then press (Home) + (Home) + (Down) and try an *Extended backward search* for text you know is in the header (assuming you created one as instructed in Chapter 5).

Searching for and Replacing text

Next to cutting and pasting, searching and replacing is is one of most important advantages a word processor has over conventional typewriters. Imagine what it would have been like in the olden days if you had been asked to write a major speech for the president of your company. At the last minute, the cranky old executive tells you to change all instances of "the company" to "the firm." And provide clean copy, of course. Panic! Administer 5cc of White Out. Today, with the *Replace* function, relief is just a few keystrokes away.

Like *Search*, WordPerfect's *Replace* function finds all words or phrases that match your search criteria. But it goes one step further and replaces the text with a word or phrase of your choice. This isn't to say that *Replace* is better than or eliminates the need for the *Search* function; both have their places in your editorial tool kit. When you want to home-in on a word, *Search* is easier and quicker to use.

Using the Replace Function

To carry out a "global search and replace" operation— that is, replace every occurrence of a word or phrase in a text—carry out the following procedure:

1. Press (Home) + (Home) + (Home) + (Up Cursor) to place the cursor at the top of the document. As in the forward and backward *Search* feature described above, WordPerfect can't locate all occurrences of a word or phrase if the cursor is already beyond the point in the document where the word or phrase resides. By starting at the top, you can't miss anything.

2. Press:

    (Alt-F2)

    WordPerfect prompts you with:

    w/Confirm (Y/N) No

    If you press (Enter) to accept the default, No, WordPerfect rips through your document, replacing every occurrence of the search criteria text (see step #3) with the specified replacement text (step #4). If you press Y for Yes, WordPerfect stops at each occurrence it finds and ask if you want to replace the text or not. If you enter Y, your text is substituted and WordPerfect continues looking through the document for the next occurrence.

While it is certainly faster to search and replace without confirming each choice, it's also much more dangerous. First, let's say you made a mistake. Instead of telling WordPerfect to find the word "any," with a space before the "a" and a space after the "y," you just told it to search for the word "any" with no leading or trailing spaces. Then let's say you instructed WordPerfect to replace "any" with "all." As explained above in the section on *Search*, without spaces in front and in back of "any," WordPerfect considers "many," anyway," and "zany" to be matches. As a result when it replaced "any" with "all," your document would acquire the word "mall," and the nonsense words "allway" and "zall."

Another reason to confirm the *Replace* operation is that there are times when you might only want to selectively substitute text. For example, you might want to leave some occurrences of the search text as is, for stylistic variation. Or, you might have a word that is used in two different senses. Let's say you're writing a computer manual, and you start off designating the carriage return key "(return)." Later, you decide to refer to the carriage return key as the "(Enter)" key. There are plenty of contexts in which "return" means "go back to," rather than the carriage return key, such as "to return to the document screen press..." If you indiscriminately replace all occurrences of "return" with "enter," your sentence will be rendered into gibberish: "to enter to the document screen press..." Therefore, when there is a possibility that the wrong text might changed, select Confirm.

3. Once you've answered the Confirm question, the lower side of the screen prompts you with:

    –> Srch:

as it did with the *Search* feature. You can change the direction of the search by pressing the up and the down arrow. An arrow pointing right means search and replace forward through the document from the current cursor position, while an arrow pointing left means search backwards through a document from the current cursor position.

Enter the word or phrase that you wish to replace. All of the rules for upper and lower case described for *Search* apply to the *Replace* function as well. Do NOT press (Enter) after you make your entry—that enters a hard return code as part of the search. Instead, press (F2) or (Esc). WordPerfect then prompts you with:

Replace with:

Enter the text, again WITHOUT pressing (Enter), for that will insert a carriage return when the word or phrase is substituted for the word or phrase being sought. Press (F2) or (Esc) to start the search.

Canceling a Search and Replace Operation

If you discover that you made a mistake and want to cancel the operation, press (F1). When you initiate the search again by pressing (Alt-F2), your last entry for the search part of the operation is displayed. You can modify it or accept it by pressing (F2) or (Esc). The replace selection, however, will be blank, and you must re-enter it.

Searching and Replacing in a Block

If you know that the text you want replaced is only located in a small chunk of text, rather than search through the whole document, block off the text as described above with the (Alt-F4) keys, then conduct a search and replace operation. The mechanics for the search and replace are the same as for a regular "global" search and replace. When the cursor reaches the end of the block, the block turns off.

Returning to the original cursor location

When WordPerfect finishes a search and replace operation, the cursor remains at the last occurrence. To return to wherever the cursor was before you began the operation, press (Ctrl-Home) twice.

Extended Replace Function

To carry out search and replace within headers, footers, footnotes, and endnotes, first move to the top of the document by pressing (Home) three times followed by the (Up Cursor). Then press the (Alt-F2) key combination to initiate the *Replace* function.

WordPerfect prompts you with:

-> Extended Srch:

Enter the text to be searched for, just as you would with a conventional search and replace operation and press (F2) or (Esc). Then enter the text you wish to substitute. WordPerfect searches *all* text in the document, including the headers, footers, etc. If you selected confirm, when a match is found in a header, footer, endnote, or footnote, the text of the note will be displayed on a blank screen, and you will asked to confirm the change. When you press Y or N, the search continues through into the main text of your document.

Note: If the last occurrence of a word is located within a header, footer, footnote, etc., WordPerfect will end the search in that screen. You are not automatically returned to the main document; press (F7) to do so.

Your Turn

The *Replace* function is one of WordPerfect's most powerful editing features. Call up your memo and play with it. See if you can sharpen your sense of how the program decides whether any text in the document matches your search criteria.

Now you should have a good idea of how to use WordPerfect's basic tools for editing text. Taken together, they may seem a bit overwhelming. But once you begin to use them one-by-one, you'll develop a natural sense of how and when each tool should be used. The next set of editing tools enable you to modify the format and appearance of individual characters, words, or the document as a whole.

EDITING FORMATS AND APPEARANCES

Changing Formats and Appearances From the Document Screen.

In the first section, you saw how to use the *Block* functions to accomplish various tasks. In this section, you learn how to change the overall appearance of an entire block with one or two key strokes. After you block off the selected text, whether it consists of one word, a sentence, a paragraph, a page, or 100 pages, you can use any of the following functions. Remember, to block off text, move the cursor to the beginning of the selected text, press (Alt-F4), then move. The block is highlighted, and the words **"Block on"** flash in the lower left-hand corner of the screen.

Center

Press (Shift-F6) and each line of the block is centered. WordPerfect asks you to confirm that you want to center the block before doing so. When WordPerfect centers a block, it inserts a hidden **[Cntr]** code before each line (see *Reveal Codes*, below). While block centering is useful for one or two lines, it is generally easier to center a full paragraph with the tab indent function (Shift-F4).

Flush Rt

Press (Alt-F6) and the block is right aligned. WordPerfect asks you to confirm before executing the command. (Note: The block may not come out perfectly right aligned, since spaces at the end of lines are moved to the right margin, and spaces count as characters. You can quickly edit a right aligned block by deleting the spaces).

When WordPerfect right aligns a block of text, it places a hidden [Flsh Rt] code in front of each line, and an end code [C/A/Flrt] at the end of each line. The significance of the coding will become clear after you read the section below on *Reveal Codes*. Using flush right with block is most useful for one or two lines; with larger blocks and pargraphs, however, it is generally better to use the indent (F4) key.

Bold:

Press (F6) and the entire block is bolded.

Underline:

Press (F8) and every character within the block is underlined.

Upper/Lowercase:

A special block function, (Shift-F3) allows you to change a block of text to all uppercase or all lowercase.

One other block feature should be mentioned: protect. When you block off text, and press (Shift-F8), WordPerfect prompts you with:

`Protect Block (Y/N)`

This keeps a block of text from getting separated across a "soft" (non-forced) page break.

Your Turn

The best way to absorb all the information you've just read is to try it with your memo file. Retrieve it, using the method explained above. Try modifying the appearance of several paragraphs of the memo using the various block functions described above. Then read the next section, which reveals the meaning of the hidden codes.

Behind the Scenes Editing :
Using Reveal Codes to Undo Formats

The most basic way to undo a format command is to switch from the document editing screen to *Reveal Codes*. As described earlier, whenever you issue a formatting command, WordPerfect creates a code or pair of codes, which send the proper commands to the monitor and the printer. These codes are invisible while you create or edit document, but can be seen in the *Reveal Codes* mode.

For example, when you press (F6) to turn on bold, type the word "Subject," and then press (F6) again to turn off bold, you simply see the word **"Subject"** in bold. When you press (Alt-F3), though, WordPerfect displays a starting and ending code, as shown in Figure 8.1. (You can toggle between document mode and *Reveal Codes* mode by repeatedly pressing (Alt-F3). Try it yourself)

The top part of the screen shows the word *"Subject"* as it appears on your screen, and the bottom part shows the codes themselves. The pair of codes, **[BOLD]** and **[bold]**, which surround the word "Subject," tell WordPerfect to turn bold on beginning with the "S" and turn it

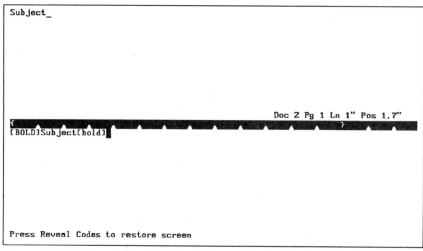

Figure 8.1 *Hidden Codes, Visible in Reveal Codes Mode (Alt-F3)*

off after the "t." Other formatting codes also appear as pairs, such as Underline, which places [UND] before text and [und] at the end of text. The majority of codes, however, appear as single codes, such as:

[Pg Num Pos]   for Page Number Position

[L/R Margin]   for Left and Right Margin

[HPg]   for Hard Page

[Suppress]   for Suppress

(See Appendix F for a complete listing of all codes used in WordPerfect.)

When you begin to add multiple formatting features, the *Reveal Codes* screen can get to be quite a mess, as demonstrated by the screen in Figure 8.2. (Dashes appear between brackets as [-]).

Why bother with the Rorschach blot on the bottom part of the screen when you can see the same thing "clean," in regular document mode, as shown in the top part of Figure 8.2?

The answer is that *Reveal Codes* is often the best way to eliminate an unwanted code. For example, if the word **Subject** is still on your

```
                        INTRODUCTION

                   GETTING DOWN TO BASICS

 ----------------------------------------------------------

HIGHLIGHTS




                                          Doc 2 Pg 1 Ln 1" Pos 1"
{                                               }
[Pg Numbering:Bottom Center][Footer A:2:Draft 1[Flsh Rt] ... ][Tab Set:0",0.5",1
",1.2",1.5",2",2.5",3",3.5",4",4.5",5",5.5",6",6.5",7",7.5",8",8.5"][Cntr][UND][
BOLD]INTRODUCTION[C/A/Flrt][HRt]
[und][HRt]
[Cntr]GETTING DOWN TO BASICS[bold][C/A/Flrt][HRt]
[HRt]
[Cntr][-][-][-][-][-][-][-][-][-][-][-][-][-][-][-][-][-][-][-][-][-][-][-][-][-
][-][-][-][-][-][-][-][-][-][-][-][-][-][-][-][-][-][-][-][-][-][-][-][-][-][-][-
-][-][-][-][-][-][C/A/Flrt][HRt]
[HRt]

Press Reveal Codes to restore screen
```

Figure 8.2 *Hidden Codes, Visible in Reveal Codes Mode (Alt-F3)*

screen in bold, switch into *Reveal Codes* mode by pressing (Alt-F3). The cursor appears as a block, highlighting each letter or code as you move the cursor keys. Slide the cursor over the [BOLD] or the [bold] code, then press the (Del) key. You'll notice the word **"Subject"** immediately switches from bold to regular intensity on the screen. It also prints in regular weight rather than in bold. Paired codes can thus be turned off by eliminating either code surrounding the text. With non-paired codes, all you have to do is highlight the code by moving the cursor keys, then press (Del).

The alternative is to try and position the cursor near the code while in regular document viewing mode and remove it with the (Del) key. If you hit the code, WordPerfect prompts you with:

Delete [X]? (Y/N) No

where X is a the code name. Unfortunately, finding the exact location of the code can be like looking for a needle in a hay stack, and you are likely to delete numerous other characters as well. Eliminating codes in *Reveal Codes* is much more precise, because you can see exactly what you're editing out.

When the cursor highlights a code, it covers all text between the left and right brackets, [ ]. For example, enter a tab set, then switch to

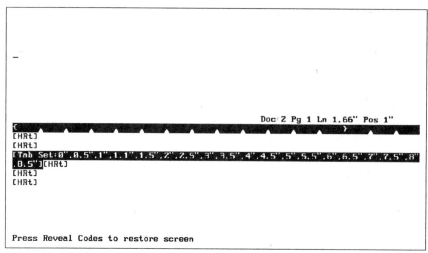

Figure 8.3 *Tab Set, Highlighted by Cursor*

Reveal Codes mode, and move the cursor to the Tab Set code. Notice how the highlight encompasses the entire code, as shown in Figure 8.3. Once highlighted, ANY code, placed intentionally or accidentally can be eliminated, copied, or moved.

Moving Through a Document in Reveal Codes

You can scroll through an entire document in *Reveal Codes* mode, using the cursor keys, the PgUp and PgDn, screen up and screen down keys. As you do so, the document, without codes appears on the top part of the screen as it would in normal viewing mode. It is generally less confusing, however, to traverse large numbers of pages in regular document mode and go to the approximate spot where you believe the code is located, and then switch into *Reveal Codes* mode.

One nice feature of *Reveal Codes* is that you can edit out or add text, too, without returning to the regular document mode. As you add characters in *Reveal Codes*, the text changes in the top portion of the screen, and the Status Line indicator shows all the vital statistics regarding the current cursor location. When you switch back into regular document mode, the new text appears as if you had typed it under "normal" circumstances.

Correcting Problems with Reveal Codes

Switching into *Reveal Codes* mode can allow you to correct certain pesky problems. For example:

A large section of text is unexpectedly underlined. The (F8) key was accidentally pressed at some point, or you forgot to toggle underline off at the end of an intentionally underlined section. Move the cursor to the place where the unwanted underline first appeared, switch into *Reveal Codes*, look for a "rogue" [UND] code and delete it. Or, move to the place where an intentional underline should be turned off. Press (F8) + (Del), and an [und] command, which turns off underline, will be inserted at the desired location.

A page with no text, but a page number, appears between two "normal" pages. You have an unwanted hard page command [HPg] sitting in your document. Move your cursor to the page in question, which will be displayed as a double-dashed line instead of the regular dotted line for soft or "regular" pages [SPg]. Move the cursor to the line immediately above the double dashes and you'll find the [HPg] command sitting there. Zap it with the (Del) key, and the blank page disappears.

The margins or indents have suddenly changed, creating inconsistent pages. Move the cursor to the problem area, switch into *Reveal Codes*, and delete the offending margin or tab command.

The page numbering is wrong. Chances are, you inserted more than one New Page Number commands in your document. This can easily happen if you're renumbering the chapters in a book, and forget to eliminate the old New Page Number codes. Press (Home) three times and then the (Up Cursor) and switch into *Reveal Codes*. Highlight the erroneous [Pg Num] code and delete it.

Using Search and Search & Replace to Find Codes

Searching for Codes

Earlier you learned how to use the *Search* function and the *Replace* function to locate specific text, and to substitute text. You can do the same thing with hidden codes, too. Instead of entering words or phrases when prompted for the search criteria, call up the *function* you wish to find. WordPerfect then knows what code you are seeking. For example, let's say that have a stray New Page Number command somewhere in your document. You can locate it by using the search command. Here's how:

1. Move the cursor to the top of the document by pressing:

   (Home) + (Home) + (Home) + (Up Cursor)

2. Press (F2) to activate the search.

3. Press (Shift-F8). WordPerfect displays an abbreviated format menu:

   1 Line; **2 P**age; **3 O**ther: **0**

4. Select 2 for *Page*, and an abbreviated *Page* options menu is displayed.

   1 Cntr **2** Force **3** Hdr **4** Ftr **5** T/B Mar **6** New PgNum

   7 PgNum Pos **8** Sz/Typ **9** Sup: **0**

   Select 6 and the code **[Pg Num]** appears after the

   —> Srch:

   prompt.

5. Press (F2) or (Esc). When WordPerfect finds the code, the cursor stops to the right of it. You can then delete the code with the (Backspace) key.

You can call up almost any function while using the *Search* option, and WordPerfect seeks out the code. Just pick out the option from the menu displayed at the bottom of the screen. If you don't see the option you want to search for, you can't use it with the *Search* option.

Seek and Destroy

The method just described takes you to the first occurrence of a code, after which it's up to you to do something about it. An alternative way to knock out an undesirable code is to use the search and replace function as a "seek and destroy" mechanism. Here's what to do:

1. Move the cursor to the top of the document by pressing:

   (Home) + (Home) + (Home) + (Up Cursor)

2. Press (Alt-F2) to activate the *Replace* operation.

3. Select Y for Confirm.

4. Press (Shift-F8). WordPerfect displays a *Format* options menu:

   1 Line; **2** Page; **3** Other: **0**

   Select 2 for *Page*, and an abbreviated *Page* options menu is displayed.

   1 Cntr **2** Force **3** Hdr **4** Ftr **5** T/B Mar **6** New PgNum

   7 PgNum Pos **8** Sz/Typ **9** Sup: **0**

Select 6. The Code **[Pg Num]** appears after the

     —> Srch:

prompt.

5. When the **Replace with:** prompt appears on the screen, press (F2) or the (Esc) key, which instructs WordPerfect to replace the New Page Number code with nothing.

6. When WordPerfect finds the first code it asks you if you want it replaced. If you respond Y, it replaces the code with "nothing," which is tantamount to deleting it. It then goes on to find any other occurrences of the code. It is advisable to use the confirm option when doing seek and destroy missions against unwanted codes, because you might have some codes that you don't want deleted, especially in the very top portion of the first page of the document.

Again, you might be wondering why you'd ever want to bother with *Search* to find a hidden code, when you can eliminate it with *Replace*. The answer is that you can potentially make things worse with *Replace* if you're not careful. If *Replace* is analogous to "seek and destroy," then think of *Search* as a reconnaissance operation; you can snoop around the hidden codes and then decide whether to attack.

Altering Paired Codes with Replace

In addition to locating and zapping codes, you can use *Replace* to find instances of text with a paired code (bold or underline) and change it. For example, if you have underlined the word *"Fact"* throughout a document, and want to make it bold instead, use the following procedure:

1. Move the cursor to the top of the document by pressing:

     (Home) + (Home) + (Home) + (Up Cursor)

2. Press (Alt-F2) to activate the *Replace* operation.

3. Select N for "No Confirm." (If there are likely to be multiple replacements, and no danger of an unwanted alteration, it's safe—and much faster—to search and replace without confirmation.)

4. At the —> **Srch:** prompt press and type:

(F8) + Fact + (F8)

Your prompt looks like:

—> Srch: [UND]Fact**[und]**

5. Press (F2) or (Esc). When the **Replace with:** prompt appears on the screen, press and enter

(F6) + Fact + (F6)

Your prompt looks like:

Replace with: [BOLD]Fact**[bold]**

6. Press (F2) or the (Esc) key. When WordPerfect finds each instance of "*Fact,*" it replaces it with **Fact.** Since you selected No Confirm, WordPerfect passes through and alters all oc-curences in the document.

The same thing could have been done if you wanted to change "Fact" (no underline) to "<u>Fact</u>" (underlined) or "<u>**Fact**</u>" (bold + underline). All you have to do is put in the appropriate codes when you structure the search and replace.

Your Turn

Look into your memo and see what WordPerfect has created behind the scenes. Try deleting some of the codes manually, and some with the *Replace* function.

If you've read *Simply WordPerfect* sequentially, you've been exposed to all of the key functions you need to create documents, from simple letters to sophisticated newsletters. The next chapter teaches you how to fine-tune your document with the speller and the thesaurus. At this point, you might be wondering about one other important editing issue that relates to appearance: changing type fonts. Because that topic can become extremely complex with WordPerfect 5.0, it appears in a special section, Appendix C, which explains how to change fonts with a laser printer. If you're going to skip ahead to the Appendices, you should probably read Appendix B first, which provides step- by-step installation for the Hewlett-Packard LaserJet Series II.

9

Fine Tuning
Your Document

THE LAST STEP

Once you've edited your document, you can put the finishing touches on it by running it through the electronic Thesaurus and Speller. In practice, if you use the Thesaurus at all, you'll probably bring it up "on the fly," to find synonyms as you write. But it's also helpful after the fact, when you proof a document and find that you need to choose a better word, or you discover that you've beaten a particular word to death 10 times per page and need some stylistic relief.

The Speller is a slightly different story. While you might occasionally use it to check words as you go along, most of your spell-checking will probably be postponed until you are ready to print. After all, if you're still tearing apart or adding words to a document, you're likely to introduce new typos and other errors, so why waste your time spell checking before you have finished your document?

This chapter is divided into two major sections, one for the Thesaurus, and one for the Speller. Unlike the Speller, which is intuitively easy to use, the Thesaurus is anything but obvious. To help learn both features, call up your memo, if you've created one, so you can see how the various options actually work— they're slick!

FINDING THE RIGHT WORD: THE THESAURUS

A Thesaurus contains lists of synonyms, words with identical meanings, and antonyms, words that mean the opposite. WordPerfect's Thesaurus provides 100,000 synonyms and antonyms for words in your text. The clever thing about the electronic Thesaurus is that you don't have to tell it what word you're looking for—WordPerfect picks up whatever word is at your cursor and instantly displays lists of words with like and opposite meanings. You can also look up words, as you would with a conventional Thesaurus.

Before proceeding, if you have a hard disk, make sure you've installed the Thesaurus file, WP{WP}US.THS, located on the disk labeled "Thesaurus." Since the Thesaurus file consumes a hefty 360,000 bytes, if disk space is at a premium, it's a prime candidate for getting axed. (Because of its memory size, if you don't think you'll use the Thesaurus even after you try it, you probably should delete the file to conserve precious disk space.)

If you don't have the Thesaurus on your system at this time, stop and install the Thesaurus. Make sure you let WordPerfect know what directory you've copied it to (see Chapter 1), by calling up the *Setup* function (Shift-F1), selecting Option 8, Location of Supplementary Files, and entering in the appropriate directory.

Using the Thesaurus

The procedure for using the Thesaurus or the Speller is different for floppy and hard disk users. The following sections cover both types of machines.

Dual Drive Floppy System

To invoke the Thesaurus with a floppy-based system, use the following steps:

1. Save your file to your data disk.
2. Remove your data disk from your B drive.
3. Insert your Thesaurus diskette into your B drive.
4. Move the cursor to the word for which you want to find a synonym.
5. Press (Alt-F1). WordPerfect displays a list of synonyms. If none are found, it indicates:

   Word Not Found,

   and gives you an opportunity to enter another word. This is explained below. To exit the Thesaurus at any time, select "0" from the Thesaurus menu, or press cancel, (F1) or exit, (F7).
6. Remove your Thesaurus disk and re-insert your data disk.

Hard Disk System

All you have to do is move the cursor to the word for which you want to find a synonym, and press (Alt-F1). The Thesaurus displays a list of potential synonyms. If none are found, it indicates:

Word Not Found

and gives you an opportunity to enter another word. See below for what to do next. To exit the Thesaurus at any time, select "0" from the Thesaurus menu, or press cancel, (F1) or exit, (F7).

The Thesaurus Screen

The Thesaurus screen consists of three columns, as shown in Figure 9.1. The screen displays three types of entries, with the following hierarchy: Headwords; Subgroups; and Reference Words.

Headwords are major entries in the Thesaurus, and appear in bold. They are organized by whatever part of speech they represent. The part of speech appears in parentheses: (a) for adjectives, (n) for nouns, and (v) for verbs. Antonyms are marked with (ant).

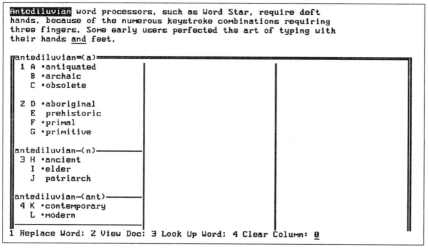

```
Antediluvian word processors, such as Word Star, require deft
hands, because of the numerous keystroke combinations requiring
three fingers. Some early users perfected the art of typing with
their hands and feet.

antediluvian=(a)
  1 A •antiquated
    B •archaic
    C •obsolete

  2 D •aboriginal
    E  prehistoric
    F •primal
    G •primitive

antediluvian-(n)
  3 H •ancient
    I •elder
    J  patriarch

antediluvian-(ant)
  4 K •contemporary
    L •modern

1 Replace Word: 2 View Doc: 3 Look Up Word: 4 Clear Column: 0
```

Figure 9.1 *Thesaurus Screen*

Subgroups are numbered sets of synonyms (such as "archaic" and "obsolete" in one group, and "primal" and "primitive" in another subgroup).

Reference words are synonyms that can also be a Headword. (While the Thesaurus has 100,000 words, there are only 10,000 headwords, words that can be looked up.) Reference words are distinguished from non-reference words by the bullet that precedes them.

In point of fact, you can forget about all of the above terms— they are only presented here in case you wish to consult the WordPerfect manual. More important than the nomenclature are the mechanics of the Thesaurus.

You can use the Thesaurus in two ways: to find a word that you can use in your document as you're composing, or to swap an existing word with a synonym. Both uses are described below.

"Free Form" Brainstorming with the Thesaurus

Let's say you're writing a sentence and stop for a moment to find another word for "trash"; you have one on the tip of your tongue, but you just can't remember it. Rather than waiting until three in the morning when it jolts you from a sound sleep, move the cursor

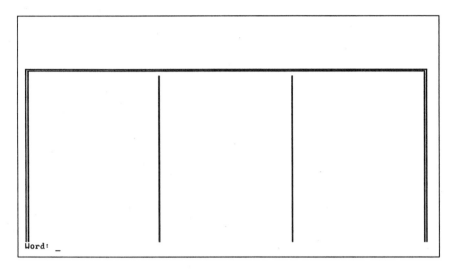

Word: _

Figure 9.2 *Brainstorming with the Thesaurus*

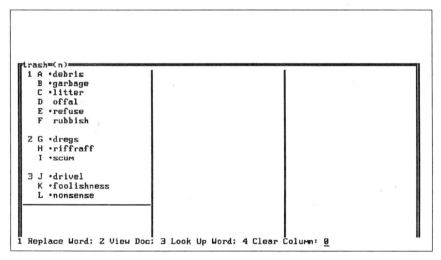

```
trash=(n)
 1 A •debris
   B •garbage
   C •litter
   D  offal
   E •refuse
   F  rubbish

 2 G •dregs
   H •riffraff
   I •scum

 3 J •drivel
   K •foolishness
   L •nonsense
```
1 Replace Word; 2 View Doc; 3 Look Up Word; 4 Clear Column: 0

Figure 9.3 *Entering a Word to be Checked*

to a blank line at the bottom of the document and press (Alt-F1) to call up the Thesaurus. WordPerfect prompts you for a word in the lower left hand corner of the screen (see Figure 9.2). Enter "trash," and a list of synonyms will be displayed, including the elusive "offal" (see Figure 9.3).

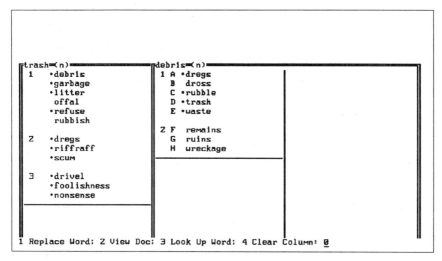

Figure 9.4 *Second Level of Synonyms*

Select option #1, Replace Word, and WordPerfect prompts you to:

Press the letter for word

That means press the letter corresponding to the desired word on the screen, "D" in this case, and it will be inserted into the document at the cursor location.

So far, no problem. But here's where things get a bit complicated. Let's say that you weren't satisfied with the first set of synonyms. You can find additional synonyms for any word that has a bullet in front of it. When you press **A**, for example, corresponding to "debris," in our example, an expanded list of synonyms appears in the second column, as shown in Figure 9.4.

Within the entries for debris, several of the entries, including "A. dregs," also have bullets in front of them. To expand them, press any of their corresponding letters. When you press "A," for dregs, the synonyms appear in the third column, as shown in Figure 9.5.

If you want to expand any bulleted entries in the third column, press their corresponding letter and the expanded list will replace the current entries in the third column. If you want to expand the

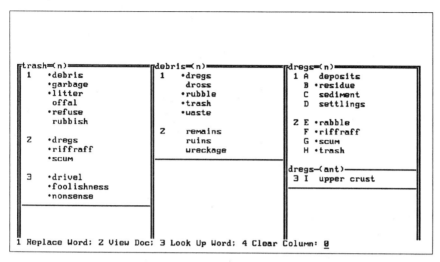

Figure 9.5 *Third Level of Synonyms*

new entries in the third column, they will be replaced by the next set of entries, and so on.

If you are duplicating the "trash" exercise, you probably notice that the alphabetic letters only appear in the column in which new entries are displayed. For example, when you press A in the first column to expand "debris," the letters jump to the second column, where the synonyms for debris appear. The letter "A" then corresponds to "dregs." When you expand "dregs," the letters jump to the third column, to correspond to a new set of entries. (You can see this progression by comparing Figures 9.3, 9.4, and 9.5.)

But what happens if the letters are in the third column, and you decide that the word your really want to use as a synonym is in the first column? Answer, use your (Left Cursor) key to move the letters to the first column. When you move the (Left Cursor) and (Right Cursor) keys, the entire column of letters "peels" off and is transported from column to column. Once you select a word and move the letters to the right column, select Option 1, Replace Word, and select the appropriate letter. The word will be placed in your text at the cursor location.

Using the Thesaurus to Check Existing Text

When you call up the Thesaurus, it first checks whatever word contains the cursor. The cursor can be anywhere within the word to be checked. If the cursor is in a blank space, the Thesaurus will look up the word to the left of the cursor.

If WordPerfect can't find any synonyms for the word on the screen, it informs you that the word was not found, then prompts you to enter a word. At this point, use the above explanation to operate the Thesaurus.

When WordPerfect does find the highlighted word, it will display the first level of synonyms, as described above. You can call up the second and third level synonyms by entering the letter of the synonym you want to expand. When you have found the "perfect replacement," select option #1, *Replace Word*, and enter the letter of the selected word, which will then be inserted into your text in place of the original word.

Looking Up Other Words

Perhaps you really don't want to use "trash" or any of its synonyms. Instead of exiting the Thesaurus, by selecting a synonym or pressing (F7), (F1), or "0," you can select another word by selecting option #3, Look Up Word. Once again, WordPerfect prompts you in the lower left-hand corner of the screen for a new word. If the word is not in the Thesaurus, WordPerfect responds with:

Word not found

and again prompts you for another word.

If the word is found, WordPerfect places the synonyms in the next blank column. If all columns are filled with previous entries, it overwrites entries in the third column. If you expand the new entries while in the third column, they replace the old entries in the third column. This makes it difficult to follow the new entries, so the best thing to do is clean out the last two columns by moving the cursor to the second column, and selecting option #4, Clear Column. The contents of the third column are instantly cleared out. First, however, the original contents of the third column slide over to the second column. If the synonyms for the word you are checking would normally fill two columns, the excess synonyms will appear in the third column. Now clean out the first column, using option #4. The contents of the second column slide over to the first. Any entries that couldn't fit in one column also "flow over" to the second and third columns.

If this seems confusing, be assured, it is. But once you try the Thesaurus a few times you'll be a pro at using it. You might it even find it a handy and useful writing tool.

speech; that is, if it is replacing a word that has an initial upper case letter, it will upper case the first letter of the synonym it inserts into the text. If it is a verb, the Thesaurus will try to match tense. If it is a noun or adjective, the Thesaurus will try to match the part of speech.

Your Turn

If you've been reading the text without trying the above example, go back and try it yourself. There are some computing actions that can only be mastered by hands-on experience. And the Thesaurus is one of them.

WORDS ON TAP: THE SPELLER

WordPerfect's spell checker contains more than 100,000 words, and can be updated or customized for your own unique needs. It is easy to use, and a fast way to clean up your documents before printing.

Dual Drive Floppy System

To start the Speller, use the following steps:

1. Save your file to your data disk.

2. Remove your data disk from your B drive.

3. Insert your Speller disk into your B drive.

4. Press (Ctrl-F2). The Speller menu appears, as described below.

5. Leave the Speller disk in your B drive during the spell checking session.

6. When the spell check is complete, replace the Speller disk with your data disk and SAVE THE FILE—whatever corrections you made must be saved in the new file.

   To exit the Speller during a checking session, press (F1) at any time. You might have to press (F1) twice, depending on what the Speller is doing.

Hard Disk System

All you have to do is press (Ctrl-F2) to display the Speller menu under your document. Each option is explained below. When you finish the spell checking, make sure you save your file to preserve the changes and corrections. To exit the Speller during a checking session, press (F1). You might have to press (F1) twice, depending on whether the Speller is waiting for input from the menu or checking a word.

```
or you discover that you've beaten a particular word to death 10

times per page and some stylistic relief.

     The Speller is a slightly different story. While you might

occassional use it to check words as you go along, most of your

spell-checking will probably be postponed until you are ready to

print.  After all, if you're still tearing apart or adding words

to a document, you'll be likely to introduce typos and other

errors, so why waste your time spell checking?

     This chapter is divided into two major sections, one for the

Thesaurus, and one for the Speller.  Unlike the Speller, which is

intuititvely easy to use, the Thesaurus is anything but obvious.

Check: 1 Word; 2 Page; 3 Document; 4 New Sup. Dictionary; 5 Look Up; 6 Count: 0
```

Figure 9.6 *Speller Main Menu*

Menu Options

When the Spell checker is invoked, the main menu is displayed underneath the text of the current screen, as shown in Figure 9.6.

Word

This instructs the Speller to check whatever word the cursor currently resides in. If the word is correctly spelled, it moves on to the next word.

Page

Select this option if you want to check the current page.

Document

This option tells the Speller to check every word in the document, from top to bottom, regardless of where the cursor is located.

New Sup. Dictionary

The Speller allows you to create your own supplementary dictionary. For most people, the main dictionary supplied by WordPerfect

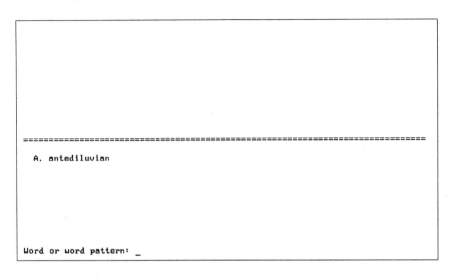

Figure 9.7 *Results of Looking up "antediluvian"*

is sufficient, given the fact that you can add your own words. If you want to get into dictionary creation, see the WordPerfect reference manual.

Look Up

If you don't want to check any specific words, but would rather look one up, select this option. The Speller prompts you to enter the word or word pattern in the lower left hand corner of the screen. If you think you know how to spell the word, enter it in its entirety. For example, let's say you want to check the spelling of the word "antediluvian." You enter it at the prompt, and WordPerfect indicates that it's correct by displaying it as in Figure 9.7. If you didn't spell it correctly, WordPerfect displays the correct spelling beneath the double dotted line. If WordPerfect finds several possible matches, it shows all of them, allowing you to select the correct one by letter.

If you're not sure exactly how to spell a word, type in as much of the word as you think is correct, and insert "wildcard" characters for the parts you are unsure of. The "?" wildcard means "any single letter," while the "*" wildcard means any number of any characters.

It works like this. Let's say you aren't sure whether "antediluvian" is spelled with an "e" or an "i" after the "d." When prompted for the word or word pattern, enter:

anted?luvian + (Enter)

This instructs the Speller to look for the exact sequence of letters you've entered, and report any word that has any single letter in the position of the question mark. The only word happens to be "antediluvian," so it displays the word on the screen, as shown in Figure 9.7. If the Speller can't find any matches, it prompts you for another word or word pattern.

What if you aren't sure about whether "antediluvian" is spelled with an "e" or an "i" after the "t," as well as an "e" or an "i" after the "d." No problem—use two "?" wildcard characters when prompted for a word or word pattern:

ant?d?luvian

You get the same results.

You could also use the "*" wildcard character as well in the last instance, entering:

ant*

which instructs the Speller to look up all words with "ant" followed by any number of any characters. While this is shorter to enter, it takes a lot longer to sort through the results. The Speller will display numerous results, as shown in Figure 9.8. Actually, the results shown in Figure 9.8 are just the tip of the iceberg; when the Speller displays:

Press any key to continue

it means there are more entries to view on the next screen. In this case, there are *21* more screens to view, for a total of *526* choices to consider!

As you can see, while it might have taken a few seconds less to input "ant*" instead of "ant?d?luvian," the savings were quickly negated by the time it takes to page through 526 entries instead of 1 entry. The moral? Be as specific as you can, narrowing down the word pattern as much as possible. And use the "*" character sparingly. To

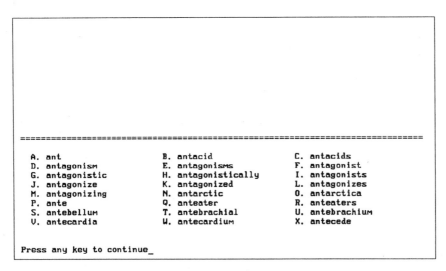

```
=========================================================================
  A. ant                 B. antacid              C. antacids
  D. antagonism           E. antagonisms          F. antagonist
  G. antagonistic         H. antagonistically     I. antagonists
  J. antagonize           K. antagonized          L. antagonizes
  M. antagonizing         N. antarctic            O. antarctica
  P. ante                 Q. anteater             R. anteaters
  S. antebellum           T. antebrachial         U. antebrachium
  V. antecardia           W. antecardium          X. antecede

  Press any key to continue_
```

Figure 9.8 *Results of Looking Up "ant*"*

return to the main speller menu, press (Enter) when prompted for the next word.

Count

This option allows you to count the number of words in a document. When the count is finished, it is displayed in the lower left hand corner of the screen. Press any key when the count is done to return to the Speller menu. You can return to your document by pressing (F7). Note that the cursor will be at the bottom of the document, rather than the position it was in when you executed the *Count* option. To return to your starting position, press (Ctrl-Home) twice.

Now that you know how to select a document, look up words, and take a word count, let's consider what happens when the Speller bumps into a word it doesn't know. The following discussion applies whether you've selected a single word check, a page check, or an entire document check.

```
page and some stylistic relief.

    The Speller is a slightly different story. While you might
occassional use it to check words as you go along, most of your
spell-checking will probably be postponed until you are ready to
print.  After all, if you're still tearing apart or adding words
to a document, you'll be likely to introduce typos and other

=============================================================================

  A. occasional




Not Found: 1 Skip Once; 2 Skip; 3 Add; 4 Edit; 5 Look Up; 6 Ignore Numbers: 0
```

Figure 9.9 *Highlighted Word and Options for Unknown Spelling*

Word Not Found: Options

If the Speller does not recognize a word, because it is misspelled or simply not in the dictionary, it highlights the word and displays a list of options underneath a double-dashed line, as shown in Figure 9.9. If you see the word correctly spelled, press the letter to which it corresponds, and the word replaces the incorrectly spelled version in your document. As with the Thesaurus, the Speller maintains case. If the word "Occassional" [sic] has an initial upper case letter in your document, when you insert the correctly spelled word, it appears with an initial upper case letter ("Occasional," correctly spelled out).

When a word isn't found, the following options are available:

Skip Once

This instructs the Speller to ignore this single occurrence of the word and continue.

Skip

This option tells the Speller to skip every occurrence of the word and continue with the spell-checking operation. This is a particularly useful option when it comes to names and technical words. If you instruct the Speller to skip all occurrences of the word, but it stops at one occurrence later on, you know that you've spelled the word differently from the first instance, which is why the Speller considers it a different word. You can then correct it or make it consistent by using the editing option below.

Add Word

There are several occasions in which you will want to add words to the Speller dictionary file.

1. You are certain that the word is correctly spelled (Good as the Speller is, you can't expect it to know *everything*, especially technical jargon peculiar to your field.)

2. You have a variation on a word already in the dictionary. While the Speller does pretty well with plurals and contractions, it does miss a few here and there.

3. You want to enter a proper name, title, or company name. Start with your own.

When you add a word to the dictionary, it is added to a file called WP{WP}US.SUP (the supplemental dictionary). The speller checks the supplemental dictionary each time it looks up a word. You can load the WP{WP}US.SUP file into WordPerfect as you would any text file and review the words you have added. You should do this occasionally to ensure that you haven't accidentally added a misspelled word (it's easy to hit option 3 for add when you meant to press number for edit). Each word should appear on a separate line, so you must delete the entire line, including the hard return, to remove a word. In order to improve the speed of the speller, you should also sort the supplemental dictionary alphabetically using the sort feature (see Appendix A). While you are editing the supplemental dictionary you can also add words. Just be sure to maintain the proper format. When you are done, resave the file in the WordPerfect directory or whatever directory you assigned for the dictionary during setup.

Edit

The *Edit* option allows you to alter the spelling of a word in your document. This may be necessary if a word is so jumbled that the Speller can't even make a recommendation, or none of the recommended alternatives are even close. (You can also enter the edit mode by pressing either the (Right Cursor) or (Left Cursor) keys. Once in edit, make your correction, then press (F7). If the Speller accepts your correction, it continues. If it still considers it misspelled, it presents another list of alternatives.

Hint 1: Sometimes it is faster to edit a word than to read through the list of alternatives, especially when the word is short and the list of alternatives is like a visual obstacle course. For instance, if you misspell "he'd" as "het," you are presented with two pages of options (see Figures 9.10a and b). You have to read through to the 25th alternative to find your word. Obviously, it's quicker just to pop into the edit mode and make the correction yourself.

Hint 2: Even if you don't know the correct spelling of a word, you may be able to recognize that it has an impossible mix of consonants and vowels. Hopefully, you can get the word close enough to a form that WordPerfect can recommend alternatives. This "one-two punch" approach is often very effective.

Look Up

This function is identical to the Look Up feature described above, with the exception that the Speller inserts the correct version into your text when you press the appropriate letter.

Ignore Numbers

This feature allows you to skip words with numbers. Numbered words can greatly slow up your search. When you select this option, you tell the Speller not to bother with letters combined with numbers for the rest of the checking session.

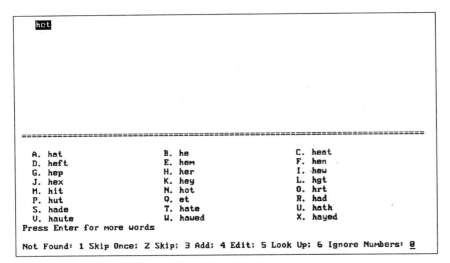

Figure 9.10a *First Set of Options for "het" Rendering of "he'd"*

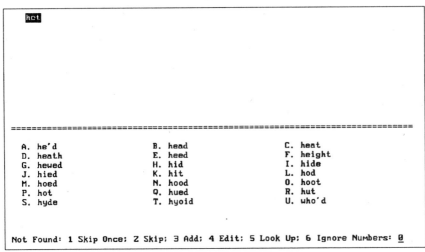

Figure 9.10b *Second Set of Options for "het" Rendering of "he'd"*

```
you discover that you've beaten a particular word to death 18

times per page and some stylistic relief.

     The Speller Speller is a slightly different story. While you

might

occassional use it to check words as you go along, most of your

spell-checking will probably be postponed until you are ready to




Double Word: 1 Z Skip; 3 Delete 2nd; 4 Edit; 5 Disable Double Word Checking_
```

Figure 9.11 *Double Word Options*

Double Word Options

In addition to the above options, the Speller offers one other set of options when it encounters a double word. As you can see from Figure 9.11, the Speller gives you five choices:

Skip

This option instructs the Speller to ignore the double word.

Delete 2nd

If the second word is a mistake and you want it removed, select this option.

Edit

This is the same editing feature as that described above. Use it to alter the second (or first) word.

Disable Double Word Checking

In some cases you will want to turn off double word checking for the rest of the document. For example, if you have columns of numbers, many of which are the same, the Speller stops incessantly and ask if you want to delete the second instance. In that case, you should probably turn off the double word checking function.

Final Caveat

The WordPerfect speller is a powerful tool, and you should spell check every document before printing. It's so fast and easy, and you'll be surprised at what your own readings miss. But it's not foolproof. WordPerfect checks the spelling of words, but not whether they are the correct or appropriate words. You must still proofread your work to ensure that you have entered the words you intended. For example, you may have intended to enter the word "bead" but accidentally typed "mead." When you spell check, the speller won't find your error, since mead is spelled correctly.

Worse, you can use the speller to insert correctly spelled, but embarrassingly incorrect, words into your document by pressing the wrong letter when selecting replacement words. One of the authors illustrated this pitfall when he submitted a manuscript in final form to his editor without paying close attention to the spell checking process. The editor wanted to know if a "house orgasm" was an original concept. No, just the danger of misspelling house "organ" and letting WordPerfect make the fix.

Your Turn

If you haven't spell checked your memo, now's the time to do it, because the next chapter will show you how to print it. The more you use the dictionary, the more you'll come to rely on it as an essential word processing tool.

10

Printing Your Document

FROM SCREEN TO PAPER

Having setup and formatted your document as described in Chapters 2 and 3, you are now ready to print. This chapter assumes the use of the simple printer installation described in Chapter 1. If you want to carry out a more complex printer installation, using multiple font cartridges, refer to Appendix A, which describes the installation of an H.P. LaserJet Series II and demonstrates most of the options.

MAIN PRINTER MENU

To start the print process, you must select the Main Print menu, shown in Figure 10.1, by pressing (Shift)-(F7).

This menu is divided into two sections. The first section, titled Print and containing numbered options from 1-7, controls the primary printing functions. The second section, titled Options, is used to alter several of the print options. Each option is described below.

Print Menu Options (Top Portion)

Full Document

The *Full Document* print option initiates printing of the complete current document, regardless of the cursor position in the document. The print job is executed immediately, using the currently selected printer and the current settings shown in section 2 of the print menu. If there are print jobs already waiting to print, the print job is added to the end of the print queue.

Page

The *Page* print option prints the current page of the current document—the page in which the cursor is currently positioned. The print job is executed immediately, using the currently selected printer and the current settings of the variable parameters in section 2 of the print menu. If there are print jobs already waiting to print, the print job is added to the end of the print queue.

Document on Disk

This option allows you to print any document saved to disk in formatted form. One of the *Setup* options called *Fast Save*, saves documents to files in unformatted form. This saves time when saving files; however, you can't use the *Print Document on Disk* option to print files saved with the *Fast Save* option. They must be first loaded into the current document and printed by selecting *Full Document* or *Page* above. You can print a formatted document prepared for another printer with this option, though WordPerfect asks you if you really intended to do that.

```
Print

     1 - Full Document
     2 - Page
     3 - Document on Disk
     4 - Control Printer
     5 - Type Through
     6 - View Document
     7 - Initialize Printer

Options

     S - Select Printer              HP LaserJet Series II
     B - Binding                     0"
     N - Number of Copies            1
     G - Graphics Quality            Medium
     T - Text Quality                High




Selection: 0
```

Figure 10.1 *Main Printer Menu*

You can either print the entire document or specify which pages you want to print in the form:

23	Print Page 23
23,45	Print Page 23 then Page 45
23-45	Print Pages 23 through 45
23-	Print Page 23 through the end of the document
-45	Print from the beginning of the document to page 45

Control Printer

This option allows you to control the printing process. When selected, this option displays a screen similar to Figure 10.2. (It varies, depending on your print queue.)

Note that the top half of the screen shows the status of the current print job, that is, the job currently being sent to the printer. Job 2 is the current print job. Any error messages or warnings are displayed at the top of the screen.

```
Print: Control Printer

Current Job

Job Number: 2                          Page Number:  2
Status:      Printing                  Current Copy: 1 of 1
Message:     None
Paper:       Standard 8.5" x 11"
Location:    Continuous feed
Action:      None


Job List

Job  Document              Destination     Print Options
 2   (Screen)              LPT 1
 3   (Screen)              LPT 1
 4   C:\5K\FONT-B.122      LPT 1           Text=Draft,Graphics=Draft

Additional Jobs Not Shown: 0




1 Cancel Job(s); 2 Rush Job; 3 Display Jobs; 4 Go (start printer); 5 Stop: 0
```

Figure 10.2 *Print Control Screen*

The center of the screen shows the queue of jobs waiting to print. Jobs 2 and 3 were initiated from the current document, while job 4 was printed from a document on file. In addition to listing the name of the job, the screen shows which printer will print the job and any special print options.

The bottom of the screen offers a small menu of *Control Printer* options. You can select any of them by entering their number or mnemonic.

Cancel

Use the *Cancel* option to cancel the current print job, any other print job (designated by number) or all pending print jobs. This option can only cancel that portion of the document not yet sent to the printer. If you have a short document or a large print buffer, you may not be able to cancel the job before the entire document is sent to the printer. In general, to truly cancel a print job, you must physically stop the printer by taking it off line first, cancel the print job and then reset the printer to clear the print buffer.

```
Print: Control Printer

Current Job

Job Number: 4                              Page Number:  1
Status:      Printing                      Current Copy: 1 of 1
Message:     None
Paper:       Standard 8.5" x 11"
Location:    Continuous feed
Action:      None


Job List

Job  Document              Destination     Print Options
  4  C:\5K\FONT-B.122       LPT 1           RUSH,Text=Draft,Graphics=Draft
  2  (Screen)               LPT 1
  3  (Screen)               LPT 1

Additional Jobs Not Shown: 0




1 Cancel Job(s); 2 Rush Job; 3 Display Jobs; 4 Go (start printer); 5 Stop: 0
```

Figure 10.3 *Rush Job Screen*

Rush

If you have more than one print job in the print queue, you can move a job to the top of the queue by selecting the *Rush* option and entering the desired job number. If there is a job currently printing that has not been completely transmitted to the printer, you are given the option of interrupting the current print job for the rush job. Figure 10.3 shows the print queue from Figure 10.2 after job 4 has been rushed to the top of the queue.

Display Jobs

If you have more print jobs in the queue than can be displayed on the Printer Control Screen, i.e., more than 3 jobs, you can display the additional jobs by selecting the *Display Jobs* option. This devotes the entire screen to listing the jobs in the queue.

Go (Start Printer)

Use the *Go* option to restart the printer after it has been stopped via the *Stop* option below or by a printer error or prompt. If you stop a print job, restart it via this option. If WordPerfect detects a serious printer error (i.e., more serious than out of paper), it stops the print process and you must select the *Go* option to restart it.

If you have selected manual feed for one of your forms during the printer installation process, WordPerfect automatically alerts you to insert the desired form the first time it is called for by the print process. The alert is simply a single beep from the computer when you try to print using the manual form. You must display the Print Control Screen to display the prompt message instructing you to insert the specified form. Then select the *Go* option to restart the printer.

Stop

Use the *Stop* option to pause during the current print job. Select *Go*, described above, to restart the print job. It is important to realize that *Stop* does not recall data already sent to the printer. If you have a short document or a large print buffer, you may not be able to stop the job before the entire document is sent to the printer. To truly pause during the print process, you must physically stop the printer by taking it off line first and then stop the print job.

Type Through

If you are using a line printer such as a daisy wheel or dot matrix that allows you to insert forms and position them precisely under the print head, you can use the *Type Through* option to turn your computer and its printer into a very expensive typewriter. This option allows you to type directly to your printer one character at a time. If you need to fill out forms this feature is invaluable. If you spent all your money and bought a sophisticated page printer such as a laser printer, sorry, but this option is not available. The reason is that you can't really position the print head on the form (laser printers don't have print heads, per se) and you certainly can't see what you are typing, since the page won't print and eject until you fill out the entire form.

View Document

WordPerfect 5.0 introduces a very sophisticated document preview feature. If you have a graphics monitor, you can view your document exactly as it will print in full graphics splendor. If you have specified different size or style fonts, they will be displayed in WYSIWYG (what-you-see-is-what-you-get) display. Furthermore, if you have incorporated any graphic elements into your document, these will be properly positioned and displayed as well. You can view the document at several different levels of magnification including: 100%, 200%, one full page on screen, and two full pages on screen. You can use the (Page Up) and (Page Down) keys to view preceding and subsequent pages. In the higher magnifications, you can also use the cursor keys to move about the page.

Note: All font attributes (bold, italic, etc) will be displayed by the *View Document* option only if the current selected printer can print the designated attributes.

Initialize Printer

This option is used to control the downloading of soft fonts to your printer. If you marked soft fonts during the printer installation, you can download them by selecting this option.

Option Menu (Lower Part of Print Menu)

Select Printer

As mentioned in Chapter 1 and discussed in detail in Appendix A, you can install several different printers or printer configurations. Once they are installed, you can select from among them by pressing S for the *Select Printer* option. The currently selected printer is marked with an asterisk as shown in Figure 10.4.

To select another printer, highlight its name and press S for Selection. The other options on the Select Printer menu are discussed in the printer installation section.

Binding Width

When you are creating two-sided pages, you should shift the even number pages to the left and the odd numbered pages to the right to allow a fixed inside margin for binding the pages together or for

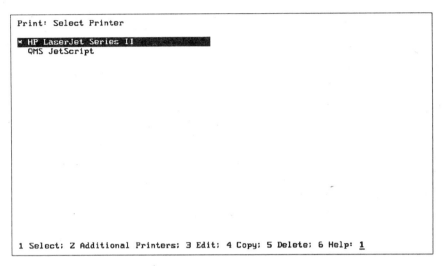

Figure 10.4 *Select Printer Screen*

punching holes for a three ring binder. This width is added to the normal left and right margins, changing the line length, so your entire document may require reformatting if you significantly change the binding width.

Number of Copies

This option allows you to specify the number of copies to be printed of the document or page. If you are printing a multi-page document, this prints out multiple sets of the document in collated order. This differs from the multiple print options on most printers which simple print multiple copies of each page as it is transmitted, leaving the collating up to you.

Graphics Quality

If your printer has variable print resolutions for graphics, you can control that feature through this option. Many of the earlier laser printers, for example, did not have enough memory to permit large 300 dot-per-inch (DPI) graphics, but they could print the same graphic at 150 DPI or 75 DPI. In addition, for draft documents, lower quality graphics will usually print more quickly. You can then print the final draft with the highest resolution available with your printer.

Text Quality

Many printers, especially dot matrix printers, have different quality text printing capability. The lower resolution type is usually referred to as Draft Quality, while the higher quality type is referred to as Near-Letter Quality. Draft quality printing is often two or three times faster than Near-Letter Quality and is therefore desirable for early drafts of a document. This option allows you to select from Draft, Medium and High quality print styles. Of course, your printer must be able to print in these different modes.

OTHER METHODS OF PRINTING

In addition to the Main Print menu described above, there are two more ways to print all or part of a document. The first is called print from *List Files*, and the second is called Block Printing. The *List Files* method is discussed in depth in the next chapter. The Block Printing method is described below.

Printing a Block of Text

You can print a block of text at any time by placing the cursor at the beginning of the block, turning on the block feature by pressing (Alt)-(F4), highlighting the desired block with the cursor keys, and then selecting the print option by pressing (Shift)-(F7). You will be asked to confirm your choice, and the block will be printed on the currently selected printer, in accordance with the currently selected print options.

Your Turn

Print your memo, or portions of it, using the functions described above. Experiment with each option until you are comfortable with the way it works.

11

Storing and Retrieving
Your Document

MAINTAINING YOUR FILES

In addition to creating and printing documents, file maintenance is an important aspect of word processing—or any computer application, for that matter. WordPerfect includes a first rate file manager, that allows you to easily store, retrieve, delete, rename, and backup files. In addition, the file manager provides extremely useful features for viewing files without retrieving them, and for searching through files to find selected text. This chapter reviews each option, and describes its use.

USING THE FILE MANAGER

To initiate the file manager, press (F5), list files. The lower left hand corner of the screen will then display the current document. If that is the directory in which you wish to manage files, press (Enter), and the List Files screen will be displayed (see Figure 11.1). If you wish to temporarily change directories, edit the directory name shown on

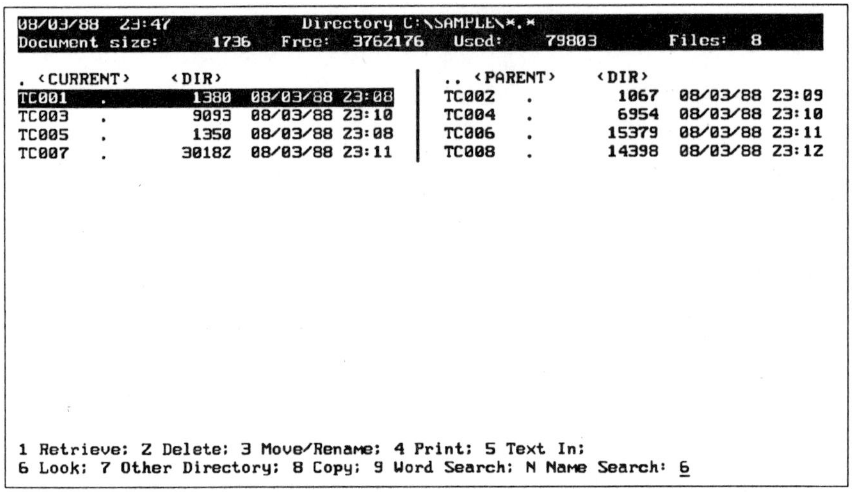

```
08/03/88  23:47              Directory C:\SAMPLE\*.*
Document size:      1736   Free:  3762176   Used:    79803        Files:  8

. <CURRENT>    <DIR>                      .. <PARENT>    <DIR>
TC001  .         1380  08/03/88 23:08     TC002  .         1067  08/03/88 23:09
TC003  .         9093  08/03/88 23:10     TC004  .         6954  08/03/88 23:10
TC005  .         1350  08/03/88 23:08     TC006  .        15379  08/03/88 23:11
TC007  .        30182  08/03/88 23:11     TC008  .        14398  08/03/88 23:12

















1 Retrieve; 2 Delete; 3 Move/Rename; 4 Print; 5 Text In;
6 Look; 7 Other Directory; 8 Copy; 9 Word Search; N Name Search: 6
```

Figure 11.1 *List FIle Screen — Invoked by Pressing* (F5) *Key*

the screen, and press (Enter). The files for that directory will be displayed, but when you exit the List Files screen, the directory will be the same as before.

If you wish to actually make another directory the current directory, enter an equal sign (=) and WordPerfect will prompt you for the name of the new directory. Enter the name, and press (Enter). The List Files screen is then be displayed, showing the files in the new directory.

The top of the screen reveals key information about your system, including:

1. The current date.

2. The current time.

3. The name of the directory.

4. The size of the current directory.

5. The amount of space free on your hard disk or floppy (data) disk.

6. The total amount of bytes occupied by the files in the current directory.

7. The number of files in the current directory.

The individual files are shown with their main file names and extensions. You can select a file for one of the file management options by moving the cursor and highlighting it. The options are listed on the bottom of the screen.

List File Options

Retrieve

This option retrieves the highlighted file into Document 1 or Document 2, depending on which document you had selected prior to using the file manager. If the retrieved file is the only document on the screen, it is considered the current document. If text already exists on the screen and you attempt to retrieve a file, WordPerfect asks you to confirm by asking:

> `Retrieve into current document (Y/N) No`

in the lower left hand portion of the screen. This confirmation is included to prevent you from accidentally combining two files on screen. Of course, there are many times when you intentionally want to insert one file into another, such as when you have created a "boilerplate" and wish to retrieve it into your document, rather than retyping it each time (see Chapter 7, for more information about this technique).

Delete

The *Delete* option erases a file. Before doing so, WordPerfect asks you to confirm your deletion, by asking:

> `Delete [highlighted file name] (Y/N) No`

If you indicate yes, the file is erased by the DOS delete/erase command. (If you were too hasty, you can always undelete them using a third party file recovery program.)

Move/Rename

This option allows you to rename files. When you highlight a file and select Option #3, WordPerfect prompts you in the lower left hand side of the screen with

New Name: [directory\highlighted file name]

Edit the file name as you choose, and press (Enter). The file will be listed with its new name.

That's the rename part. The move part comes in if you alter the directory in front of the file name. For example, if you want to move the file TC003.SAM from the directory named C:\SAMPLE to the directory named C:\WORD, you would simply edit the directory name, C:\SAMPLE and change it to C:\WORD or enter the new directory name by itself at the prompt. When you press (Enter), TC003.SAM will be transferred to C:\WORD and deleted from the C:\SAMPLE directory listing. In this regard, Move is a "move and delete" function.

Finally, you can rename a file *and* transfer it to another directory. Let's say that you want to transfer the file named C:\SAMPLE\TC003.SAM to the directory called C:\WORD, and rename it INTRO.SAM. At the new name prompt, edit both the directory and the file name so that they read:

New Name:C:\WORD\INTRO.SAM

When you press (Enter), TC00.SAM will be transferred to C:\WORD, and renamed INTRO.SAM.

Print

This is probably the easiest way to print a document. Highlight it, then press 4. In the lower right hand corner of the screen, WordPerfect will prompt you for the pages to print. If you want to print (All) pages, the default, press (Enter) and the document will be printed in its entirety.

You can also print selected pages either as a continuous range, or in discontinuous chunks. For example, a designation of

23	means print page 23.
23,35	means print pages 23 and 35.
34-	means print everything from page 34 to the end of the document.
34-39	means print pages 34 through 39.
-12	means print all pages from the start of the document through page 12

You can also combine any of the above. For example, 23,34-39,45- means print page 23, 34 through 39, and 45 to the end of the document.

Text in

This is a quick way to format an ASCII (DOS) text file and import it into your document. It's quicker and easier than using the function key *Text/In Out* option (Ctrl-F3), as described in Chapter 3.

Look

This feature lets you examine the contents of a file without actually retrieving it. You can also examine the contents of various directories. *Look* is extremely useful because it allows you to quickly examine many different files without waiting for WordPerfect to load them. Also, when you are already using two documents at once, it functions as a quasi third document allowing you to read the file but not edit it.

Let's say you are working on documents 1 and 2, and you need to check a third file to see if you covered a certain topic. Press (F5), select the third file, and scroll through in *Look* mode. When you find what you're looking for, return to document 1 or 2. Note, however, that you can't cut and paste from or to the file in *Look* mode—it is strictly view only. Here are some rules for using *Look*.

Viewing files

When you highlight a file and select 6, the contents of the document appear in a special format, as shown in Figure 11.2. The directory, file name, and file size appear in the highlighted bar at

```
Filename C:\WP122\CH8-A.122                        File size:     48744
YOUR EDITING TOOL KIT
     There are many ways to edit a document, some of which you've
already encountered earlier, such as Reveal Codes and the Block
functions.  In this chapter, we'll revisit those and other
features and explore how they can be used to alter your text.
The chapter is divided into two basic sections: editing text, and
editing formats/appearances.  The former refers to word,
sentence, and paragraph changes; the latter is concerned with
undoing or modifying various format changes.



I EDITING TEXT
     The real power of a word processor is the ability to easily
and instantly juggle words, sentences, paragraphs, and pages
without resorting to scissors and tape, correcting tape, or
correction fluid.  This involves six basic actions: 1) deleting
text; 2) cutting and pasting text; 3) copying text; 4) inserting
text; 5) searching for text; and 6) searching for and replacing
text.  This section explains how each action is used in editing a
document.

Press Exit when done                    (Use Cursor Keys for more text)
```

Figure 11.2 *Document in Look Mode* (F5) + 6)

the top of the screen. The document shows various formatting features, such as tabs, indents, bold, underline, etc., but it can only appear for viewing in single line spacing.

While viewing a document, there are certain restrictions:

1. You can move up or down through the document, but not left or right. Up or down movement is achieved by using the cursor keys, the (PgUp) and (PgDn) keys, and the screen up (+) and screen down (-) keys.

2. To continuously scroll from top to bottom without having to press any cursor movement keys, press S. To stop the forward scrolling, press S again.

3. You can use forward or backward *Search*, but not *Replace* or any other feature that alters the text. *Search* itself has a few wrinkles when used in *Look* mode. After pressing *Search*, enter the text as you normally would. But you MUST press (F2) to initiate the search; pressing (Esc) negates the search operation.

When a search is successful, WordPerfect highlights the found text, but the cursor only goes to the line on which the text occurs. You cannot search for text that wraps from one line to another; when you try to enter a hard return, WordPerfect will simply continue the search with whatever text you have already entered as the search criteria.

To continue searching for other occurrences of the text, press (F2) and repeat the operation. To continue scrolling through the text, press any of the scrolling keys described above. Do not press (F1), (Esc), or (F7)—you will immediately return to the List Files screen.

If the search is unsuccessful, WordPerfect beeps. You can then proceed to scroll through the document or try another search.

Finally, you can only search for words, not codes. Remember, *Look* is strictly for viewing. If you try to alter text, WordPerfect either does nothing, scrolls continuously, or returns you to the List Files screen.

4. To voluntarily return to the List Files screen, press:

(F1), (Enter), (Esc), or (F7)

Then press (F7) to return to your document.

Viewing Directories

If you want to view the contents of a directory, highlight the words CURRENT <DIR>, which will always appear above the first file on the left side of the List File screen. At the bottom of the screen, WordPerfect displays the current directory name. Edit the name to the directory you wish to view, then press (Enter). The new directory will then be displayed. You can use *Look* to peer into any of the files.

If you are using a floppy disk system and are reviewing the directory of your data disks, and trying to locate a particular file, you can use the CURRENT <DIR> to update the directory listing each time you swap data disks. When you press CURRENT <DIR> without changing the directoy name, WordPerfect rereads the current directory and relists the files. If you have changed data disks, the new list of file names will be displayed.

Note that when you use *Look* to view the files of another directory, your current directory hasn't changed. In other words, if your current directory is called C:\SAMPLE, and you use *Look* to view the contents of C:\WORD, when you press (F1) or (F7), you return to your document, and the current directory is still C:\SAMPLE. The only way to change the current directory from within WordPerfect is by pressing the = sign and entering a new directory after pressing (F5), as described above, or by selecting Option #7 from the file manager, as described below.

Finally, you can use the "?" and "*" wildcard characters when viewing the contents of a directory. The "?" wildcard means any single character, while the "*" means any number of characters.

When you highlight the words CURRENT <DIR> the directory name in the lower left hand corner of the screen lists the directory followed by a backslash and "*.*." The string "*.*" means any file name followed by any extension, i.e. all files. You can refine that portion to generate a more selective listing.

For example, let's say that in the directory C:\WORD, you only want to view the files with the extension "REJ." In this case, when prompted for a directory, you would enter:

C:\WORD*.REJ (Enter)

This means display files that have *any* main name, but only REJ as an extension. Conversely, you might want to find files with the same main name, say "CHAP1," but different extensions. In that case, you'd enter:

C:\WORD\CHAP1.* (Enter)

to specify the main name, and include any extension. To further refine your viewing, you might be interested in files with specific combinations of letters in the extension. Perhaps you want to find all files that have an extension consisting of "R" plus *one* letter or number. You would enter:

C:\WORD*.R? (Enter)

The "?" character says include any *single* character. Thus, R1, R2, and RA would be selected, but not REJ or R12. If you had used the "*" character, as in:

C:\WORD*.R* (Enter)

extensions with one or more characters starting with the letter R are also displayed.

As you can see, between the two wildcard characters, you can be as broad or specific as you like, and can zero in on any file or set of files.

Other Directory

Use this option to change the current directory. When you press 7, WordPerfect prompts you for a new directory in the lower left hand corner of the screen. Edit the current directory name, or enter a completely new one. When you press (Enter), the contents of the new directory will be displayed in the List Files screen.

If the directory you enter does not exist, WordPerfect asks if you want to create it. Type Y to confirm, and N if you change your mind. (It's easy to make a mistake typing in the name of a directory. If WordPerfect prompts you to create a new directory, and you know the directory you entered exists already, that's a sure sign you've made a typo. Enter N, and select Option #7 to start over again.)

Copy

This option lets you copy the highlighted file to another directory, or a floppy disk. It is extremely useful for backing up your work, especially if you're using a hard disk. Remember, no hard disk is infallible, and it pays to frequently copy valuable files to floppies...just in case. (Unfortunately, many people do not get into a regular backup routine until *after* disaster strikes and they must recreate their files. Why become a statistic? Use the *Copy* function on a regular basis. Remember, the WordPerfect backup feature only makes a copy of the *current* file, and only keeps it until the machine is turned off. If your hard disk crashes, ALL your files may be lost.)

To use the *Copy* option, highlight the file to be copied and select Option #8. WordPerfect prompts you with:

Copy this file to:

Enter the drive and the directory, as in C:\WORD or the floppy drive name, as in "B:" Press (Enter) to copy the file. If the file already exists in the other directory or on the floppy, WordPerfect asks if you want to replace it. Respond with a Y if you do, which is probably be the case if you're updating a backup file.

Here is a useful variation. You can copy the file to another directory, but assignit a different name when it gets there. For instance, if you highlight the file called TC003.SAM, and want to copy it to the C:\WORD directory as TC003.REJ, at the **Copy this file to:** prompt you would type:

C:\WORD\TC003.REJ (Enter)

When the file is copied to C:\WORD, the contents will remain the same, but the name will be new. You can do the same thing when copying to a floppy disk:

B:\TC003.REJ (Enter)

Word Search

This option allows you to check through all the files listed and search for text, just as you would use the search function with a document. When you use it, WordPerfect places an asterisk next to the byte size of all files in which the specified text was found. If no text is found, WordPerfect flashes:

* Not Found *

and the screen lists all files in the directory.

When carrying out a search, by selecting options 2 and 3 below you can use the wildcard characters "?" and "*" in selecting text to be found. As with file transfers (see above), "?" means a single character, while "*" means any number of characters. If you are looking for the word "bicycle" OR the plural form, "bicycles" you could enter the word "bicycle*", since the asterisk means any number of characters.

Likewise, let's say you have numerous documents with the words "model 200," "model 205," and "model 208," as well as "model 400, ""model 410," and "model 600." If you want to find those files that contain "model 200," "model 205," and "model 208," you could conduct several searches, or just one search by entering the criteria as "model 20?" This tells WordPerfect to only list files that have "model 20 plus any character in the last place." If you want to locate files with all models, you might enter "model *"

Another set of useful searching tools includes the "logical operators" AND, represented by a semicolon (;) and OR, represented by a comma (,). For example, "model 20?;model 40?" means find all files containing both model 200 and model 400 regardless of the last digit in either one (204, 208, 404, 407, etc). The search criteria "model 20?",model "40?" means mark a file if it has *either* model 200 or model 400 in the text.

As with the document search function, you must try to hone in as closely as possible to the desired text, bearing in mind that if you seek a precise phrase you must enter it *exactly* as it actually appears in the files. Otherwise, you won't find anything. On the other hand, if the search is too broad, WordPerfect may include too many files in the search results.

By thinking out your search strategies and using the wildcards carefully, you can pinpoint exactly the files you are seeking.

The *Word Search* function has four options.

Document summary

Ignore this, unless you're using the Document Summary feature, as explained in the *Setup* section (Chapter 3).

First Page

This instructs WordPerfect to look for the desired pattern only on the first page of each document. Enter the text you are seeking when prompted in the lower left hand corner with word pattern.

Entire Doc

This is the same as the previous entry, except that it searches the entire document for the word or phrase you are seeking.

Conditions

This option allows you to refine your search. Once WordPerfect has selected a file or a group of files, it returns to the List Files screen,

```
Word Search

  1 - Perform Search on          7 Marked File(s)

  2 - Undo Last Search

  3 - Reset Search Conditions

  4 - File Date                   No
        From (MM/DD/YY):          (All)
        To   (MM/DD/YY):          (All)

                    Word Pattern(s)

  5 - First Page
  6 - Entire Doc                  model 100
  7 - Document Summary
        Creation Date (e.g. Nov)
        Descriptive Name
        Subject/Account
        Author
        Typist
        Comments

  Selection: 1
```

Figure 11.3 *Search Conditions Menu*

with an asterisk after the byte size indicator of each file containing the text you are seeking. If you want to refine your search, select *Word Search* again, but this time choose *Conditions* from the *Word Search* menu. The *Condition* option shown in Figure 11.3 will be displayed. Note: for routine word processing, chances are that a "top level" search will suffice to find what you are looking for, and you may never have to venture into the *Condition* option. The following explanations are provided for those who may need more sophisticated file searches.

The following options are available on the Conditions menu.

Perform Search On

This option is only significant after you have done a successful search. The number of files identified during the search is listed. For example, if six of the eight files in your directory have the specified text, the number showing after this option would be six. If you want to further refine the search *on those six files*, you must select this option. Otherwise, WordPerfect performs your next search on all eight files originally in the directory.

Another way of looking at this option is that it remembers which files it found, and performs the next search as if these were the only files in the directory.

Undo Last Search

If you want to start from scratch, using all files in the directory, rather than the number of files matching the previous search, select this option. The number immediately changes back to the number of files *in your previous search*. For example, let's say you refined your search on the six files during the first search. Your second search turned up four files, so four files would be listed after the *Perform Search On* option. When you select *Undo Last Search*, the number of files moved back up to six. Press *Undo Last Search* again, and the number changes back up to eight, the number of files in the directory.

The *Undo Last Search* option allows you to call up three levels of searches. In point of fact, though, you will rarely use more than the first level of searching, so you may never have to use *Perform Search On* or *Undo Last Search*.

Reset Search Conditions

This resets all conditions back to the original search defaults.

File Date

Use this option to restrict the search to files created within a certain date range. For example, to select files created between 07/02/88 and 07/04/88, select *Conditions* from the *Word Search* menu, press (Enter) twice, and then enter the beginning date (in the format shown: MM/DD/YY). Press (Enter) again, and do the same for the ending date. Press (Enter) to complete the action.want to select a specific day, use the same beginning and ending date. For a broader sweep, you can simply enter 7//88 (i.e., no day), and WordPerfect searches all files in July. Similarly, //88 finds all files dated 1988.

```
┌─────────────────────────────────────────────────────────────────────┐
│  Word Search                                                          │
│                                                                       │
│     1 - Perform Search on              6 Marked File(s)               │
│                                                                       │
│     2 - Undo Last Search                                              │
│                                                                       │
│     3 - Reset Search Conditions                                       │
│                                                                       │
│     4 - File Date                      No                             │
│            From (MM/DD/YY):            (All)                          │
│            To   (MM/DD/YY):            (All)                          │
│                                                                       │
│                     Word Pattern(s)                                   │
│                                                                       │
│     5 - First Page                     model 200                      │
│     6 - Entire Doc                           _                        │
│     7 - Document Summary                                              │
│            Creation Date (e.g. Nov)                                   │
│            Descriptive Name                                           │
│            Subject/Account                                            │
│            Author                                                     │
│            Typist                                                     │
│            Comments                                                   │
│                                                                       │
│  Selection: 5                                                         │
└─────────────────────────────────────────────────────────────────────┘
```

Figure 11.4 *Search Conditions for First Page of Search*

First Page

This has the same effect as the *First Page* option of the *Word Search*
menu. The difference is that it restricts the search to the first page
(or first 4000 characters) of the files listed in the *Perform Search On*
option. In other words, if *Perform Search On* indicates it is operating
on the six files found in the last search, the search will be restricted
to the first page of those files. If you select *First Page* from the main
word search menu, you will always be searching the first page of
ALL files in the directory.

After you select *First Page*, the cursor moves to the right of the
option (see Figure 11.4). Enter the pattern to be found and press
(Enter).

To begin the actual search, press (Enter) when the cursor returns to
the Selection line at the bottom of the screen. The search will be
carried out, and the new marked file or files will be displayed on the
screen. To refine the search at a another level, Select 9 from the List
Files menu, then select *Conditions*, and repeat the procedure.

Entire Doc

This is the same as the *First Page* Option, but it applies to the entire document. You enter your search words in the same fashion when you select the option.

Document Summary

Use this only if you've included a document summary, as explained in the explanation of the *Setup* function (Chapter 4).

N Name Search

This is the last option on the List File menu. When you select this option, you can type in a portion of the name of the file to be highlighted. For example, if you type "Chap," the cursor moves to the first file with "C" in it. When you type "h" it moves to the first file with "Ch," and so on. If you have a short listing, it is definitely faster just to move the cursor and highlight the desired file. If you have a very long list, this may be a more efficient way to highlight the file you want to act upon.

Mark Files

WordPerfect provides a useful function for executing several of the File List functions on a group of files by first marking the files and then calling the desired function. To mark a group of files, highlight each file to be included and press (Shift-8). This marks the highlighted files with an asterisk after the byte size indicator. (You might not see it at first, since the screen is busy—refer to Figure 11.5.)

The following functions can then be used with the group of marked files:

Delete

When you select delete, WordPerfect will ask you to confirm the mass deletion by asking:

```
Delete marked files (Y/N) No
```

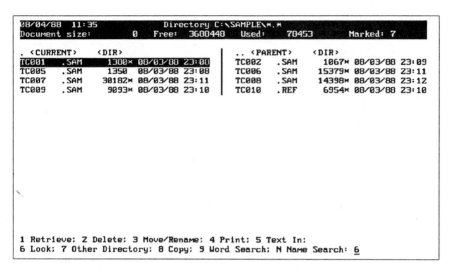

Figure 11.5 *Marked Files (Note asterisk next to byte size)*

If you say yes, they will all be deleted. If you say no, WordPerfect asks if you want to delete the SINGLE file underneath the highlight. Answer Y or N.

CAUTION! This is a very powerful and potentially dangerous feature. If you are not on your toes when you use it, you could wipe out many hours or days worth of hard work!

Move/Rename

You can't rename a group of files, but you can move them to another directory or a floppy disk. (Remember, once moved, they are deleted from the current directory and transferred to the new directory.) WordPerfect prompts you with:

Move marked files (Y/N) No

If you answer Y, it will prompt you with:

Move marked files to:

Enter the directory or the floppy drive. Make sure you include a colon after the drive letter. Otherwise you will copy the file to a new file named "A" or "B" in the current directory.)

If you enter N when asked if you want to Move marked files, WordPerfect assumes that you want to rename or move the single file under the highlight.

Print

When you select *Print*, WordPerfect will ask if you want to

Print marked files (Y/N) No

Pressing Y will print all pages of all files.

Copy

As with the other options that work with a marked group of files, WordPerfect asks if you want to

Copy the marked files (Y/N) No

If you respond Y, it will prompts you with:

Copy all marked files to:

Enter the name of the directory or floppy drive (Make sure you include a colon after the drive name.)

Your Turn

The *List File* options are very powerful and very useful. Try using each of the options described above. When you begin using WordPerfect on a regular basis, you'll pick and choose those that can make your daily word processing go more smoothly.

Appendix

Other WordPerfect Features

So far, everything you've read in this book has focused on the basic tools you need for routine word processing. In addition, WordPerfect offers a wealth of other powerful features that you may or may not want to learn after you become more familiar with the basic word processing tools. The following discussion is meant to give you a brief taste for how several of the features work. If your appetite is whetted, and you feel like you can absorb yet more information, you can turn to the WordPerfect reference manual and learn how to use these and other features yourself. By now you've probably come to realize that trial and error is the best way to get a handle on any WordPerfect feature (or for that matter, *any* software program, whether it's a word processor, a database, or a spreadsheet).

MACRO GENERATOR

A macro is a file that allows you to execute a series of commands with just two keystrokes. The commands can include the input of text, or any of the WordPerfect functions. For example, let's say you constantly type in the name, "Amalgamated Refrigeration Installation and Repair Corporation, Inc." Instead of retyping this monster each time you need it, create a macro that types if for you. Here's what to do:

1. Shift into macro definition mode by pressing (Ctrl-F10).

2. The lower part of the screen prompts you to:

    Define macro:

    Press (Alt) plus a selected key. In this case, choose "A," as a mnemonic for "Amalgamated." WordPerfect then prompts you for a description. Type in:

    Amalgamated Inc.

    or anything else that describes what the macro does.

3. WordPerfect then flashes the words "**Macro Def**" in the lower left hand corner of the screen. At this point, WordPerfect "watches over your shoulder" and records any keystrokes (including mistakes you make). Carefully type in:

    Amalgamated Refrigeration Installation and Repair Corporation, Inc.

    Then turn off the macro recorder by pressing (Ctrl-F10) again. The **Macro Def** message will clear the screen.

4. The next time you press (Alt-A), Amalgamated Refrigeration Installation and Repair Corporation, Inc. will be typed in for you at the current cursor location.

Now let's write a macro that executes a command. In this case, you'll automate the process of changing from single to double space.

1. Turn on the macro recorder (Ctrl-F10).

2. When prompted to define the macro, press (Alt) + D (or any letter of your choosing. "D" makes sense to remind you that this is the macro for double spacing.)

3. Type:

Double space (Enter)

when prompted for a description.

4. Press:

(Shift-F8) + 1 + 6 + 2 (F7) + (F7)

These are the keystrokes you use to set double spacing.

5. Press (Ctrl-F10) to stop the macro recorder.

6. Each time you press (Alt-D), the format changes to double spacing.

The subject of macros could fill a whole book. To learn how to edit macros and use some of the powerful special macro commands, look at your WordPerfect reference manual. Also a complete selection of 450 pre-written macros on disk and a detailed discussion of macro programming logic is available in *WordPerfect Power Pack* from Brady Books.

MAIL MERGE

The "mail merge" function allows you to combine the contents of a "primary file," say a letter, with the contents of a "secondary file," such as an address list. You can either create the primary or the secondary merge file first, depending on your needs. The primary file is coded so that each line of the address appears in the proper position. There are many types of merges, as explained in the WordPerfect reference manual. Here's the most common one.

Primary File: A Letter

Type a letter, but leave out the specific addressee and the name following the "dear." Instead, insert the merge codes F1 through F5. F1 corresponds to the first line of an address in your secondary file (i.e. the addressee's name). F2 refers to the second line (company or institutional name), while F3 is street address and F4 is the city, state, and zip. Finally, F5 is used for the name following the greeting. It is critical that the codes in the primary letter file correspond to the lines in the secondary address file. The technique for creating a secondary address file is explained below.

The merge codes for the primary letter file are most easily inserted by pressing (Shift-F9), which brings up the following Merge Code menu at the bottom part of the screen:

^C:^D;^E;^F;^G;^N;^O;^P;^Q;^S;^T;^U;^V;

Since you're interested in the ^F code, press F. WordPerfect prompts you for the field (line) number. If it is the first line of the address, type 1. WordPerfect inserts ^F1^. Press (Enter) to move to the next line. For the second line of the address (company name) type the field number as 2?, which will appear in your text as ^F2?^. The reason is that you may have some people who have company or institutional affiliations, and some who don't. The "?" character tells WordPerfect to close up the space if nothing is on second line of an address. Repeat the procedure used in line one for lines three and four of the address.

Now type "Dear," followed by a fifth ^F and a comma (,). Type the body of the letter. Then press

(Home) + (Home) + (Down Cursor)

to reach the end of your letter. Insert a space with the (Enter) key, and type the following code:

^T^N^P^P

by pressing the (Ctrl) key and typing the letter. These codes instruct WordPerfect to merge the letter and address file at the printer (^T), to go on to the next address when finished (^N), and to continue using the letter as the primary file (^P). When you're finished, your letter should have the code arrangement shown in Figure A.1.

Save your letter with the (F7) key, but don't exit WordPerfect— you have to type an address list, which constitutes the secondary file. Each address will be "merged" into the letter, based on your coding. The result will look like a genuine personal letter.

```
                                        August 4, 1988


^F1^
^F2^
^F3^
^F4^

Dear ^F5^,

[Text of letter]




                                        Sincerely




                                        ^T^N^P^P
                                        Doc 2 Pg 1 Ln 5.16" Pos 6.8"
```

Figure A.1 *Letter With Merge Codes*

Secondary File: Address List

Create an address list, placing each line of the address on a separate line in your document, followed by the code ^R after each line. You can insert the ^R code and a hard return by pressing (F9) key. Be sure to enter each record (complete address) in exactly the same order as you set up the fields in your letter:

name

company

street

city-state-zip,

appellation

on separate lines.   After typing in the name that follows the "Dear", insert a ^R and go to the next line. If a particular address does not have an entry for a specific field, such as company name, you MUST enter a blank line including a ^R to indicate that the field is empty. At the end of the complete address (a single record), enter a ^E character by pressing (Ctrl-E) or using (Shift-F9) function key combination. The ^E tells WordPerfect this address is complete. It is imperative that you

```
┌─────────────────────────────────────────────────────────────────────────────┐
│ Mr. Richard Beckswith^R                                                       │
│ Admiral Food Company^R                                                        │
│ 1 Penn Sq^R                                                                   │
│ Chaicago, IL 60612^R                                                          │
│ Richard^R                                                                     │
│ ^E                                                                            │
│ ===============================================================================│
│ Ms. Marsha Bulfinch^R                                                         │
│ ^R                                                                            │
│ 1 Feroy St^R                                                                  │
│ Cambridge, MA 02138^R                                                         │
│ Marsha^R                                                                      │
│ ^E                                                                            │
│ ===============================================================================│
│ Mr. Herbert Thurston^R                                                        │
│ Thurston Hotels^R                                                             │
│ 22 Main St.^R                                                                 │
│ Philadelphia, PA 19072^R                                                      │
│ Herb^R                                                                        │
│ ^E                                                                            │
│                                                                               │
│                                                                               │
│ C:\WP122\SECOND                              Doc 1 Pg 2 Ln 1" Pos 1"          │
└─────────────────────────────────────────────────────────────────────────────┘
```

Figure A.2 *Merge Codes for Address List (Secondary File)*

place the ^E after each address, with no extra characters or spaces or lines, or the mail merge won't work properly. To make a secondary merge file easier to read, you can insert a hard page code (Ctrl-Enter) after the ^E code instead of the hard return (Enter). This will place a double dashed line between each address record and allow you to scan through your secondary merge file address by address by pressing (PgUp) and (PgDn).

A typical address should look like the samples shown in Figure A.2.

Merging the Primary and Secondary

Once you create and save your primary and secondary files to disk, clear the screen, then press (Ctrl-F9) to display the following menu:

1 Merge **2** Sort **3** Sort Order: **0**

Select 1 for merge, WordPerfect prompts you for the name of the primary file. Type in the name and press (Enter). WordPerfect then prompts you for the name of the Secondary file. Type in the name and press (Enter).

Each letter will be printed individually, with the name and address of everyone in the secondary file. There are many other merge options available. If you're interested, consult your WordPerfect reference manual.

SORT

WordPerfect has a built-in sorting feature that allows you to sort lines of text and paragraphs. While it is not meant to replace a relational database, it can be very useful in sorting lists of items, addresses, etc.

While there are many sort options, you can perform a simple alphabetic sort with the following procedure:

1. Type a list.

2. Press (Ctrl-F9). The following menu will be displayed.

3. Select the *Sort* option:

    1 Merge   **2 S**ort   **3** Sort Order: **0**

4. WordPerfect asks you for the name of the "input file." Press (Enter) to sort the document displayed on the screen.

5. WordPerfect asks you for the name of the "output file." Press (Enter) to accept the default of screen.

6. The *Sort* options menu will be displayed, with numerous options (see Figure A.3). The default sort order is alphabetic from A to Z. Press 1 to select *Perform Action* with the default sort order.

7. To sort paragraphs or addresses, select item 7, *Type*, from the *Sort* menu, and select Option #3, **Paragraphs**. Then select Option #1, *Perform Action*.

CAUTION: Make sure each paragraph or address ends with at least TWO hard returns (i.e., press (Enter) twice).

Refer to the manual if you need more than the basic alphabetic sort.

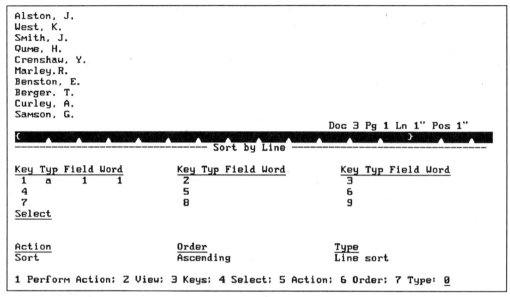

Figure A.3 *Sort Menu*

OUTLINER

Many people find it helpful to organize their thoughts into an outline before proceeding to write. WordPerfect offers a built in outliner to help you. While it does not offer the power of a full-featured, stand alone outliner, or programs based around an outliner, such as Framework, it is a useful tool and easy to learn.

To create an outline:

1. Press (Shift-F5). Select Option #4, outline.

2. The screen blanks except for the word Outline in the lower left hand corner to remind you that you are in outline mode.

3. Press (Enter), and the Roman numeral I will appear on the screen. Press (F4) indent, then enter your text.

4. When you press (Enter) again, Roman numeral II will appear. If you have a sub-section for "I", press the (Tab) key, and the "II" will change to an "A". Type your text and press (Enter). On

the next line, a "II" will appear. If have a subpoint for "A," press (Tab) twice until "1." appears. Type your text and press (Enter) when you are finished. You can continue six levels under point "A," or add a "B" level. Or you can go on to "II." The result will look something the outline shown in Figure A.4.

5. When you are finished, press (Shift-F5) to turn the outliner off and return to normal text entry mode.

There are many predefined options for changing the numbering styles of the outline. You can also invent your scheme. Refer to the manual for instructions in changing styles.

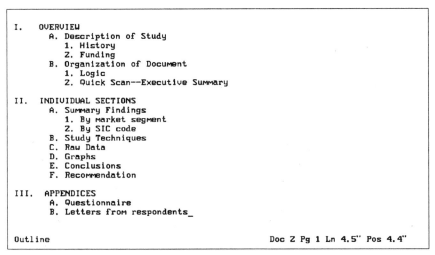

```
I.    OVERVIEW
      A. Description of Study
         1. History
         Z. Funding
      B. Organization of Document
         1. Logic
         Z. Quick Scan--Executive Summary

II.   INDIVIDUAL SECTIONS
      A. Summary Findings
         1. By market segment
         Z. By SIC code
      B. Study Techniques
      C. Raw Data
      D. Graphs
      E. Conclusions
      F. Recommendation

III.  APPENDICES
      A. Questionnaire
      B. Letters from respondents_


Outline                                    Doc Z Pg 1 Ln 4.5" Pos 4.4"
```

Figure A.4 *Sample Outline*

GRAPHICS

WordPerfect allows you to insert into your document predefined graphic elements, such as 1-2-3 graphs, images created in other programs or entered through a scanner, or "clip art" files supplied with the program. Refer to your manual for a list of the supported graphic sources. The following procedure explains how to insert a 1-2-3 Graph into a document.

Inserting a Lotus 1-2-3 Graph

If you have created and saved a Lotus 1-2-3 graph (with the .PIC file extension) and wish to include it in a document, use the following procedure.

1. Select *Graphics* by pressing (Alt-F9).

2. Select a box type. (Option 1, *Figure*, is recommended for this exercise.)

3. Select the Create option (#1) and you will be presented with a menu prompting you to define the figure. You will have to enter the following six elements:

    1. Filename. Enter the name of the 1-2-3 file, including the extension.

    2. Caption. Type in the desired caption, which will appear underneath the figure. The caption automatically wraps, according to the size of the figure.

    3. Type. Two graphic types are significant: paragraph and page. The paragraph type automatically moves with the text surrounding it, so that if you insert or delete text in front of a paragraph-type graphic, the graphic maintains its position relative to the text. The second type, page, works just the opposite, maintaining its position on the page, while allowing the text to move around it. For this exercise, select paragraph.

    4,5. Position. Enter the desired position on the page.

    6. Size. Enter a desired height and width or both, or leave it set for autosizing, which maintains proper proportions. (For this exercise, we recommend not adjusting the size.)

    7. Wrap text around box. The default setting, YES, tells WordPerfect to allow text to flow around the graphic, as opposed to overwriting the text with the graphic. Leave the wrap option set for YES.

    8. Edit. This option allows you to manipulate the graphic within its box. *Move* allows you to shift the graphic horizontally and vertically; *Scale* allows you to change its dimensions; and *Rotate* allows you to change its orientation.

Once you've set the options, press (F7) to exit. You can then view your graphic by previewing the document (Shift-F7) + 6. If you do not have a graphics monitor, you will have to print the document.

The same principle applies to all graphics, including the clip art images supplied with the program. You might want to try inserting and manipulating a clip art image in a document for practice. Refer to your manual for using the rich array of graphics features that WordPerfect 5.0 offers.

Appendix

Installing the H.P. Laserjet
Series II

OVERVIEW

WordPerfect can be customized for hundreds of printers, to take advantage of their special features. It does an exceptionally good job of this with laser printers in general, and the H.P. LaserJet Series II in particular. This chapter provides detailed instruction for installing a LaserJet Series II with a font cartridge and a soft font. The steps described apply to *any* printer; if you don't have font cartridges or envelope feeding capabilities with your printer, simply skip those steps of the installation procedure—you'll find instructions for terminating the installation process at key points. This chapter assumes that you have a computer with a hard disk—consult the WordPerfect manual for modifying the instructions if you have a floppy system. While you can use the LaserJet with a floppy-based system, as you begin to add soft fonts, you will find it extremely slow, as well as a disk juggling act.

BASIC CONCEPTS

Drivers

WordPerfect uses a number of "drivers," software files that enable the software to communicate with the printer. The drivers are contained on the disks labeled Printer 1-4. Each of the disks contains drivers for a different group of printers:

Printer 1 — H.P. LaserJet and compatible printers

Printer 2 — PostScript laser printers, and a selection of letter quality printers

Printer 3 — Most dot matrix printers

Printer 4 — Older and some obsolete printers

During the installation procedure, you have the opportunity to select your printer from the appropriate printer disk. You can change or add additional printers at any time.

Multiple Printers

WordPerfect allows you to install several different printer drivers on your system. You can then select different ones for specific types of print jobs. For example, you might have a laser printer connected to your serial port and a dot matrix printer connected to your parallel port. By installing the drivers for both printers, you can produce draft material on the dot matrix printer and final output on the laser printer simply by issuing a few commands from the print menu.

The installation for a second or third printer is the same as the one you're about to read about in this chapter; once you get the hang of it, you'll be able to install a new printer yourself in a matter of minutes. The only limitation on the number of printers you can install is the amount of disk space you're willing to devote to printer drivers.

What You Need To Know Before You Begin

Before you can install your H.P. Laserjet Series II or other printer, you need to know some specific information. The necessary data is summarized in Table B.1 below and can generally be found in your printer's manual. If you have difficulty gathering the information, contact your dealer or the person in your department who sets up your computers.

Armed with the information contained in Table B.1, you're ready to install your printer. During the course of the following instructions for installing an H.P. LaserJet Series II printer, cartridge font and soft font installation are discussed, as is the procedure for setting up an envelope form. You may not have or need all the options we describe, but by reading about them, you'll learn all the steps involved in installing a full-featured printer. You can select from among them as you install your printer, using only those applicable to your situation.

TABLE B.1 PRE-INSTALLATION INFORMATION

Memory

Amount of *available* RAM _____

Disk Space (For hard disk users)

2 Megabytes of Hard Disk (Y/N)_____

Display

Monitor type _____

Graphics adapter _____

Printer:

Make/Model # _____

    Font Cartridges _____

    Soft Fonts_____

Printer Interface (Serial/Parallel) _____

    If Serial Interface:

    Baud Rate _____

    Parity (none, even, odd)_____

    Stop Bits (1 or 2) _____

    Data Bits (7 or 8) _____

Forms Feed (Continuous/Manual Feed Sheet Feeder)

    If Sheet Feeder: _____

    Brand Name _____

Number of Paper Bins _____

THE INSTALLATION PROCESS

Step #1: Selecting a Printer

1. Turn on your computer and start WordPerfect 5.0 from whatever directory your program files are located. If WordPerfect is in a directory called C:\WP50, the commands are:

   CD \WP50

   WP

2. Call up the Main Print menu by pressing (Shift-F7); that is, press and hold the (Shift) key while pressing the (F7) key. The Main Printer menu will appear (see Figure B.1.)

3. Press S to choose the *Select* option. You will be presented with the Printer Selection menu shown in Figure B.2a.

4. If this is the first time you are installing a printer, your screen appears blank as in Figure B.2a. (If you have already installed printers, they will be listed on the menu, as shown in Figure B.2b.)

   Press 2 to select the *Additional Printer* option. If you have not copied all the printer disks to your hard disk (which is generally a waste of space) you will be presented with the Printer files not found message shown in Figure B.3.

   Press 2 to select the *Other Disk* option. You will be prompted to enter the name of the disk or directory where WordPerfect can find the Printer files. Enter the letter FOLLOWED BY A COLON corresponding to the drive you are using, as in A: or B:.

   WordPerfect then presents you with a list of the printer drivers contained on the Printer 1 disk as shown in Figure B.4.

```
Print

        1 - Full Document
        2 - Page
        3 - Document on Disk
        4 - Control Printer
        5 - Type Through
        6 - View Document
        7 - Initialize Printer

Options

        S - Select Printer
        B - Binding                 0"
        N - Number of Copies        1
        G - Graphics Quality        Medium
        T - Text Quality            High




Selection: 0
```

Figure B.1 *Main Print Menu*

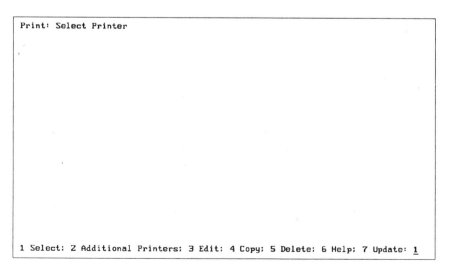

Figure B.2a *Select Printer Screen — First Time Installation*

```
Print: Select Printer

* HP LaserJet Series II









1 Select; 2 Additional Printers; 3 Edit; 4 Copy; 5 Delete; 6 Help; 7 Update: 1
```

Figure B.2b *Select Printer Screen — Printer Already Installed*

```
Select Printer: Additional Printers

Printer files not found

     Use the Other Disk option to specify a directory for the printer
     files.  Continue to use this option until you find the disk with the
     printer you want.








1 Select; 2 Other Disk; 3 Help; 4 List Printer Files; N Name Search: 1
```

Figure B.3 *Message to Indicate Drive for Printer Disk*

5. Use your (Up Cursor) and (Down Cursor) keys to move the highlight bar to the name of your printer. If the name of your printer does not appear on the list, replace the Printer 1 disk with the Printer 2 disk and press 2 to select the *Other Disk* option again. Repeat the process with each of the Printer disks until you find your printer by name. If you still can't find your printer, call WordPerfect and ask which printer driver you should use for your particular printer.

Use the cursor to highlight your printer, press 1 or S for the *Select* option. You will be shown the default printer driver file name. Press (Enter) to accept the name and WordPerfect then copies the printer drivers to your hard disk. After the drivers are copied, the screen displays a list of helpful hints for using the new printer driver. It also displays a countdown as it updates the internal fonts of the selected printer. When the countdown is complete, press (F7) and WordPerfect displays the options for the selected printer in "edit mode" as shown in Figure B.5.

EXIT OPPORTUNITY: At this point, you can accept the printer options as they are and end the printer installation procedure by pressing (F7) twice. Otherwise, you can edit the options as described below.

Step 2: Editing Your Printer Definition

As you can see in Figure B.5, there are seven basic options, each of which has several sub-options under it. These are discussed in the sequence in which it appears on the screen. If you don't need to use a certain option, skip it and move on to the next.

Name

WordPerfect supplies a default name for your printer when you first install it. In the case of the LaserJet, the name is "HP LaserJet Series II." You can edit it or insert any name you choose, up to 36 characters. For instance, you may want to supply a more descriptive name such as "My Laser Printer" or "Phil's Dot Matrix Printer." The

```
Select Printer: Additional Printers

   Dataproducts LZR-1Z30
   Destiny Laseract I
   HP LaserJet
   HP LaserJet 2000
   HP LaserJet Series II
   HP LaserJet+, 500+
   Kyocera F-1000A/1010/2010/3010
   LaserImage 1000
   Mannesmann Tally MT910
   NEC Silenturiter LC-860+
   Okidata LaserLine 6
   Olympia Laserstar 6
   Panasonic KX-P4450 Laser Partner




 1 Select; 2 Other Disk; 3 Help; 4 List Printer Files; N Name Search: 1
```

Figure B.4 *Additional Printers Menu*

```
Select Printer: Edit

         Filename              HPLASEII.PRS

    1 - Name                   HP LaserJet Series II

    2 - Port                   LPT1:

    3 - Sheet Feeder           None

    4 - Forms

    5 - Cartridges and Fonts

    6 - Initial Font           Courier 10 pitch (PC-8)

    7 - Path for Downloadable
          Fonts and Printer
          Command Files



 Selection: 0
```

Figure B.5 *Printer Edit Menu*

choice is up to you. Whatever name you choose is displayed on the Printer Selection menu when you select printers in the future.

Port

"Port" refers to the way the computer and printer are connected. There are two types of ports: parallel and serial. Parallel means that the data is transferred from computer to printer 8 bits at a time; serial means that the data is transmitted one bit after another. Parallel connections are therefore faster than serial connections. The computer can have several parallel and serial ports. Parallel ports are referred to as LPT1:, LPT2:, etc. Serial ports are called COM1:, COM2:, and so on. If you don't instruct the computer otherwise, it assumes that your printer is connected to LPT1:, which makes LPT1: the "default" port. If, however, your printer is connected to LPT2: or COM1: or COM2:, you must inform WordPerfect of the change. If you're not sure, check your printer manual, or contact your dealer or the person who sets up computers in your company. Select 2 while in the editing menu, and the Printer Port Menu shown in Figure B.6 will be displayed at the bottom.

Enter the number corresponding to the desired port. If the printer is connected to a parallel port such as LPT2:, you don't have to do anything more than enter the number—the screen then redisplays the Edit Menu (Fig B.5). If the printer is connected to a serial port, however, you also have to provide WordPerfect with additional information. Figure B.7 shows the Serial Port Parameters menu including the default values for the H.P LaserJet Serial II.

You should refer to the data about your printer that you collected in Table B.1 and edit those parameters that need to be changed. When you are satisfied with the Serial Port parameters, press (F7), the Exit key, to save the changes and return to the Edit menu (Figure B.5).

Caution: If you press the (Esc) key, you will not save the changes you have made.

Sheet Feeder

If you are using a sheet feeder, which automatically loads individual

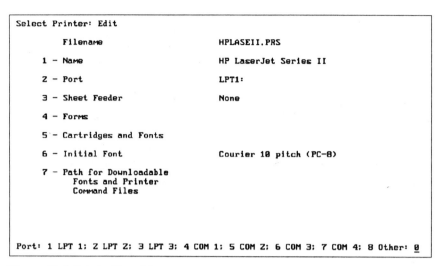

Figure B.6 *Printer Port Menu*

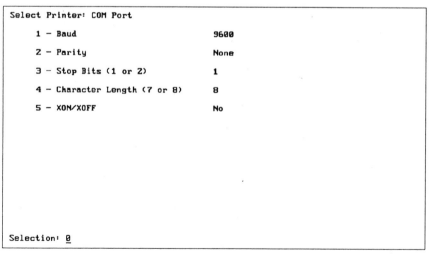

Figure B.7 *Serial Port Parameters*

sheets of paper or envelopes into the printer, you have to enter
certain information about the device. Again, you must insert the
Printer 1 disk into Drive A or B as described above and select the
sheet feeder by name from the list of available feeders. If the list
doesn't contain your sheet feeder, try disks 2 through 4. If you still
can't find the name of your sheet feeder, call WordPerfect and ask
which sheet feeder driver to use for your device. The LaserJet Series
II does not need a separate sheet feeder, since it effectively has one
built in, although several external models are available. If, however, you are using a "Classic" LaserJet or LaserJet PLUS, which
generally require an external envelope and bulk sheet feeder for
volume work, you may wish to select a sheet feeder. Use the H.P.
LaserJet Sheet Feed Driver from Disk 1, as shown in Figure B.8.

You will be shown a Help and Hints Screen (see Figure B.9) that
describes the assignment of paper bins. Make a note of the bin
assignments, as you will need it later. You can always review this
screen by selecting the *Edit* option under the Printer Selection menu
and asking for Help.

Press (F7) to exit the Sheet Feeder Selection sub-menu and return to
the Edit menu.

Form Description

A form is a description of the paper on which you plan to print. It
includes the size of the paper, its "orientation" (whether it prints
lengthwise in Portrait orientation or widthwise in Landscape orientation), and other aspects of the page. These are described below in
the section on adding forms.

Adding a Form: Legal-Size Paper

When you first select the *Forms* option, you will be presented with
the default forms (Standard and All Other) on the Forms menu. See
Figure B.10.

To add legal-size paper and the legal-size paper tray to your list of
available forms and feeding devices, select 1 for the *Add* option. You
will be presented with a list of common form types. See Figure B.11.

```
Select Printer: Sheet Feeder

  BDT MF 830 (6 Bin)
  Dataproducts LZR-1230 (Multi-Bin)
  HP LaserJet
  HP LaserJet 2000
  HP LaserJet 500+
  KX-P4450 Laser Partner
  Kyocera F Series
  Mannesmann Tally MT910
  Mechanical
  Zyiad PaperJet 400
```

```
1 Select; 2 None; 3 Help; N Name search: 1
```

Figure B.8 *Sheet Feeder Selection Menu*

These are the names you are presented with when selecting from among your forms for a particular document. You can either select one of the existing names or add one of your own, by selecting the O option for *Other* and inserting your own name at the prompt. In this example, the name "Legal" is inserted for the title of the form

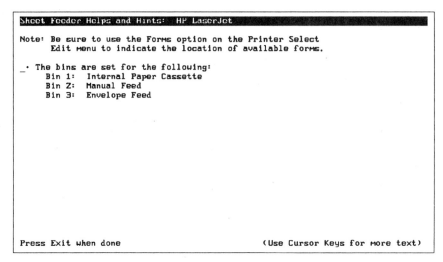

```
Sheet Feeder Helps and Hints:  HP LaserJet

Note: Be sure to use the Forms option on the Printer Select
      Edit menu to indicate the location of available forms.

 _ • The bins are set for the following:
      Bin 1:  Internal Paper Cassette
      Bin 2:  Manual Feed
      Bin 3:  Envelope Feed
```

```
Press Exit when done                    (Use Cursor Keys for more text)
```

Figure B.9 *Sheet Feeder Help and Hints Screen*

```
Select Printer: Forms

                                       Orient Init              Offset
Form type               Size           P L    Pres Location  Top    Side

Standard                8.5" x 11"     Y Y    Y    Contin    0"     0"
[ALL OTHERS]            Width ≤ 8.5"          N    Manual    0"     0"










If the requested form is not available, then printing stops and WordPerfect
waits for a form to be inserted in the ALL OTHERS location.  If the requested
form is larger than the ALL OTHERS form, the width is set to the maximum width.

1 Add; 2 Delete; 3 Edit: 3
```

Figure B.10 *Forms Menu*

representing standard 8 1/2 x 14 inch paper. To add this form, press 9 or O for *Other*. At the prompt "Other form type:" type Legal and press (Enter). You will be presented with the form description menu shown in Figure B.12. You can now enter the five characteristics that define the form. Each are described below.

```
Select Printer: Form Type

     1 - Standard

     2 - Bond

     3 - Letterhead

     4 - Labels

     5 - Envelope

     6 - Transparency

     7 - Cardstock

     8 - [ALL OTHERS]

     9 - Other




Selection: 1
```

Figure B.11 *Form Type Menu*

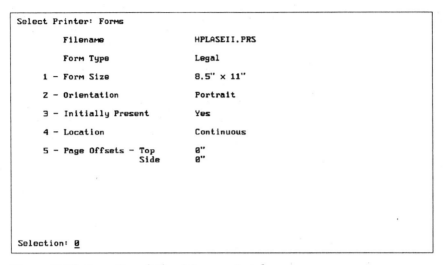

```
Select Printer: Forms

        Filename              HPLASEII.PRS

        Form Type            Legal

    1 - Form Size            8.5" x 11"

    2 - Orientation          Portrait

    3 - Initially Present    Yes

    4 - Location             Continuous

    5 - Page Offsets - Top   0"
                      Side   0"




Selection: 0
```

Figure B.12 *Form Description Menu — Legal*

```
Select Printer: Form Size
                            Inserted
                            Edge

    1 - Standard            8.5"    x    11"

    2 - Standard Wide       11"     x    8.5"

    3 - Legal               8.5"    x    14"

    4 - Legal Wide          14"     x    8.5"

    5 - Envelope            9.5"    x    4"

    6 - Half Sheet          5.5"    x    8.5"

    7 - US Government        8"      x    11"

    8 - A4                   210mm   x    297mm

    9 - A4 Wide             297mm   x    210mm

    0 - Other

Selection: 1
```

Figure B.13 *Form Size Menu*

Form Size

The *Form Description* menu allows you to describe the form in great detail. The first requirement is to select the form size from the Form Size menu. See Figure B.13.

Here you would select Option #3 for legal-size paper (8 1/2 x 14 inches).

Orientation

The orientation determines if the paper is treated as being fed lengthwise into the printer (Portrait) or widthwise (Landscape). In the case of the H.P. LaserJet, this determination is not made on the basis of the actual method of feeding the paper, since it can only be fed in lengthwise, but rather by the availability of Portrait or Landscape fonts. Since the LaserJet Series II has both Portrait and Landscape fonts, select Both. If you are using another printer, you must determine if you can either insert the paper widthwise or print on it with a Landscape font. Then make the appropriate indication at the orientation option.

Initially Present

The *Initially Present* option determines whether WordPerfect prompts you to insert the paper when it is needed, or whether it assumes that the requested paper is available when required. Asking WordPerfect to prompt you to insert the requested forms is somewhat awkward in operation, since the program only prompts you with a beep and then requires you to select the printer option menu, (Shift-F7) + 4, to determine the cause of the beep and view the prompt. Fortunately, this problem is somewhat alleviated with the H.P. LaserJet, since it has its own method for determining whether the requested paper is available in the current paper tray (in this case the legal size tray.) The LaserJet can sense the presence of the legal paper tray, and requests you to insert it if it is not there. Because of this ability, select Yes for the *Initially Present*, even if you don't have the legal tray inserted at all times— the LaserJet printer will tell you when to make the change.

Location

Next, you must tell WordPerfect what type of feeding mechanism the selected form option is using, and where it can be found. When you select this option, WordPerfect displays the following menu.

Location: 1 Continuous; **2 B**in Number; **3 M**anual: **0**

You can tell WordPerfect that you will be manually inserting the requested form (Option #3), in which case it prompts you as described above. You can tell WordPerfect that the form is available in a particular paper bin (Option #2—remember the bin number from the sheet feeder installation procedure? this is where you'll use it). Or you can tell WordPerfect that the form is continuous and available from the default bin (Option #1).

In the case of our example with the legal form, you want to be able to use the legal tray in the default bin location. You can either select "Continuous," which selects the default bin (# 1) or you can select "Bin #1," which was previously defined by the sheet feeder driver as continuous. Either selection works.   Manual selection is be considered later in this chapter under the discussion of envelope forms.

Page Offset

The final option is the selection of the *Page Offset*. Think of this as sort of a "super margin" setting. All other margin settings are determined from the page offset setting. If, for example, you are setting up a letterhead form with two inches of company logos and other heading material, you might want to set the *Top Offset* to 2 1/2 inches. This means that the printing area of the form will start two-and-a-half inches from the top of the page before you set your top margin in a particular document. Remember that the system will also automatically add one inch (the default) to the top of each document, and that margin will be added to the *Top Offset*. Therefore the first character will actually be printed *three-and-a- half inches* from the top of the paper if you make no change to the *Top Margin* option in the page format settings (Shift-F8) + 2. Likewise you can set the *Side Offset* to compensate for unusual side margins of the form.

The other use of the Offset function is for sheet feeders that regularly insert forms with the print head located at some position other than the top left margin. For example, if your sheet feeder always extends the paper one inch above the print head, you can't print on the first one inch. You must tell WordPerfect that the paper is in effect one inch shorter than specified. This is done by setting the *Top Offset* to one inch.

Likewise, if the sheet feeder centers the paper across the printer platen so that the left edge is indented several inches from the left edge, you can set the *Side Offset* so that the margins are calculated from the correct edge of the paper. You can even set negative offsets if the sheet feeder positions the paper below or to the left of the initial print head position. This will then be considered by WordPerfect when calculating the actual margins.

After you set all the above form options, press (F7) to exit the Form Menu and view the new form. See Figure B.14.

EXIT OPPORTUNITY: If you are satisfied with the forms as specified, you can press the (F7) key to exit the forms definition mode. Otherwise, you might want to go on to create a manually fed envelope form.

Creating an Envelope Form

Most people will want to be able to print envelopes with their LaserJets. The Series II has both a manual feed for envelopes and an envelope tray. The manual feed method is discussed here, since it complements the above discussion of the legal paper form. While the process of adding an envelope form is the same as that used for adding a legal form, many of the specific options are different. In addition, at the time of this writing, WordPerfect has a problem with the way it handles envelopes for the H.P. LaserJet, and a "work around" is necessary. More on this later.

To begin, select Option #4 (*Forms*) from the *Printer Edit* menu again and then select 1 for *Add*. Select *Envelope* from the *Form Type* menu. You will next be presented with the *Form Description* menu. In the

```
Select Printer: Forms
                                  Orient Init          Offset
Form type            Size         P L    Pres Location Top    Side

Legal                8.5" x 14"   Y N    Y    Contin   0"     0"
Standard             8.5" x 11"   Y Y    Y    Contin   0"     0"
[ALL OTHERS]         Width ≤ 8.5"        N    Manual   0"     0"








If the requested form is not available, then printing stops and WordPerfect
waits for a form to be inserted in the ALL OTHERS location.  If the requested
form is larger than the ALL OTHERS form, the width is set to the maximum width.

1 Add; 2 Delete; 3 Edit: 3
```

Figure B.14 *Forms Menu*

same fashion as described above, you must edit the description to fit the LaserJet Series II for each option described below.

Form Size

Here is where you run into a small, but easily remediable problem. The form size for the Envelope option is described as 9.5" x 4". While at first this seems correct for a standard commercial #10 envelope, it is in fact *backwards*. The LaserJet Series II inserts the envelopes *short* edge first. Therefore, the size should be 4" x 9.5". Fortunately, WordPerfect provides for such variations. Select O for the *Other* option and enter the form size as Width: 4" and Length: 9.5". See Figure B.15.

Orientation

Next, you must select the printing orientation. Since you will be inserting the envelope sideways, you must also print sideways. Therefore select the *Landscape* option.

```
Select Printer: Form Size
                                Inserted
                                Edge

        1 - Standard            8.5"    x    11"

        2 - Standard Wide       11"     x    8.5"

        3 - Legal               8.5"    x    14"

        4 - Legal Wide          14"     x    8.5"

        5 - Envelope            9.5"    x    4"

        6 - Half Sheet          5.5"    x    8.5"

        7 - US Government        8"     x    11"

        8 - A4                  210mm   x    297mm

        9 - A4 Wide             297mm   x    210mm

        0 - Other

Width: 4"        Length: 9.5_
```

Figure B.15 *Form Size Selection Menu — Envelope*

Initially Present

Since you will be using the manual feed technique, you would think that the *Initially Present* option should be set for No. As mentioned above, however, the H.P.LaserJet has its own method for determining whether the correct form is present and it is more efficient than WordPerfect's. Therefore, set this option to Yes.

Location

Earlier in this chapter, it was explained that one of the options for the LaserJet sheet feeder is the setting of Bin #3 for Envelope Feed. (Refer back to Figure B.9). At this time, you want to actually assign the envelope form to Bin #3. Select Option #4 for Location, then Option #2 for Bin number and enter 3 for the assigned bin number. See Figure B.16.

Page Offset

The *Page Offset* option comes in very handy when dealing with envelopes, especially when dealing with the center feed mecha-

```
Select Printer: Forms

        Filename              HPLASEII.PRS

        Form Type             Envelope

   1 - Form Size              4" × 9.5"

   2 - Orientation            Landscape

   3 - Initially Present      Yes

   4 - Location               Bin 3

   5 - Page Offsets - Top     0"
                      Side    0"




Selection: 0
```

Figure B.16 *Forms Description Menu — Envelope*

nism of the Series II. While the specific *Offset* setting depends to a degree on personal taste, keep two concepts in mind. First, the offsets are set from the top and the left as the paper moves through the printer. Since the envelope moves through the LaserJet sideways, the *Top Offset* and the *Side Offset* are logically reversed. The *Top Offset* determines what in effect is part of the left margin setting, while the *Side Offset* determines the vertical position on the envelope.

In addition, you must remember to take into account the margin settings. If you are going to treat the address portion of a letter as a separate document with the default margins, you must add them to the offsets when calculating the position on the envelope. More importantly, if you place the address of a memo on a separate page at the end the memo (a good and easy practice), you must take into consideration the margins assigned to that memo, if different than the defaults. Therefore, if you have two different sized letterheads, with different margins, you may want to create two different envelope forms with different offsets to correspond to the different margin settings of their associated letterhead. After setting the offsets, press (F7) twice to exit the forms menu.

This concludes the forms selection process. You are now ready to select the font cartridges and soft fonts for you printer.

Cartridges and Soft Fonts

If you have optional font cartridges or soft fonts, you must tell WordPerfect what they are. Thereafter, WordPerfect allows you to select from among the various fonts available on your printer. See Appendix C for details on selecting fonts. When you installed the H.P. LaserJet Series II, the printer driver informed WordPerfect that the printer has 6 internal or "resident" fonts and two line draw options:

> Courier 10 pitch (PC-8)
>
> Courier 10 pitch (Roman-8)
>
> Courier Bold 10 pitch (PC-8)
>
> Courier Bold 10 pitch (Roman-8)
>
> Line Printer 16.66 pitch (PC-8)
>
> Line Printer 16.66 pitch (Roman-8)
>
> Solid Line Draw 10 and 12 pitch

Courier 10 Portrait is defined as the default or *Base Font.* To select one of the other resident fonts as the document *Base Font,* select the *Initial Font* from the *Format, Document* menu, (Shift-F8), then highlight the desired font with the cursor keys, and press 1 for Select. More on font selection and *Base Fonts* later.

In any case, WordPerfect needs to know which fonts are available and where they are located. Suppose that you want to use the fonts available on the H.P. font cartridge F, which contains a variety of Times Roman and Helvetica proportional fonts. WordPerfect not only needs to know which fonts are available, but also how to handle the complex task of character spacing associated with different sized proportional fonts. All this information is contained in yet another resource file on the Printer disks 1-4. Here's how it works.

To install the F cartridge, you must first select the Cartridges and Soft Fonts option from the Printer Edit menu. If you haven't

```
Select Printer: Cartridges and Fonts

Font Category                    Resource                      Quantity

Cartridge Fonts                  Font Cartridge Slot                 2
Soft Fonts                       Memory available for fonts      350 K












1 Select Fonts; 2 Change Quantity; N Name search: 1
```

Figure B.17 *Cartridge and Soft Font Selection Menu*

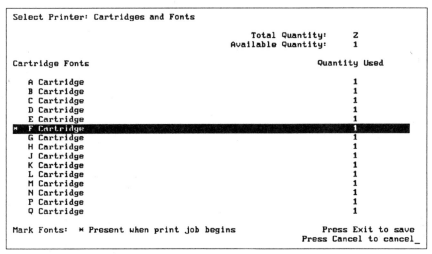

```
Select Printer: Cartridges and Fonts
                                      Total Quantity:       2
                                  Available Quantity:       1

Cartridge Fonts                                       Quantity Used

    A Cartridge                                            1
    B Cartridge                                            1
    C Cartridge                                            1
    D Cartridge                                            1
    E Cartridge                                            1
  * F Cartridge                                            1
    G Cartridge                                            1
    H Cartridge                                            1
    J Cartridge                                            1
    K Cartridge                                            1
    L Cartridge                                            1
    M Cartridge                                            1
    N Cartridge                                            1
    P Cartridge                                            1
    Q Cartridge                                            1

Mark Fonts:  * Present when print job begins       Press Exit to save
                                                   Press Cancel to cancel_
```

Figure B.18 *Font Cartridge Selection Menu*

installed the Printer 1 disk files on your hard disk (a waste of space), you will be prompted to insert the Printer 1 disk into drive A: or B: and tell WordPerfect which drive the disk is in. Be sure to include the colon after the drive letter. You will then be presented with the Cartridge and Fonts Selection Menu shown in Figure B.17.

Note that you can change the number of available cartridge slots and printer memory. Unless you have added additional memory to your LaserJet Series II, however, or you are installing a compatible laser printer with more than two cartridge slots, you needn't change either quantity.

To select a font cartridge for installation, use the cursor to highlight the *Cartridge Font* option and choose 1 for *Select Fonts*. You will be presented with the menu of font cartridges available for the H.P. LaserJet Series II. The list of available fonts is determined by the fonts WordPerfect selects to support. If you are using a font cartridge that is not on the list, call WordPerfect to determine the best method for either using another driver, obtaining a special driver, or altering one of the existing drivers.

Since the F cartridge is on the list, you need only highlight its name and enter an asterisk by pressing (Shift-8). The asterisk indicates that the font cartridge will be ready for use when the print job begins. You must have the cartridge properly installed before attempting to print. Note that the available quantity of cartridge slots has dropped by one, indicating that you only have one left to select. See Figure B.18.

Here's where things get a bit tricky. You can actually increase the number of cartridges beyond the two slots available on the Series II if you have *more* than 2 cartridges, and you can select all of them as being present when the job begins. In that case, though, YOU are responsible for ensuring that 1) you only use fonts from *two* cartridges in any single document, and 2) that the correct pair of cartridges are inserted in the printer prior to starting a print job that calls for them (i.e., prior to printing the document in which the particular font cartridges were specified).

When you are done marking all the cartridges, press (F7) twice to get back to the Edit menu. You may have to wait a moment while WordPerfect updates its available font file.

Initial Font

Although you have installed the new F font cartridge, your documents will still print in Courier 10 until you tell the printer to either change the *Base Font* for a particular document, or you reset the *Printer, Initial Font*. By resetting the *Initial Font* to Times Roman 10 Point, you automatically set the default, *Base Font* for each new document as Times Roman 10 Point.

To do this, select 6 for the *Initial Font* option from the Printer Edit menu, use the (Up Cursor) or (Down Cursor) to highlight the font you want to become the new default *Base Font* and press 1. The next time you print a document, it prints in Times Roman 10, unless you change the *Base Font* to Courier 10 or some other font by pressing (Ctrl-F8) + 4, highlighting the desired new *Base Font*, and pressing 1 to select it. The new *Base Font* will only be in effect for the current document; all other documents will be printed in Times Roman 10, unless you change their *Base Font*, or reset your *Initial Font*. Note that you can also reset the *Initial Font* for an individual document from the *Format, Document* menu (Shift-F8).

Path for Downloadable Fonts and Printer Command Files

If you are going to use soft fonts (fonts that are stored on disk files and "downloaded" into the printer's memory before use), you must tell WordPerfect where to find the soft font files. You must also install the soft fonts in a directory on your hard disk according to the manufacturer's directions; each manufacturer uses a different technique for creating and storing fonts.

Once the soft fonts are properly installed on your hard disk, select Option #7 from the *Edit* menu. Enter the complete path for the directory in which you have placed your soft fonts including the drive letter (e.g. "C:\FONTS").

Next, go back and Select Option #5, *Cartridges and Fonts,* described above. This time, however, highlight the *Soft Font* option and press 1 to begin the font selection process. You will be prompted to place the Printer disk in drive A: or B: (unless you've installed it on your hard drive) and indicate which drive you used. Again, don't forget the colon following the drive letter. WordPerfect presents you with the names of all the fonts available from Hewlett-Packard at the time your copy of 5.0 was shipped. Select the fonts from the Soft Font disk sets that you want to use. You can select them as either *Present When the Print Job Begins* by marking them with an asterisk or *Can be Loaded During Print Job* by marking them with a plus sign (the "+" from the alphabetic portion of the keyboard.) The former assumes that you have already downloaded the font as a Permanent Font (see your H.P. manual if you are uncertain). The latter instructs WordPerfect to download the font as required by the document being printed.

It is easiest to let WordPerfect do the work for you, so you're probably best off marking the desired fonts with a plus sign to designate the font as *Can be Loaded During Print Job*. After you have marked all the fonts you wish to select, exit the print menu system by pressing (F7). You are now ready to try out the power of the WordPerfect 5.0 printer system.

Note: the number of fonts that can be assigned an "*" depends on how much memory you have in your printer. As you mark fonts with "*" the amount of available memory is shown in the upper right-hand corner of the screen. When the memory becomes insufficient to store the fonts you want to be available when the print job begins, WordPerfect simply won't let you assign an "*." You can always assign a "+," though, so the font is available when it's needed. You can always upgrade your memory, if you need more. Contact your dealer for more information. Once you've upgraded, you must tell WordPerfect how much memory is available, by changing by selection Option #5 from the Edit menu, *Cartridges and Fonts*. Move the cursor to Soft Fonts, then select #2, *Change Quantity*, from the menu below. Enter the new amount of memory, in kilobytes (a kilobyte is a 1,000 bytes). For example, if you've added a 2 megabyte memory board to your printer, you will have a total of 2,512,000 bytes—the built in 512,000 bytes plus the 2,000,000 bytes you are adding. You would therefore enter 2512. Press (Enter) after you enter the new memory amount. Then press (F7) once to return to the *Edit* menu. You can now add more permanent soft fonts as desired.

At this point, you have a fully installed HP LaserJet, and you can print in a variety of fonts, as well as on envelopes fed one-at-a time through the manual paper feed. The next Appendix explains the art of changing Fonts with WordPerfect 5.0 and your HP LaserJet Series II printer.

Appendix

Changing Fonts

OVERVIEW

One way to jazz up your documents is to bold text, or use different fonts. A font is a group of characters related by certain characteristics, such as style (Courier, Times Roman, Helvetica); weight (bold, regular, light); and size (10, 12, or 14 points). Figure C.1 shows a variety of type fonts.

Some printers have a variety of built-in fonts, and allow you access to still more fonts by using plug-in font cartridges or fonts that reside on disk, called "soft fonts." The HP LaserJet Series II, for example, allows you to use two plug-in cartridges at a time, and to download whatever soft fonts you have installed on your computer.

The key to using the full potential of WordPerfect 5.0's font selection and printing capabilities is to understand a few of the fundamental ideas on which it is based. The information WordPerfect needs about each font is transferred from the Printer disk to your computer during the installation procedure (see Appendix B), and

```
This is 12 point Courier.
```
This is 12 point Times.

This is 12 point Palatino.

This is 12 point Helvetica.

This is 12 Avant Garde.

This is 12 Franklin Gothic.

Figure C.1 *Type Font Samples*

contains the physical dimensions of each character in the selected fonts.

Each printer has a default font that is used until you specify another. WordPerfect calls the default font for the selected printer its *Base Font*, which defines a family of type styles. In other words, you can describe all the variations of bold, italics, underline, outline, and shadow—in terms of their relation to the to the *Base Font*. For example, if you select a Times Roman Font (any size) as a *Base Font*, when you instruct WordPerfect to italicize a particular word, it inserts the command to use the italics version of Times Roman. If your printer is capable of printing italics, it does so. If not, it finds the nearest substitute. If no substitutes for italics are available, it may underline the word instead.

Similarly, you can instruct WordPerfect to use the next larger or smaller size of the same type as the *Base Font*, by simply inserting the command code for Large or Small font size. Again, if your printer is capable of printing a larger or smaller version of the *Base Font*, it does so. If not, WordPerfect finds the closest substitute.

In addition to offering variations on the *Base Font* capabilities, WordPerfect can instantly reformat documents if the *Base Font* is changed. Suppose you had set up a document with the *Base Font* of Courier 10, and you used several variations, such as bold, italics, and small. Now you decide that you want to print the document in Times Roman 12 point proportional type. In earlier versions of WordPerfect and most other word processors, you would have to go back and reset each of the font changes to correspond to the new font and its variations. With WordPerfect 5.0, however, all you need to do is position the cursor at the beginning of the document and reset the *Base Font* to Times Roman 12 point. Since all the variations are defined relative to the *Base Font*, they are all changed to variations of Times Roman 12 point. Furthermore, WordPerfect repaginates the entire document for the spacing requirements of the new proportional font, without any effort on your part.

SELECTING YOUR BASE FONT

As you can see from the above discussion, a great deal depends on your selection of the *Base Font*. When you first open a document, the *Base Font* is assumed to be the *Initial Font* for the currently selected printer. (See Appendix B for more information on Initial Fonts.) Suppose that you are using an H.P. LaserJet Series II printer with a full complement of resident Courier fonts and the Z1 font cartridge, which supports a variety of Times Roman and Helvetica fonts. How do you tell WordPerfect that you don't want to accept the Initial Font (probably Courier 10) as your *Base Font*, but want Helvetica 10 instead? It's quite simple. Move the cursor to the very beginning of the document by entering:

(Home) + (Home) + (Home) + (Up Cursor)

Then open the Font Menu by pressing:

(Ctrl-F8)

You will be presented with the following menu at the bottom of the screen:

1 **S**ize; 2 **A**ppearance; 3 **N**ormal; 4 **B**ase Font;
5 **P**rint Color: **0**

```
Select Printer: Initial Font

* Courier 10 pitch (PC-8)
  Courier 10 pitch (Roman-8/ECMA)
  Courier Bold 10 pitch (PC-8)
  Courier Bold 10 pitch (Roman-8/ECMA)
  Helv 08pt (Z1A)
  Helv 10pt (Z1A)
  Helv 10pt Bold (Z1A)
  Helv 10pt Italic (Z1A)
  Helv 12pt (Z1A)
  Helv 12pt Bold (Z1A)
  Helv 12pt Italic (Z1A)
  Helv 14pt Bold (Z1A)
  Line Draw 10 pitch
  Line Printer 16.66 pitch (PC-8)
  Line Printer 16.66 pitch (Roman-8/ECMA)
  Solid Line Draw 10 pitch
  Tms Rmn 08pt (Z1A)
  Tms Rmn 10pt (Z1A)
  Tms Rmn 10pt Bold (Z1A)
  Tms Rmn 10pt Italic (Z1A)
  Tms Rmn 12pt (Z1A)

1 Select; N Name search: 1
```

Figure C.2 *Menu of Available Fonts*

Select Option #4 for *Base Font*. You will be shown all the fonts for the currently selected printer available for the orientation of the current Form. If you are working on a Portrait Form, you will be shown only Portrait fonts. See Figure C.2.

The currently selected *Base Font* will be marked with an asterisk. To change to another *Base Font*, use the (Up Cursor) and (Down Cursor) to highlight the desired font and press 1 to select it. You can confirm that the new *Base Font* command has been inserted into your document by shifting into *Reveal Codes* by pressing (Alt-F3).

While you can select any of the available fonts as the *Base Font*, remember that all the other fonts that you can use in your document must be described as specific variations on the *Base Font*. For example, if you select Helvetica Bold as your *Base Font*, you can't use Helvetica medium later on, since "unbold" is not one of the variations supported by WordPerfect. Instead, you should select Helvetica Medium as you *Base Font* and then select the desired bold font as a variation of the *Base Font*.

You can change the selected *Base Font* within a document in the same fashion. Suppose you want to use a Helvetica 8 point italic font for a "Continued on Page 3" note at the end of a newsletter column

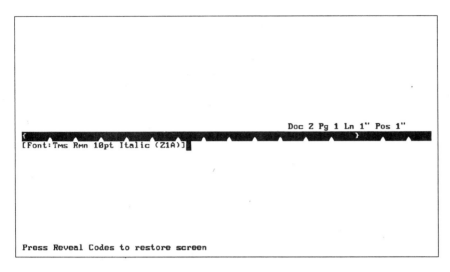

Figure C.3 *Reveal Code Showing Base Font*

in a document that is otherwise set in Times Roman 10 point type. You can't describe the Helvetica font as a variation on the Times Roman font, so you must change the *Base Font* to Helvetica 8 point just before the new text and re-select the Times Roman font just after it.

Variations on the Base Font

Once you select a *Base Font*, you can make several variations in it. The variations fall into two types: *Size* and *Appearance*. To access the variations, press (Ctrl-F8) and then select either 1 or S for Size, or 2 or A for Appearance. When you select the *Size* option, the following choices are available

1 Su**p**rscpt; **2** Su**b**scpt; 3 **F**ine; 4 **S**mall; 5 **L**arge;

6 **V**ry Large; 7 **E**xt Large: **0**

The *Appearance* option offers the following selections:

1 Bold; 2 **U**ndrln; **3 D**bl Und; **4 I**talc; **5 O**utln; 6 **S**hadw;

7 Sm **C**ap; **8 R**edln; **9** Stkout: **0**

This is Helvetica 14 point medium.

This is Helvetica 14 point Bold variation.

This is Helvetica 14 point Underline variation.

This is Helvetica 14 point Italic variation.

This is Helvetica 14 point Outline variation.

THIS IS HELVETICA 14 POINT SMALL CAPS VARIATION.

Figure C.4 *Variations on Helvetica Font*

To select a particular variation, enter the desired options. For example, to select *Large* type, enter 5 (or L). Figure C.4 shows examples of all the basic variations and a few of the combinations available for a 14 point Helvetica font as the *Base Font*.

As you can see, the *Base Font* and variations concept provides considerable flexibility for defining the fonts in a document. If you add the possible combinations and the ability to change the *Base Font* within a given document, you can create the most complex documents.

Changing the Base Font for Existing Text

To select a variation of the *Base Font* for existing text, place the cursor on the first letter of the text to be changed. Press (Alt-F4) to start the *Block* command. Use the cursor keys to highlight the text to be altered and then press (Ctrl-F8). You will be presented with an abbreviated Font Menu at the bottom of the screen. Select either *Size* or *Appearance* as desired and then select the variation you desire from the menu. For example, to italicize a block of text:

1. Press (Alt-F4) to start the Block command.
2. Highlight the text to be changed.
3. Press (Ctrl-F8) to bring up the abbreviated Font Menu.
4. Press 2 to select *Appearance.*
5. Press 4 to select *Italcs.*

Changing Fonts for New Text

When you are changing fonts for new text, you have two choices: you can either select a new *Base Font* or you can describe the new font as a variation on the existing *Base Font.* If the current *Base Font* is a better basis for your total font selection and you can use it to describe the new font, leave the current *Base Font* as defined. To do this, simply position the cursor in the location you wish to inset the new text in the new type font and press (Ctrl-F8). Select either the *Size* or *Appearance* options form the main Font menu, and then select the desired attribute as described above. You can then begin entering the new text, and it will print in the variation selected.

If you shift into *Reveal Codes* by pressing (Alt-F3), you can see the new text entered in between the code to turn on the variation and the code to turn it off again. You can continue to insert text between these two codes and it will continue to be printed in the selected variation.

To terminate the variation, either select the *Normal* option from the main Font menu (press (Ctrl-F8) + 3) or use the cursor key to move the current cursor position to the right of the variation off code. Any further text entered prints in the font selected before the variation was started (usually the *Base Font* unless you have other variations also in use).

Changing the Initial Font

When you installed your printer, you were asked to select an *Initial Font.* The Initial Font is the font assumed to be the *Base Font* for a document that does not have another *Base Font* setting. If you wish to change the *Initial Font* for a given document, use the following procedure:

1. Start up the *Format Document* menu by pressing (Shift-F8) + 3 + 3.

2. Select the desired *Initial Font* by highlighting its name and pressing 1 or S.

3. Press (F7) twice to exit from the *Initial Font* selection process and save your selection.

Changing Printers

When you change the printer selection, you can have a dramatic impact on the way a document appears. In addition to the obvious physical change you get if you are selecting a different printer, you are quite likely to change both the *Initial Font* as well as the number and types of available fonts. Changing the *Initial Font* for the printer affects any document that does not contain another *Base Font* or *Document, Initial Font* setting. As mentioned above, the *Base Font* for a document is assumed to be the *Printer, Initial Font* for the currently installed printer, unless another *Base Font* has been selected from the main *Font* Menu, (Ctrl-F8), or another *Document, Initial Font* has been specified from the *Document Format* menu, (Shift-F8) +3 +3.

In addition to the implicit change to the *Base Font*, a change in selected printers can significantly alter the fonts available for printing a particular document. WordPerfect uses its intelligent print drivers to select the closest font for any fonts or variations that are requested but unavailable on the new printer. This permits you to print the document in as close a font as was initially selected.

The concept of base fonts and font variations can be somewhat confusing. The best way to sort out the options is to try your own variations. Once you get the hang of it, you'll have a remarkable capability at your fingertip.

WordPerfect
File Summary

Location	File Name	File Size	Description
WordPerfect 1	WP.EXE	245K	Main program file
	WPHELP.FIL	48K	Help data file
	WPHELP2.FIL	52K	Help data file
WordPerfect 2	WP.FIL	299k	Program overlay file
	KEYS.MRS	5K	Keyboard macro resource file
	WPSMALL.DRS	14K	Condensed driver resource file. Subset of WP.DRS
	WP.MRS	4K	Macro editing resource file
	STANDARD.PRS	1K	Generic print driver
Speller	WP{WP}US.LEX	292K	Main English dictionary (United States)
	SPELL.EXE	38K	Speller utility program used to create and manage user dictionaries

Location	File Name	File Size	Description
Thesaurus	WP{WP}US.THS	362K	Main English thesaurus (United States)
Fonts/Graphics	GRAB.COM	15K	Screen capture utility
	WP.DRS	73K	Full driver resource file. Superset of WPSMALL.DRS
	*.FRS		Font resource files containing specialty display fonts
	*.WPD		Special drivers for graphics monitors
	*.WPG		Sample Clip-Art
Learning	INSTALL.EXE	27K	Hard disk installation utility
	TUTOR.COM	42K	Tutorial program
	*.WKB		Workbook learning files
	*.STY		Sample style sheets
	*.TUT		Tutorial data files
	*.WPG		Sample graphic files
	*.WPM		Sample macros
	LEARN.BAT		Batch file used to start the tutorial program
Conversion	CONVERT.EXE	81K	Document conversion program
	GRAPHCNV.EXE	71K	Graphic conversion program

Location	File Name	File Size	Description
	MACROCNV.EXE	23K	Macro conversion program
	CURSOR.COM	1K	Utility for changing cursor size and shape
	CHARACTR.DOC	53K	Printer test document displaying full character set
	PRINTER.TST	18K	Printer test document
	CHARMAP.TST	15K	Printer test document
	STANDARD.CRS	2K	Document conversion resource file
	LIBRARY.STY	1K	Library of style sheets
	*.WPK		Sample keyboard maps
	README	11K	Documentation for conversion files & macros (DOS version)
	README.WP	12K	Documentation for conversion files & macros (WP version)
Printer 1	WPRINT1.ALL	357K	Printer drivers for HP LaserJet and compatible printers
Printer 2	WPRINT2.ALL	329K	Printer drivers for PostScript laser printers and a selection of letter quality printer
Printer 3	WPRINT3.ALL	323K	Printer drivers for dot matrix printers

Location	File Name	File Size	Description
Printer 4	WPRINT4.ALL	140K	Printer drivers for variety of old and obsolete printers
PTR Program	PTR.EXE	204K	Printer driver utility program, used to create and edit printer driver resource files
	PTR.HLP	139K	PTR help data file

Appendix

WordPerfect
Command Summary

Feature	Keystrokes
Appearance Attributes	Ctrl-F8 + 2
Automatically Format & Rewrite	Shift-F1 + 3 + 1
Backspace	<—(Backspace)
Backup	Shift-F1 + 1
Base Font	Ctrl-F8 + 4
Beep Options	Shift-F1 + 5 + 1
Binding	Shift-F7 + B
Block	Alt-F4
Block Protect (Block on)	Shift-F8
Bold	F6 or Ctrl-F8 + 2 + 1
Cancel	F1
Cancel Print Job(s)	Shift-F7 + 4 + 1
Cartridges and Fonts	Shift-F7 + S + 3 + 5
Case Conversion (Block on)	Shift-F3
Center	Shift-F6
Center Page Top to Bottom	Shift-F8 + 2 + 1
Colors/Fonts/Attributes (screen)	Shift-F1 + 3 + 2
Columns (Text and Parallel)	Alt-F7
Control Printer	Shift-F7 + 4
Copy File	F5 + (Enter) + 8

Feature	Keystrokes
Create Directory	F5 + =
Date	
Code	Shift-F5 + 2
Format	Shift-F5 + 3
Text	Shift-F5 + 1
Date/Outline	Shift-F5
Decimal/Align Character	Shift-F8 + 4 + 3
Define (Mark Text)	Alt-F5 + 5
Delete	
Character Left	Backspace
Character Right	Del
Directory	F5,(Enter) + 2
File	F5 + (Enter) + 2
to End of Line (EOL)	Ctrl-End
to End of Page (EOP)	Ctrl-PgDn
Word	Ctrl-Backspace
Word Left	Home + Backspace
Word Right	Home + Delete
Display All Print Jobs	Shift-F7 + 4 + 3
Display Pitch	Shift-F8 + 3 + 1
Display Setup	Shift-F1 + 3
Document Comments	Ctrl-F5 + 5
Document Format	Shift-F8 + 3
Document Summary	Shift-F8 + 3 + 5
DOS Text File	
Retrieve (CR/LF to [HRt])	Ctrl-F5 + 1 + 2
Retrieve (CR/LF to [SRt])	Ctrl-F5 + 1 + 3
Save	Ctrl-F5 + 1 + 1
Double Underline	Ctrl-F8 + 2 + 3
Endnote	Ctrl-F7 + 2
Endnote Placement Code	Ctrl-F7 + 3
Enter (or Return)	<—| or (Enter)
Exit	F7
Extra Large Print	Ctrl-F8 + 1 + 7
Fast Save	Shift-F1 + 4
Figure (Graphics)	Alt-F9 + 1
Filename on Status Line	Shift-F1 + 3 + 4

Feature	Keystrokes
Fine Print	Ctrl-F8 + 1 + 3
Flush Right	Alt-F6
Footers	Shift-F8 + 2 + 4
Footnote	Ctrl-F7 + 1
Force Odd/Even Page	Shift-F8 + 2 + 2
Format	Shift-F8
Forms	Shift-F7 + S + 3 + 4
Generate (Mark Text)	Alt-F5 + 6
Generate Tables, Indexes etc.	Alt-F5 + 6 + 5
Generic Word Processor Format	Ctrl-F5 + 3
"Go" (Start Printer)	Shift-F7 + 4 + 4
Go to DOS	Ctrl-F1 + 1
Graphics	Alt-F9
Graphics Quality	Shift-F7 + G
Graphics Screen Type	Shift-F1 + 3 + 5
Hard	
Page	Ctrl-(Enter)
Return	<—| or (Enter)
Return Display Character	Shift-F1,3,6
Space	Home,Space Bar
Headers	Shift-F8,2,3
Help	F3
Home	Home
Horizontal Line (Graphics)	Alt-F9 + 5 + 1
Hyphenation	Shift-F8 + 1 + 1
Hyphenation Zone	Shift-F8 + 1 + 2
—>Indent	F4
—>Indent<—	Shift-F4
Index	
Define	Alt-F5 + 5 + 3
Mark	Alt-F5 + 3
Initial Settings (Format)	Shift-F8 + 3 + 2
Initial Settings (Setup)	Shift-F1 + 5
Insert	Ins
Insert, Forced	Home + Home + Ins
Italics	Ctrl + F8 + 2 + 4
Justification	Shift-F8 + 1 + 3

Feature	Keystrokes
Kerning	Shift-F8 + 4 + 6 + 1
Keyboard Layout	Shift-F1 + 6
Large Print	Ctrl-F8 + 1 + 5
Line	
Draw	Ctrl-F3 + 2
Format	Shift-F8 + 1
Height	Shift-F8 + 1 + 4
Numbering	Shift-F8 + 1 + 5
Spacing	Shift-F8 + 1 + 6
List	
Define	Alt-F5 + 5 + 2
Mark (Block on)	Alt-F5 + 2
List Files	F5 + (Enter)
Location of Auxiliary Files	Shift-F1 + 7
Look	F5 + (Enter) + 6
Macro	Alt-F10
Macro Define	Ctrl-F10
<—Margin Release	Shift-Tab
Margins	
Left/Right	Shift-F8 + 1 + 7
Top/Bottom	Shift-F8 + 2 + 5
Math/Columns	Alt-F7
Menu Letter Display	Shift-F1 + 3 + 7
Merge	Ctrl-F9 + 1
Codes	Shift-F9
Move	Ctrl-F4
Block (Block on)	Ctrl-F4 + 1
Page	Ctrl-F4 + 3
Paragraph	Ctrl-F4 + 2
Rectangle (Block on)	Ctrl-F4 + 3
Rename (List Files)	F5 + (Enter) + 3
Sentence	Ctrl-F4 + 1
Tabular Column (Block on)	Ctrl-F4 + 2
Name Search (List Files)	F5 + (Enter) + N
New Page Number	Shift-F8 + 2 + 6
Normal Text (Turn off Attributes)	Ctrl-F8 + 3
Number of Copies	Shift-F7 + N

Feature	Keystrokes
Other Directory	F5 + (Enter) + 7
Outline	Shift-F5 + 4
Outline (Font Attribute)	Ctrl-F8 + 2 + 5
Page Format	Shift-F8 + 2
Page Numbering	Shift-F8 + 2 + 7
Paragraph Number	Shift-F5 + 5
Paragraph Numbering Definition	Shift-F5 + 6
Paper Size/Type	Shift-F8 + 2 + 8
Password	Ctrl-F5 + 2
Print	Shift-F7
Block (Block on)	Shift-F7 + Y
Color	Ctrl-F8 + 5
Full Document	Shift-F7 + 1
List Files	F5 + (Enter) + 4
Page	Shift-F7 + 2
Printer	
Command	Shift-F8 + 4 + 6 + 2
Settings	Shift-F7 + S + 3
Repeat Value	Esc
Replace	Alt-F2
Replace, Extended	Home + Alt-F2
Retrieve	
Block (Move)	Ctrl-F4 + 4 + 1
Document	Shift-F10
Document (List Files)	F5 + (Enter) + 1
Rectangle (Move)	Ctrl-F4 + 4 + 3
Tabular Column (Move)	Ctrl-F4 + 4 + 2
Reveal Codes	Alt-F3
Rewrite	Ctrl-F3 + 0
Rush Print Job	Shift-F7 + 4 + 2
Save	F10
Screen	Ctrl-F3
—>Search	F2
—>Search, Extended	Home + F2
<—Search	Shift-F2
<—Search, Extended	Home + Shift-F2
Select Printer	Shift-F7 + S

Feature	Keystrokes
Setup	Shift-F1
Shadow	Ctrl-F8 + 2 + 6
Shell	Ctrl-F1
Side-by-Side Column Display	Shift-F1 + 3 + 8
Size Attribute	Ctrl-F8 + 1
Small Caps	Ctrl-F8 + 2 + 7
Small Print	Ctrl-F8 + 1 + 4
Sort	Ctrl-F9 + 2
Spell	Ctrl-F2
Split Screen	Ctrl-F3 + 1
Stop Printing	Shift-F7 + 4 + 5
Strikeout	Ctrl-F8 + 2 + 9
Style	Alt-F8
Subscript	Ctrl-F8 + 1 + 2
Superscript	Ctrl-F8 + 1 + 1
Suppress (Page Format)	Shift-F8 + 2 + 9
Switch	Shift-F3
Tab Align	Ctrl-F6
Tab Set	Shift-F8 + 1 + 8
Text Box (Graphics)	Alt-F9 + 3
Text In (List Files)	F5 + (Enter) + 5
In/Out	Ctrl-F5
Text Quality	Shift-F7 + T
Thesaurus	Alt-F1
Thousand's Separator	Shift-F8 + 4 + 3
Typeover	Ins
Typeover, Forced	Home + Ins
Undelete	F1
Underline	F8 or Ctrl-F8 + 2 + 2
Underline Spaces/Tabs	Shift-F8 + 4 + 7
Units of Measure	Shift-F1 + 8
User-Defined Box (Graphics)	Alt-F9 + 4
Vertical Line (Graphics)	Alt-F9 + 5 + 2
Very Large Print	Ctrl-F8 + 1 + 6
View Document	Shift-F7 + 6
Widow/Orphan Protection	Shift-F8 + 1 + 9
Window	Ctrl-F3 + 1

Feature	Keystrokes
Word/Letter Spacing	Shift-F8 + 4 + 6 + 3
Word Search	F5 + (Enter) + 9
Word Spacing Justification Limits	Shift-F8 + 4 + 6 + 4
WordPerfect 4.2 Format	Ctrl-F5 + 4

Cursor Control

Beginning of Document (Before Codes)	Home + Home + Home + (Up Cursor)
Beginning of Document (Before Text)	Home + Home + (Up Cursor)
Beginning of Line (Before Codes)	Home + Home + Home + (Left Cursor)
Beginning of Line (Before Text)	Home + Home + (Left Cursor)
Character Left	(Left Cursor)
Character Right	(Right Cursor)
End of Document	Home + Home + (Down Cursor)
End of Line	Home + Home + (Right Cursor) or End
Go To	Ctrl-Home
Line Down	(Down Cursor)
Line Up	(Up Cursor)
Page Down	PgDn
Page Up	PgUp
Screen Down	Home + (Cursor Down) or + (Num Pad)
Screen Left	Home + (Left Cursor)
Screen Right	Home + (Right Cursor)
Screen Up	Home + (Up Cursor) or - (Num Pad)
Word Left	Ctrl- (Left Cursor)
Word Right	Ctrl- (Right Cursor)

Appendix

WordPerfect Codes

285

[Def Mark:List] ....List Definition
[Def Mark:ToC] ....Table of Contents Definition
[End Def] ....End of Index, List, or Table of Contents
[End Opt]..........................Endnote Options
[Endnote] ....Endnote
[Endnote Placement] ....Endnote Placement
[Ext Large] ....Extra Large Print
[Figure] ....Figure Box
[Fig Opt] ....Figure Box Options
[Fine] ....Fine Print
[Flsh Rt] ....Begin Flush Right
[Footnote].........................Footnote
[Font] ....Base Font
[Footer] ....Footer
[Force]...............................Force Odd/Even Page
[Form] ....Form (Printer Selection)
[Ftn Opt]...........................Footnote/Endnote Options
[Full Form].......................Table of Authorities, Full Form
[HLine] ....Horizontal Line
[Header]............................Header
[HPg]................................Hard Page
[HRt] ....Hard Return
[Hyph on] ....Hyphenation on
[Hyph off]........................Hyphenation off
[HZone] ....Hyphenation Zone
[—>Indent] ....Indent
[—>Indent<—] ....Left/Right Indent
[Index] ....Index Entry
[ISRt].................................Invisible Soft Return
[Italc] ....Italics
[Just] ....Right Justification
[Just Lim] ....Word/Letter Spacing Justification Limits
[Kern]................................Kerning
[L/R Mar] ....Left and Right Margins
[Lang] ....Language
[Large] ....Large Print
[Line Height] ....Line Height
[Ln Num] ....Line Numbering
[<—Mar Rel] ....Left Margin Release

[Mark:List] ....List Entry
[Mark:ToC] ....Table of Contents Entry
[Math Def] ....Definition of Math Columns
[Math Off] ....End of Math
[Math On] ....Beginning of Math
t ....Subtotal Entry
+..Calculate Subtotal
T ....Total Entry
=..Calculate Total
* ....Calculate Grand Total
[Note Num] ....Footnote/Endnote Reference
[Outln]................................Outline (attribute)
[Ovrstk] ....Overstrike
[Paper Sz/Typ] ....Paper Size and Type
[Par Num] ....Paragraph Number
[Par Num Def] ....Paragraph Numbering Definition
[Pg Num] ....New Page Number
[Pg Num Pos] ....Page Number Position
[Ptr Cmnd] ....Printer Command
[RedLn] ....Redline
[Ref] ....Reference (Automatic Reference)
[Set End Num] ....Set New Endnote Number
[Set Fig Num] ....Set New Figure Box Number
[Set Ftn Num] ....Set New Footnote Number
[Set Tab Num] ....Set New Table Box Number
[Set Txt Num] ....Set New Text Box Number
[Set Usr Num] ....Set New User-Defined Box Number
[Shadow] ....Shadow
[Sm Cap]..............................Small Caps
[Small] ....Small Print
[SPg].....................................Soft New Page
[SRt] ....Soft Return
[StkOut] ....Strikeout
[Style] ....Styles
[Subdoc] ....Subdocument (Master Documents)
[SubScrpt] ....Subscript
[SuprScrpt] ....Superscript
[Suppress] ....Suppress Page Format
[T/B Mar] ....Top and Bottom Margins

[Tab] ....Tab
[Tab Opt] ....Table Box Options
[Tab Set] ....Tab Set
[Table] ....Table Box
[Target] ....Target (Auto Reference)
[Text Box] ....Text Box
[Txt Opt]............................Text Box Options
[Und] ....Underlining
[Undrln] ....Underline Spaces/Tabs
[Usr Box] ....User-Defined Box
[Usr Opt] ....User-Defined Box Options
[VLine]...............................Vertical Line
[Vry Large] ....Very Large Print
[W/O] ....Widow/Orphan
[Wrd/Ltr Spacing] ....Word and Letter Spacing

Index

D

Data
  directory for, 8-9, 13, 25, 26
  entered in parallel columns, 138
Dates
  Date command (Shift-F5) for, 63-65
  formats for, 88
  in headers and footers, 112
  searching files by, 221
Decimal points
  setting tabs for, 105
  Tab Align command (Ctrl-F6) for, 66
Deleting
  backup files, 80
  blocks of text, 156-157
  Cancel command (F1) to undo, 48-49
  endnotes, 153
  files, in File Manager, 211, 223-224
  footnotes, 149
  formatting codes, 172
    search-and-replace functions for, 175-176
  keys for
    by character, 40-41
    by page, 42-43
    by word, 41-42
Del [Delete] key, 41
Desktop publishing systems, justified text imported into, 100
Dictionaries
  in Spell checker, 188
  supplementary, 189-190, 194
  in Thesaurus, 180
Directories, 25

  for auxiliary files, 91
  changing, 217
  creating, 11-12
  List Files command (F5) for, 65-66
  PATH command for, 12-17
  viewing, 215-217
  WordPerfect installed in, 7-9
Disks *See also* Floppy disks; Hard disks
  printing documents from, 200-201
Displays
  of columns, 139
  cursor on, 35-36
  of jobs in print buffer, 203
  menus on, 34
  personalizing, 81-82
    automatic format and rewrites, 82
    black and white, 86
    colors, fonts and attributes, 82-84
    columns, 85-86
    comments, 84-85
    filenames on Status Line, 85
    graphics screen types, 85
    hard carriage returns, 85
    menus, 85
  Status Line on, 31-33
  in View Document option, 204-205
Documents
  backups for, 78-81
  comments added to, 61-63
  directory for, 8-9, 13, 25, 26
  format options for, 70, 94-95, 120

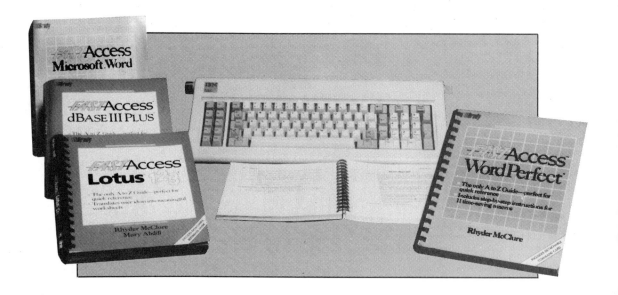

Inside the Norton Utilities™

The Official Guide.

by Rob Krumm
with an Introduction by Peter Norton

More than a million PC users depend on the Norton Utilities to make their computers reliable, efficient tools. The official guide to these best-selling programs, *Inside the Norton Utilities* shows you the most efficient way to use:

- Norton Utilities—the original
- Norton Utilities Advanced Edition—faster, and with new features
- Norton Commander—for high speed computer management
- Norton Editor—a programmer's tool in the Norton tradition

With this book you'll learn to fill the gaps in DOS's functionality. You'll explore memory and hard disk organization. You'll learn how to use the Norton Utilities, and, more importantly, how the Norton Utilities work with your data.

Inside the Norton Utilities covers formatting disks and erasing and copying files and disks. Then it shows you how to undo it all using UnErase and other Norton Utility functions. Working with Inside the Norton Utilities you'll learn how DOS stores data and gain greater control over your files. You'll stop losing data accidentally, and you'll stop disasters before they happen.

Rob Krumm runs a computer school in Walnut Creek, California. He is the author of *Getting The Most Out Of Utilities On IBM PC* and *Understanding and Using dBASE III Plus*. His columns and commentaries regularly appear in the *San Francisco Examiner* and Computer Currents.

ISBN: 0-13-467887-7 • $19.95

‖‖Brady

ABOUT THE AUTHORS

Steven J. Bennett is a professional writer and computer consultant. Educated at the University of Rochester and Harvard University, he has edited and written numerous medical and scientific publications, and has authored a number of business books, including *Playing Hardball With Soft Skills* (Bantam), *Executive Chess* (New American Library), and *Think To Win* (New American Library). He has also co-authored ten computer books: 1-2-3 *Ready-to-Run* (Brady), *dBASE III Plus to Go* (Brady), *The HAL Handbook* (Brady), 1-2-3 *Power Pack* (Brady), *WordPerfect Power Pack* (Brady), *Instant Byline* (Brady), *Instant PageMaker* (Brady), *Instant Ventura Publisher* (Brady), *Hewlett-Packard Laser Printer Power Pack* (Brady), and *The LASERJET Handbook* (Brady).

Peter G. Randall is the president of Ariel Enterprises, Inc., a software development and consulting firm. Prior to the start-up of Ariel, he served as the president of ESIS International, an international marketing subsidiary of Cigna Corporation. Mr. Randall, who holds a B.S.E. in systems engineering from Princeton University and an M.B.A. from the Wharton School of Business, has written more than thirty major application programs for use in business. He has co-authored ten computer books: *1-2-3 Ready-to-Run* (Brady), *dBASE III Plus to Go* (Brady), *The HAL Handbook* (Brady), *1-2-3 Power Pack* (Brady), *WordPerfect Power Pack* (Brady), *Instant Byline* (Brady), *Instant PageMaker* (Brady), *Hewlett-Packard Laser Printer Power Pack* (Brady), and *The LASERJET Handbook* (Brady).